THE LAST MAN — Unmanned

Brian K. Vaughan
Writer

Pia Guerra
Penciller

José Marzán, Jr.
Inker

Pamela Rambo
Colorist

Clem Robins
Letterer

J.G. Jones
Original series covers

Y: THE LAST MAN created by Brian K. Vaughan and Pia Guerra

Heidi MacDonald
Steve Bunche
Editors-original series

Zachary Rau
Assistant Editor-original series

Scott Nybakken
Editor

Robbin Brosterman
Design Director – Books

Louis Prandi
Publication Design

Karen Berger
Senior VP – Executive Editor, Vertigo

Bob Harras
VP – Editor-in-Chief

Diane Nelson
President

Dan DiDio and **Jim Lee**
Co-Publishers

Geoff Johns
Chief Creative Officer

John Rood
Executive VP – Sales, Marketing and Business Development

Amy Genkins
Senior VP – Business and Legal Affairs

Nairi Gardiner
Senior VP – Finance

Jeff Boison
VP – Publishing Operations

Mark Chiarello
VP – Art Direction and Design

John Cunningham
VP – Marketing

Terri Cunningham
VP – Talent Relations and Services

Alison Gill
Senior VP – Manufacturing and Operations

Hank Kanalz
Senior VP – Digital

Jay Kogan
VP – Business and Legal Affairs, Publishing

Jack Mahan
VP – Business Affairs, Talent

Nick Napolitano
VP – Manufacturing Administration

Sue Pohja
VP – Book Sales

Courtney Simmons
Senior VP – Publicity

Bob Wayne
Senior VP – Sales

Y: THE LAST MAN — UNMANNED

DC Comics, 1700 Broadway, New York, NY 10019
A Warner Bros. Entertainment Company
Printed in the USA. Eleventh Printing.
ISBN: 978-1-56389-980-5
Cover illustration by J.G. Jones.
Logo design by Terry Marks.

Library of Congress Cataloging-in-Publication Data

Vaughan, Brian K.
  Y, the last man. Vol. 1, Unmanned / Brian K. Vaughan, Pia Guerra, José
Marzán, Jr.
    p. cm.
  "Originally published in single magazine form as Y: The Last Man 1-5."
  ISBN 978-1-56389-980-5 (alk. paper)
  1. Graphic novels. I. Guerra, Pia. II. Marzán, José. III. Title. IV. Title:
Unmanned.
  PN6728.Y2V382 2012
  741.5'973–dc23
                              2012024702

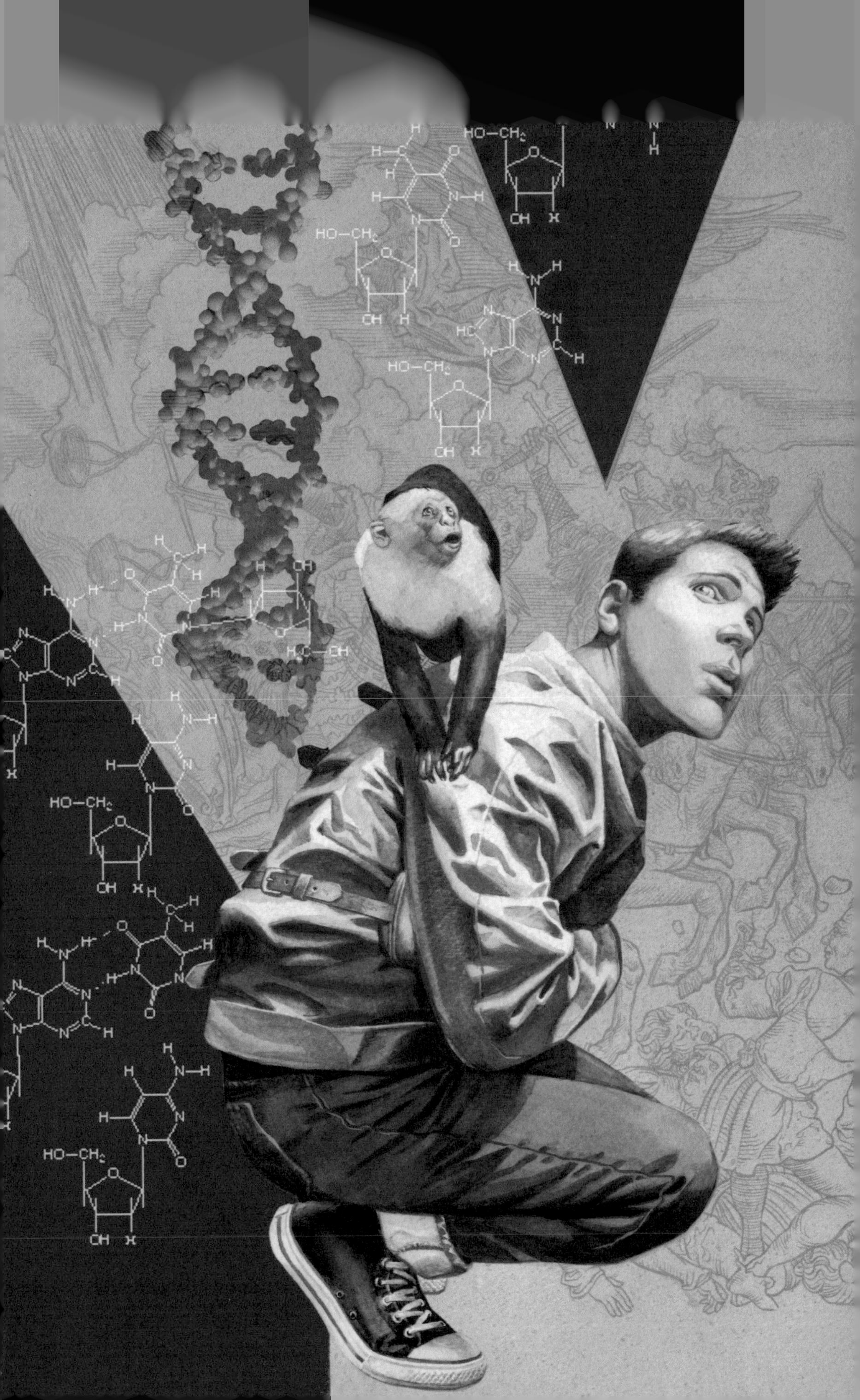

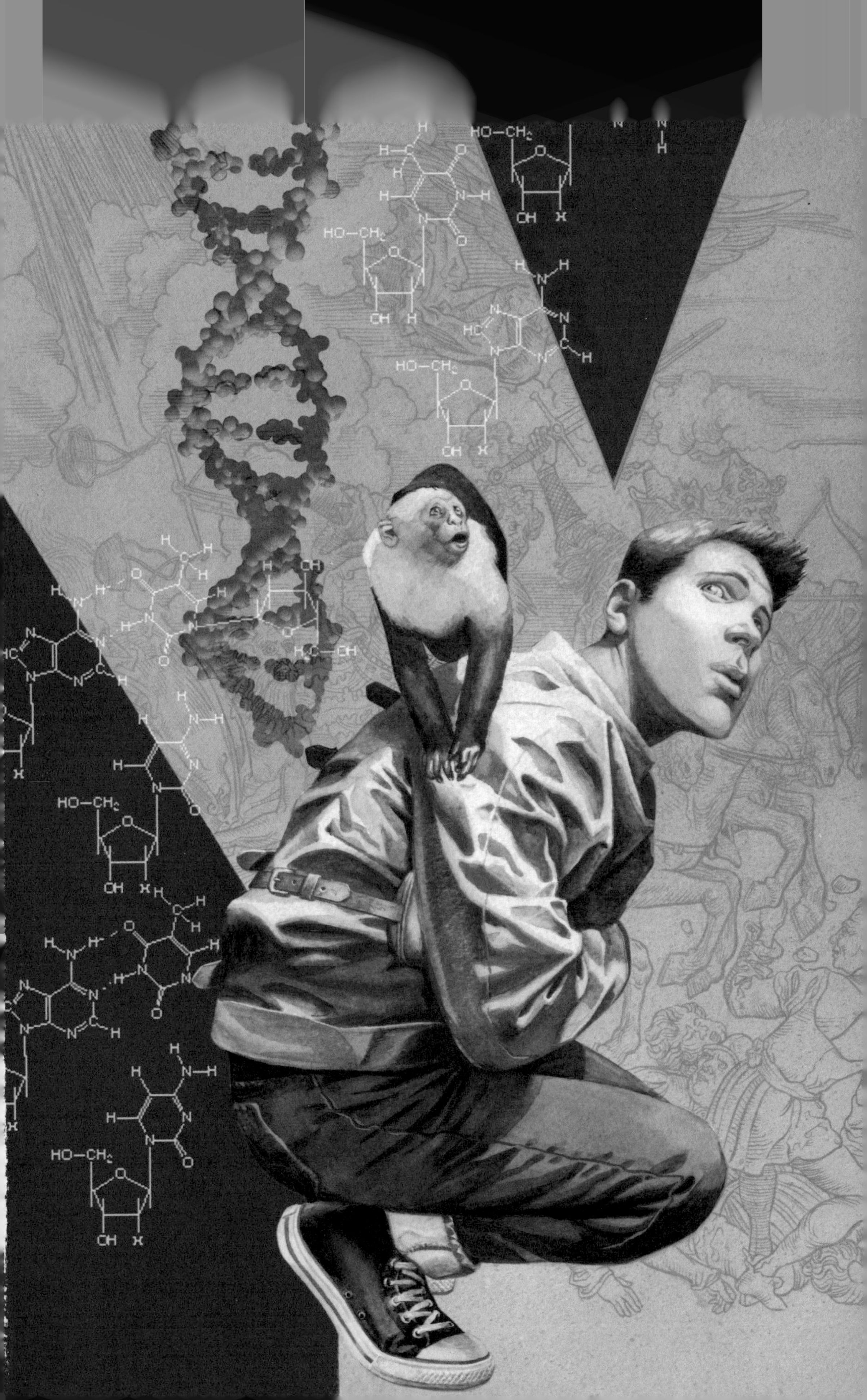

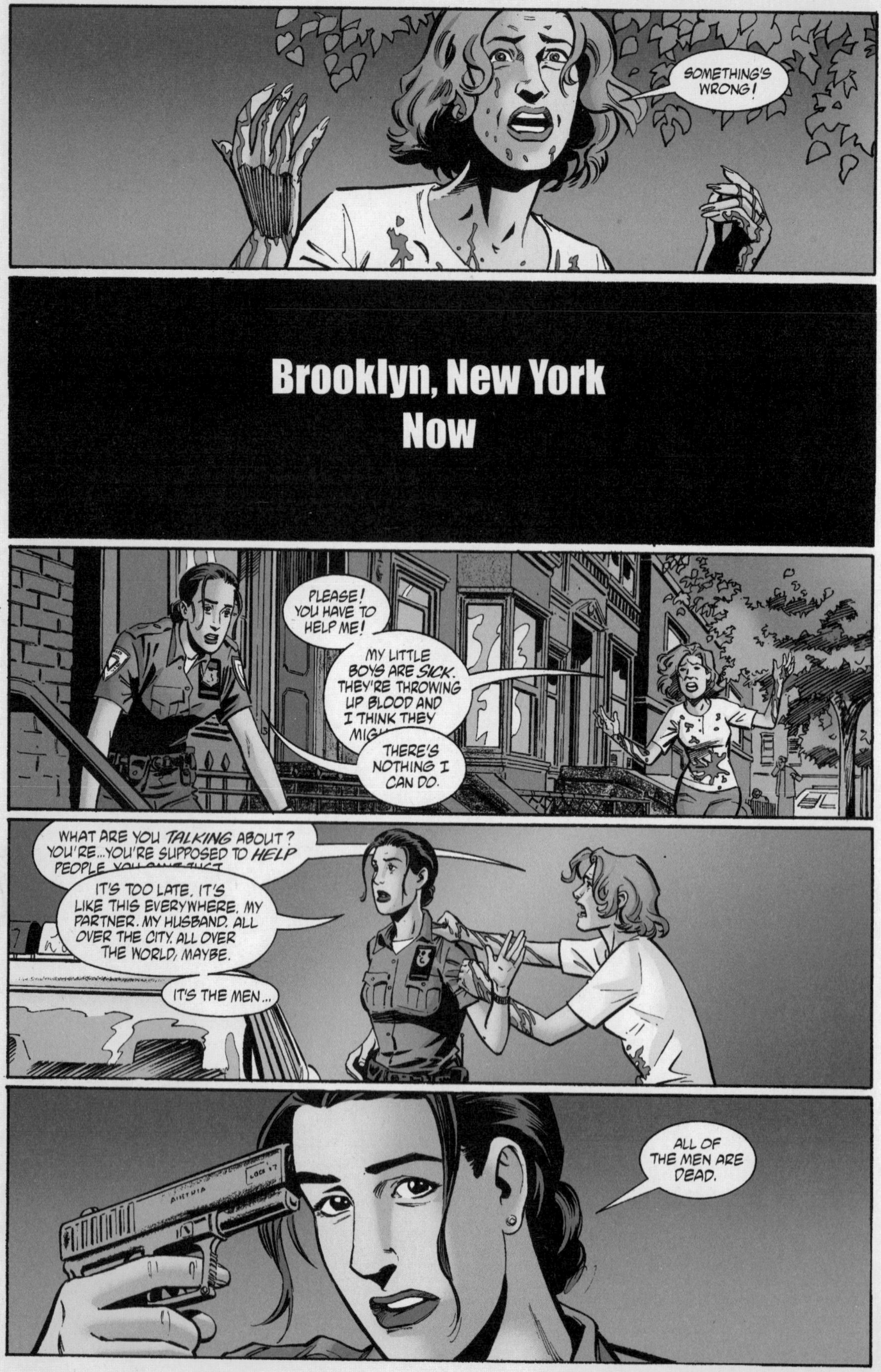
SOMETHING'S WRONG!
Brooklyn, New York
Now
PLEASE! YOU HAVE TO HELP ME!
MY LITTLE BOYS ARE SICK. THEY'RE THROWING UP BLOOD AND I THINK THEY
THERE'S NOTHING I CAN DO.
WHAT ARE YOU TALKING ABOUT? YOU'RE...YOU'RE SUPPOSED TO HELP PEOPLE.
IT'S TOO LATE. IT'S LIKE THIS EVERYWHERE. MY PARTNER. MY HUSBAND. ALL OVER THE CITY. ALL OVER THE WORLD, MAYBE.
IT'S THE MEN...
ALL OF THE MEN ARE DEAD.

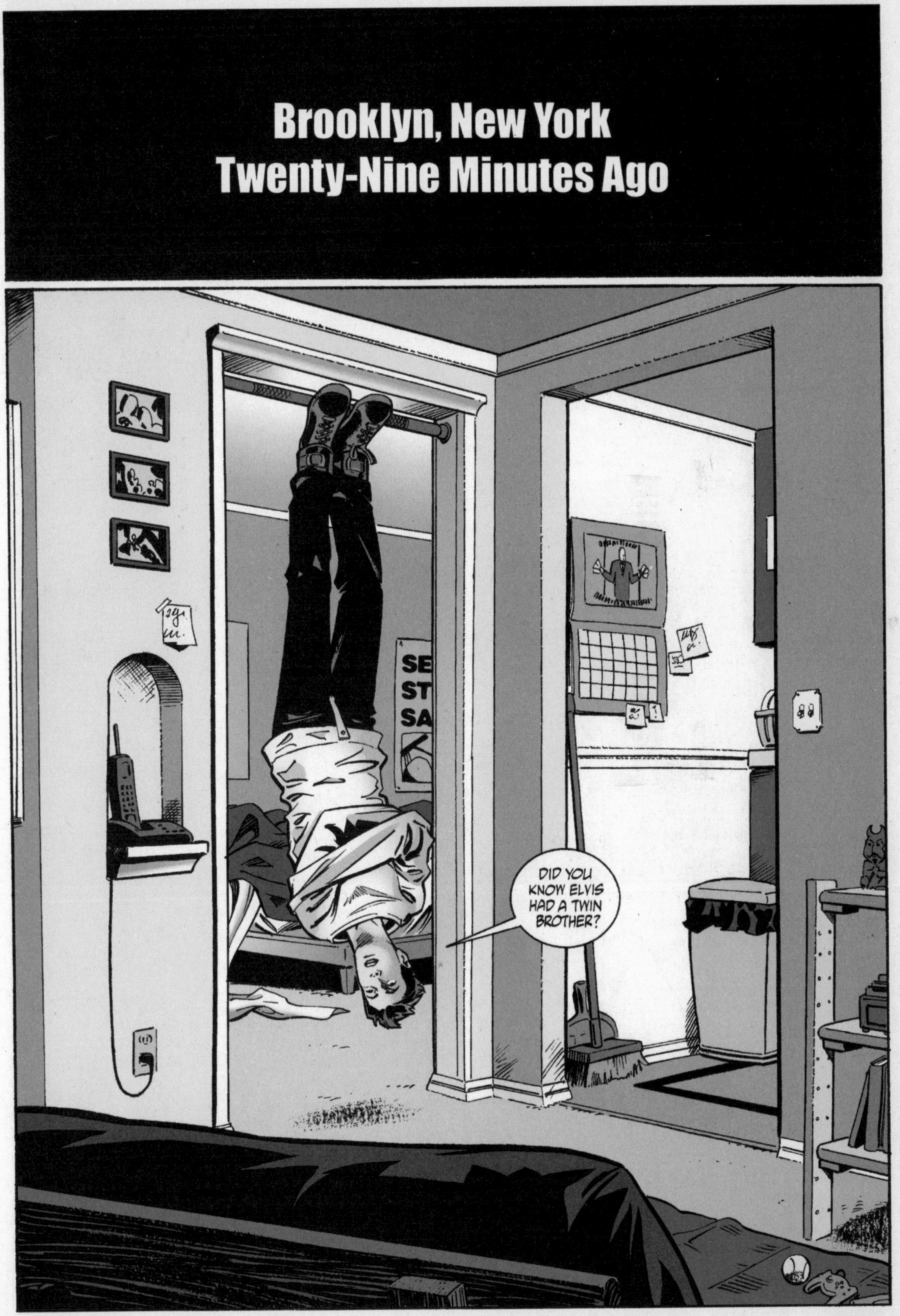
Brooklyn, New York
Twenty-Nine Minutes Ago
DID YOU KNOW ELVIS HAD A TWIN BROTHER?

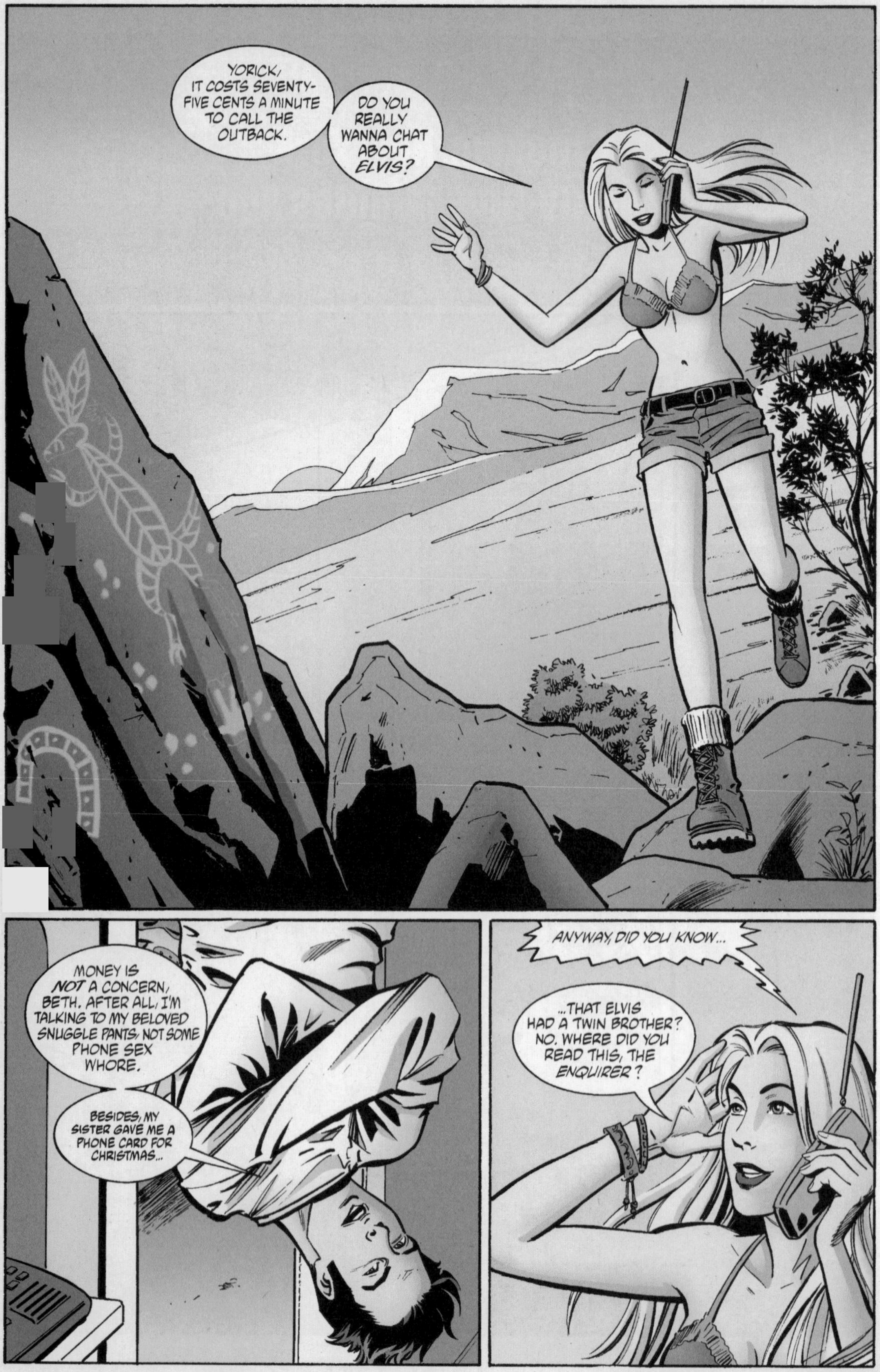
YORICK, IT COSTS SEVENTY-FIVE CENTS A MINUTE TO CALL THE OUTBACK.
DO YOU REALLY WANNA CHAT ABOUT *ELVIS?*
MONEY IS *NOT* A CONCERN, BETH. AFTER ALL, I'M TALKING TO MY BELOVED SNUGGLE PANTS, NOT SOME PHONE SEX WHORE.
BESIDES, MY SISTER GAVE ME A PHONE CARD FOR CHRISTMAS...
ANYWAY, DID YOU KNOW...
...THAT ELVIS HAD A TWIN BROTHER? NO. WHERE DID YOU READ THIS, THE *ENQUIRER?*

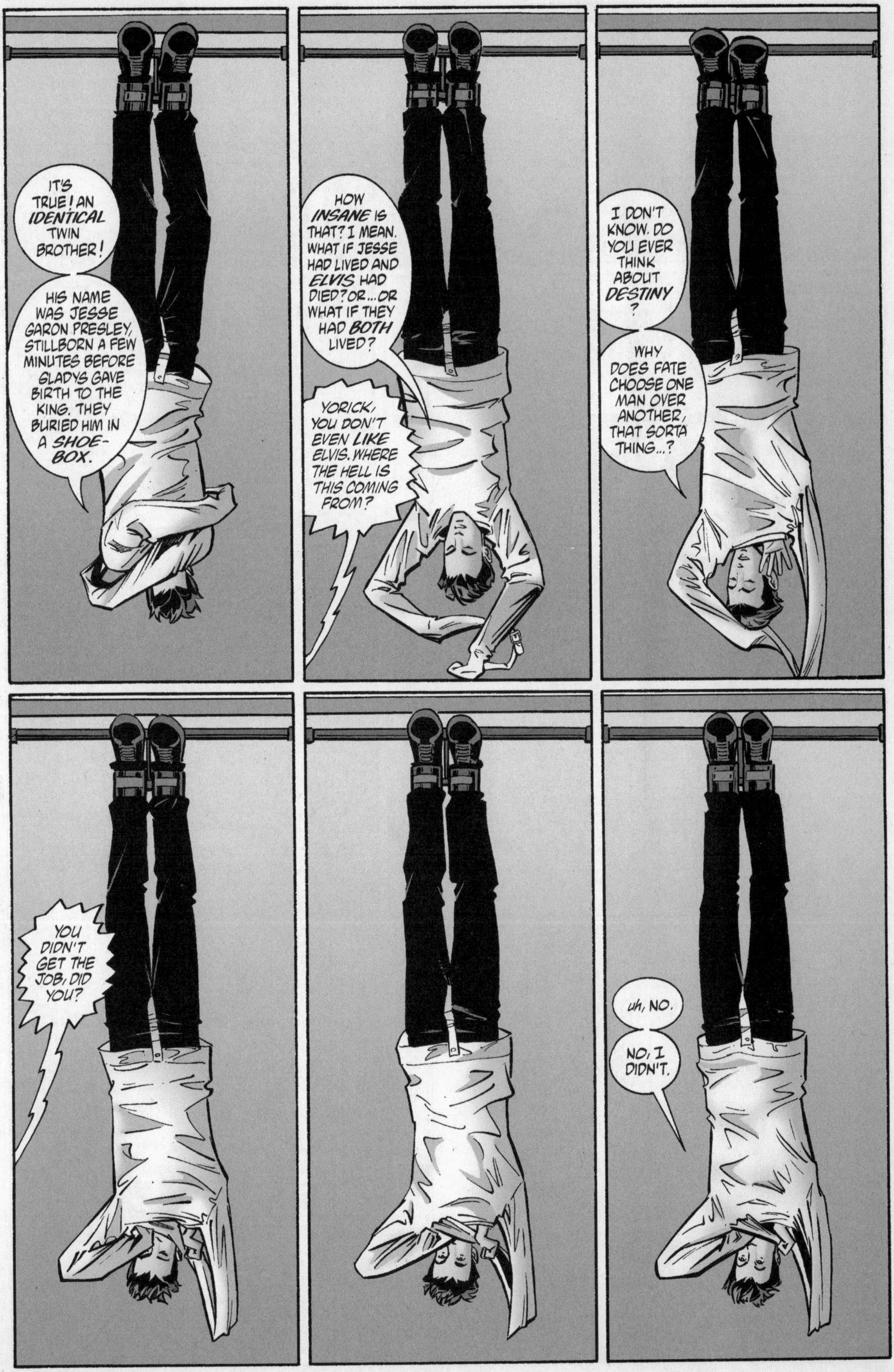
IT'S TRUE! AN IDENTICAL TWIN BROTHER!
HIS NAME WAS JESSE GARON PRESLEY, STILLBORN A FEW MINUTES BEFORE GLADYS GAVE BIRTH TO THE KING. THEY BURIED HIM IN A SHOE-BOX.
HOW INSANE IS THAT? I MEAN. WHAT IF JESSE HAD LIVED AND ELVIS HAD DIED? OR...OR WHAT IF THEY HAD BOTH LIVED?
YORICK, YOU DON'T EVEN LIKE ELVIS. WHERE THE HELL IS THIS COMING FROM?
I DON'T KNOW. DO YOU EVER THINK ABOUT DESTINY?
WHY DOES FATE CHOOSE ONE MAN OVER ANOTHER, THAT SORTA THING...?
YOU DIDN'T GET THE JOB, DID YOU?
uh, NO.
NO, I DIDN'T.

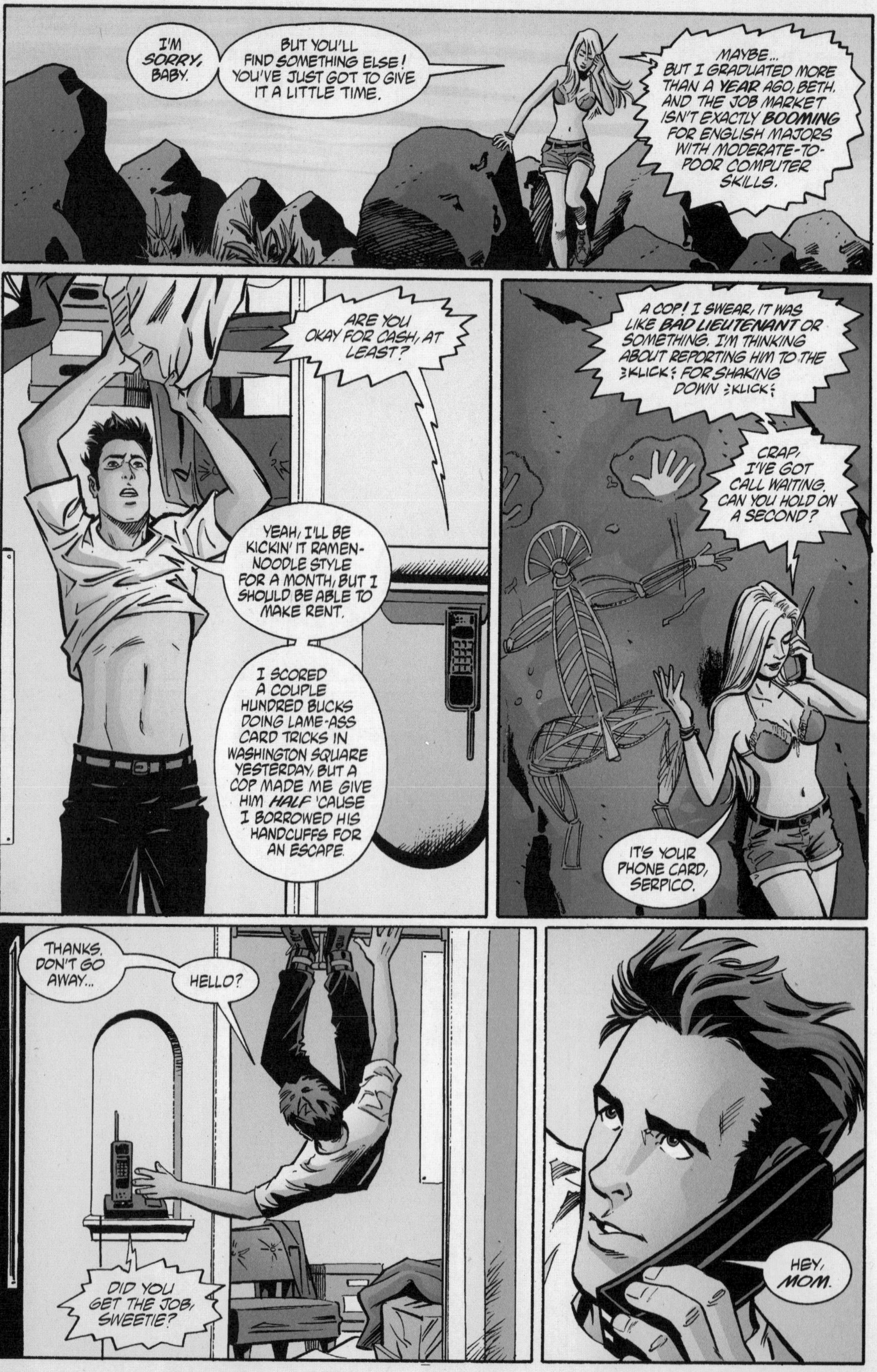
I'M SORRY, BABY.
BUT YOU'LL FIND SOMETHING ELSE! YOU'VE JUST GOT TO GIVE IT A LITTLE TIME.
MAYBE... BUT I GRADUATED MORE THAN A YEAR AGO, BETH. AND THE JOB MARKET ISN'T EXACTLY BOOMING FOR ENGLISH MAJORS WITH MODERATE-TO-POOR COMPUTER SKILLS.
ARE YOU OKAY FOR CASH, AT LEAST?
YEAH, I'LL BE KICKIN' IT RAMEN-NOODLE STYLE FOR A MONTH, BUT I SHOULD BE ABLE TO MAKE RENT.
I SCORED A COUPLE HUNDRED BUCKS DOING LAME-ASS CARD TRICKS IN WASHINGTON SQUARE YESTERDAY, BUT A COP MADE ME GIVE HIM HALF 'CAUSE I BORROWED HIS HANDCUFFS FOR AN ESCAPE.
A COP! I SWEAR, IT WAS LIKE BAD LIEUTENANT OR SOMETHING. I'M THINKING ABOUT REPORTING HIM TO THE ⋮KLICK⋮ FOR SHAKING DOWN ⋮KLICK⋮
CRAP, I'VE GOT CALL WAITING. CAN YOU HOLD ON A SECOND?
IT'S YOUR PHONE CARD, SERPICO.
THANKS. DON'T GO AWAY...
HELLO?
DID YOU GET THE JOB, SWEETIE?
HEY, MOM.

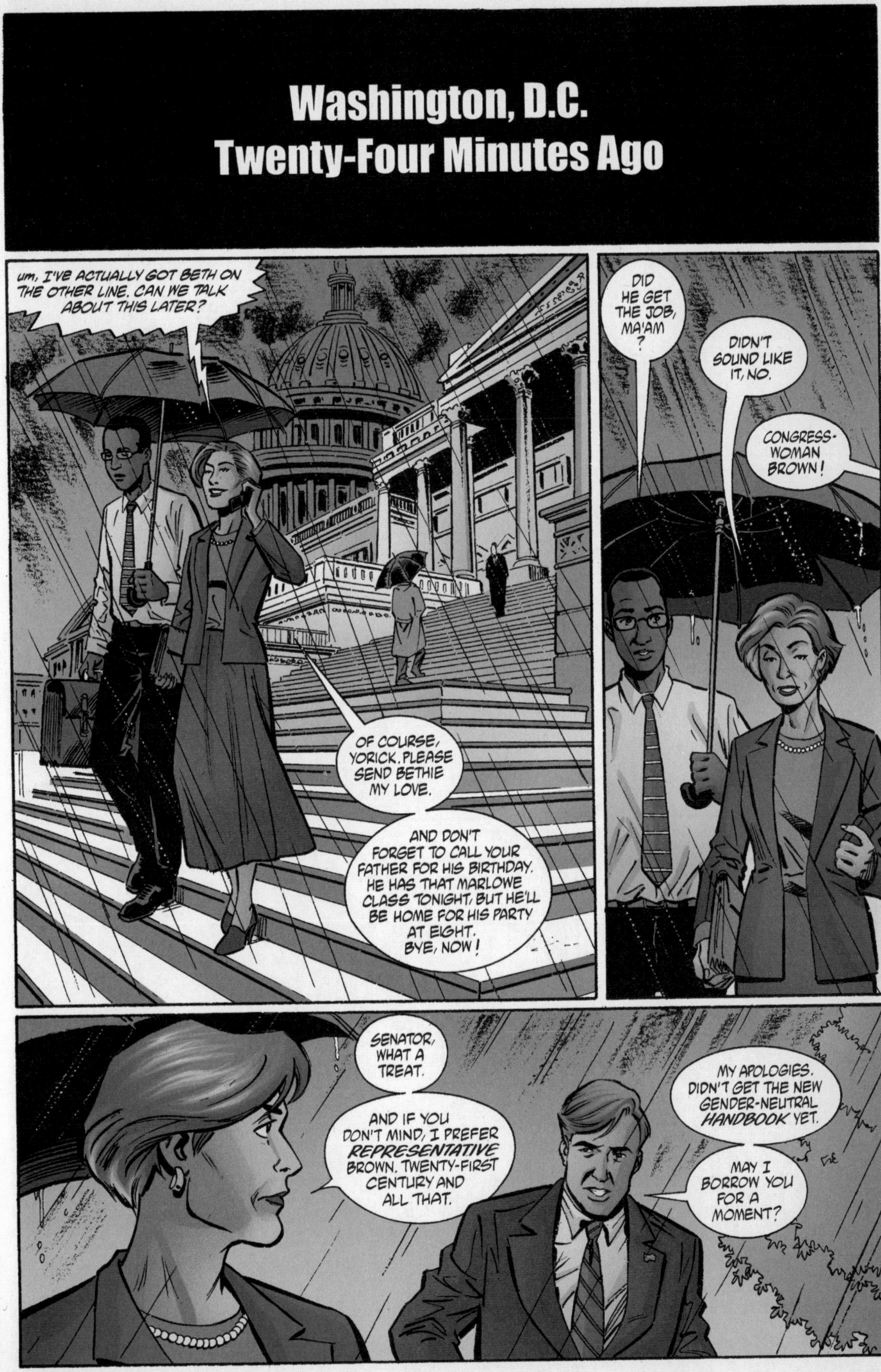
Washington, D.C.
Twenty-Four Minutes Ago
um, I'VE ACTUALLY GOT BETH ON THE OTHER LINE. CAN WE TALK ABOUT THIS LATER?
OF COURSE, YORICK. PLEASE SEND BETHIE MY LOVE.
AND DON'T FORGET TO CALL YOUR FATHER FOR HIS BIRTHDAY. HE HAS THAT MARLOWE CLASS TONIGHT, BUT HE'LL BE HOME FOR HIS PARTY AT EIGHT. BYE, NOW!
DID HE GET THE JOB, MA'AM?
DIDN'T SOUND LIKE IT, NO.
CONGRESS-WOMAN BROWN!
SENATOR, WHAT A TREAT.
AND IF YOU DON'T MIND, I PREFER REPRESENTATIVE BROWN. TWENTY-FIRST CENTURY AND ALL THAT.
MY APOLOGIES. DIDN'T GET THE NEW GENDER-NEUTRAL HANDBOOK YET.
MAY I BORROW YOU FOR A MOMENT?

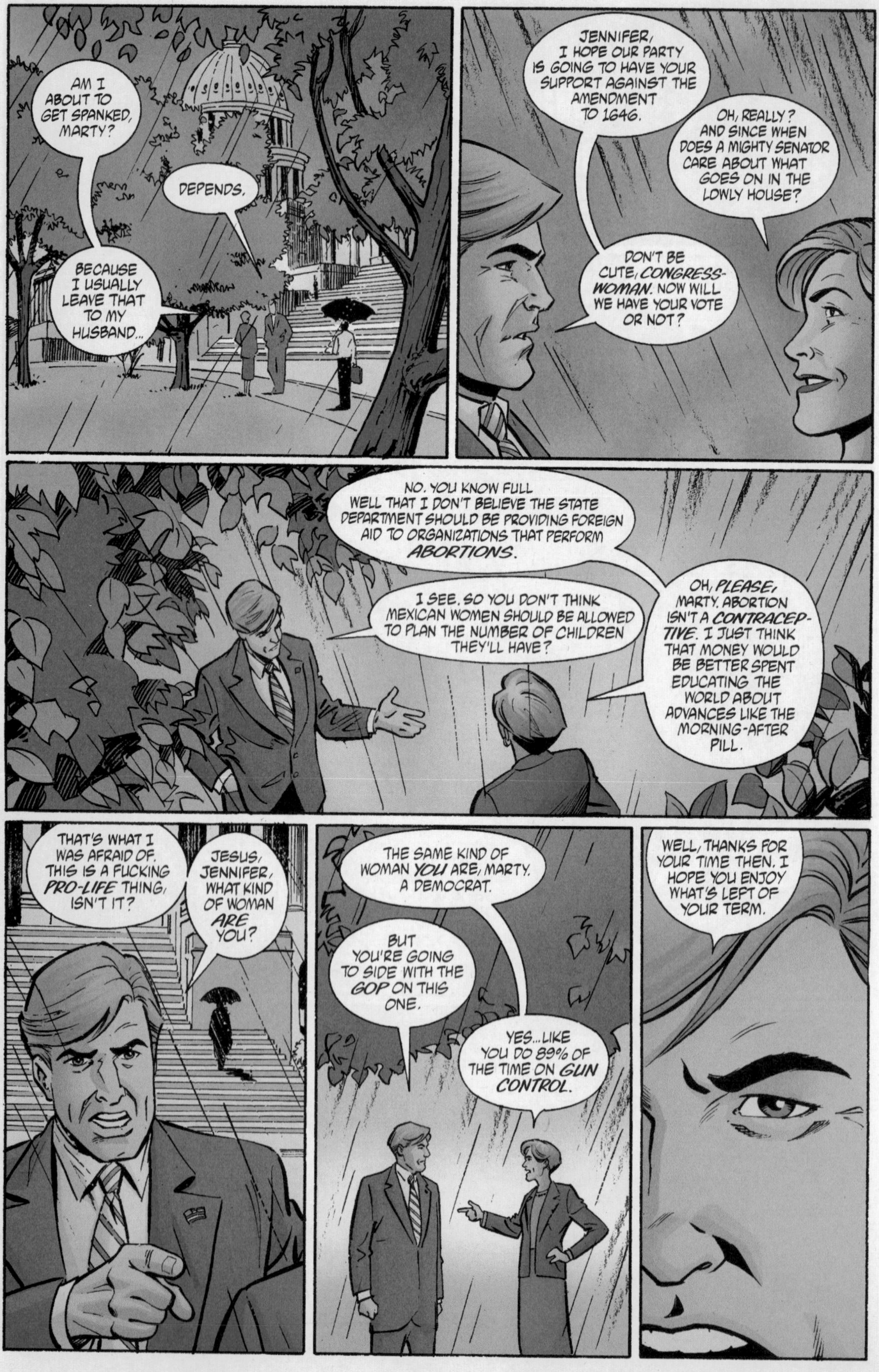
AM I ABOUT TO GET SPANKED, MARTY?
DEPENDS.
BECAUSE I USUALLY LEAVE THAT TO MY HUSBAND...
JENNIFER, I HOPE OUR PARTY IS GOING TO HAVE YOUR SUPPORT AGAINST THE AMENDMENT TO 1646.
OH, REALLY? AND SINCE WHEN DOES A MIGHTY SENATOR CARE ABOUT WHAT GOES ON IN THE LOWLY HOUSE?
DON'T BE CUTE, CONGRESS-WOMAN. NOW WILL WE HAVE YOUR VOTE OR NOT?
NO. YOU KNOW FULL WELL THAT I DON'T BELIEVE THE STATE DEPARTMENT SHOULD BE PROVIDING FOREIGN AID TO ORGANIZATIONS THAT PERFORM ABORTIONS.
I SEE. SO YOU DON'T THINK MEXICAN WOMEN SHOULD BE ALLOWED TO PLAN THE NUMBER OF CHILDREN THEY'LL HAVE?
OH, PLEASE, MARTY. ABORTION ISN'T A CONTRACEP-TIVE. I JUST THINK THAT MONEY WOULD BE BETTER SPENT EDUCATING THE WORLD ABOUT ADVANCES LIKE THE MORNING-AFTER PILL.
THAT'S WHAT I WAS AFRAID OF. THIS IS A FUCKING PRO-LIFE THING, ISN'T IT?
JESUS, JENNIFER, WHAT KIND OF WOMAN ARE YOU?
THE SAME KIND OF WOMAN YOU ARE, MARTY. A DEMOCRAT.
BUT YOU'RE GOING TO SIDE WITH THE GOP ON THIS ONE.
YES...LIKE YOU DO 89% OF THE TIME ON GUN CONTROL.
WELL, THANKS FOR YOUR TIME THEN. I HOPE YOU ENJOY WHAT'S LEFT OF YOUR TERM.

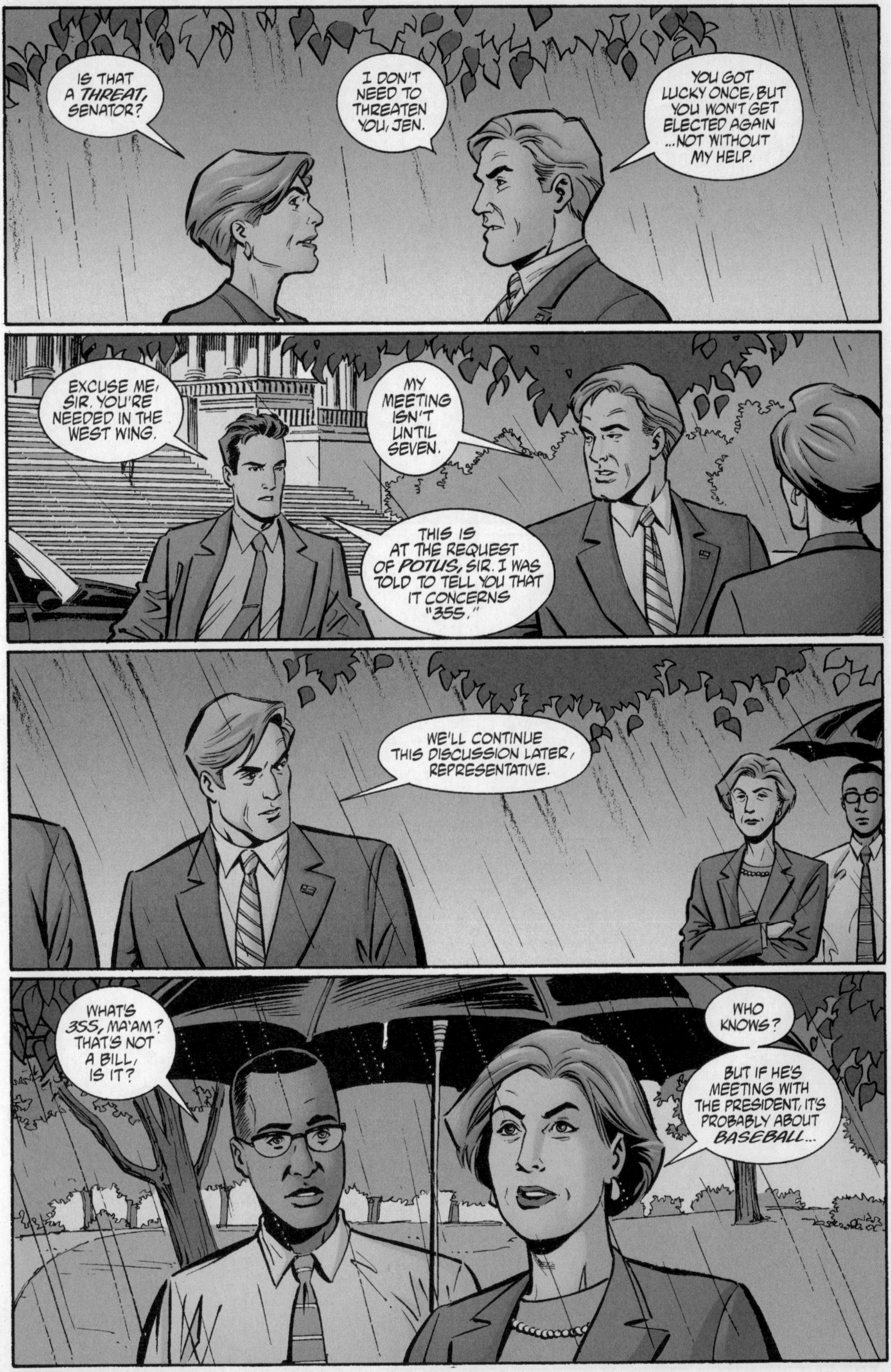
IS THAT A THREAT, SENATOR?
I DON'T NEED TO THREATEN YOU, JEN.
YOU GOT LUCKY ONCE, BUT YOU WON'T GET ELECTED AGAIN ...NOT WITHOUT MY HELP.
EXCUSE ME, SIR. YOU'RE NEEDED IN THE WEST WING.
MY MEETING ISN'T UNTIL SEVEN.
THIS IS AT THE REQUEST OF POTUS, SIR. I WAS TOLD TO TELL YOU THAT IT CONCERNS "355."
WE'LL CONTINUE THIS DISCUSSION LATER, REPRESENTATIVE.
WHAT'S 355, MA'AM? THAT'S NOT A BILL, IS IT?
WHO KNOWS?
BUT IF HE'S MEETING WITH THE PRESIDENT, IT'S PROBABLY ABOUT BASEBALL...

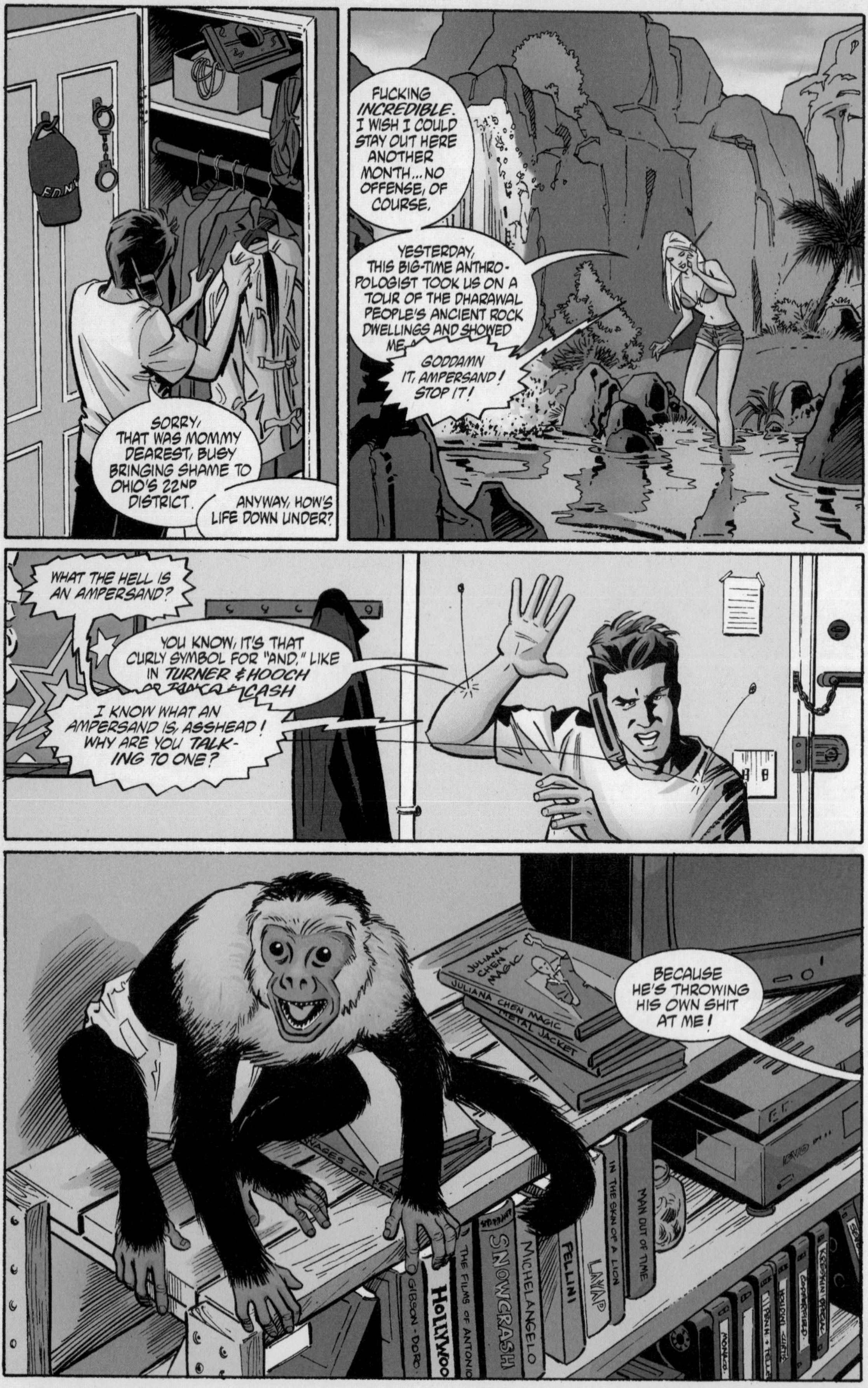
FDNY
SORRY, THAT WAS MOMMY DEAREST, BUSY BRINGING SHAME TO OHIO'S 22ND DISTRICT.
ANYWAY, HOW'S LIFE DOWN UNDER?
FUCKING INCREDIBLE. I WISH I COULD STAY OUT HERE ANOTHER MONTH... NO OFFENSE, OF COURSE.
YESTERDAY, THIS BIG-TIME ANTHROPOLOGIST TOOK US ON A TOUR OF THE DHARAWAL PEOPLE'S ANCIENT ROCK DWELLINGS AND SHOWED ME
GODDAMN IT, AMPERSAND! STOP IT!
WHAT THE HELL IS AN AMPERSAND?
YOU KNOW, IT'S THAT CURLY SYMBOL FOR "AND," LIKE IN TURNER & HOOCH
I KNOW WHAT AN AMPERSAND IS, ASSHEAD! WHY ARE YOU TALKING TO ONE?
BECAUSE HE'S THROWING HIS OWN SHIT AT ME!
JULIANA CHEN MAGIC
JULIANA CHEN MAGIC
METAL JACKET
IN THE SKIN OF A LION
MAN OUT OF TIME
FELLINI
MICHELANGELO
SNOWCRASH
THE FILMS OF ANTONIO
GIBSON · DORO

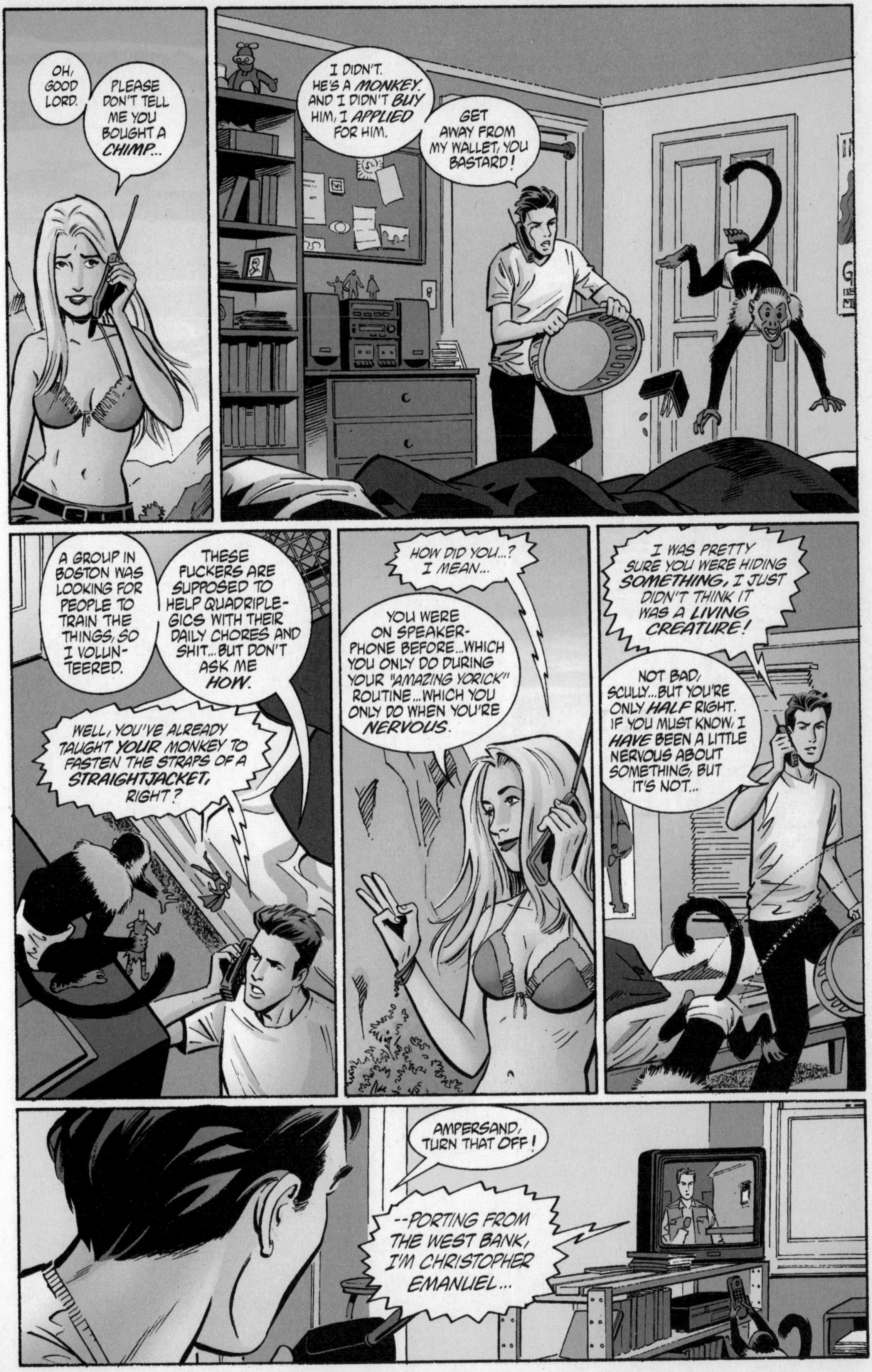
OH, GOOD LORD.
PLEASE DON'T TELL ME YOU BOUGHT A CHIMP...
I DIDN'T. HE'S A MONKEY. AND I DIDN'T BUY HIM, I APPLIED FOR HIM.
GET AWAY FROM MY WALLET, YOU BASTARD!
A GROUP IN BOSTON WAS LOOKING FOR PEOPLE TO TRAIN THE THINGS, SO I VOLUNTEERED.
THESE FUCKERS ARE SUPPOSED TO HELP QUADRIPLEGICS WITH THEIR DAILY CHORES AND SHIT...BUT DON'T ASK ME HOW.
WELL, YOU'VE ALREADY TAUGHT YOUR MONKEY TO FASTEN THE STRAPS OF A STRAIGHTJACKET, RIGHT?
HOW DID YOU...? I MEAN...
YOU WERE ON SPEAKERPHONE BEFORE...WHICH YOU ONLY DO DURING YOUR "AMAZING YORICK" ROUTINE...WHICH YOU ONLY DO WHEN YOU'RE NERVOUS.
I WAS PRETTY SURE YOU WERE HIDING SOMETHING, I JUST DIDN'T THINK IT WAS A LIVING CREATURE!
NOT BAD, SCULLY...BUT YOU'RE ONLY HALF RIGHT. IF YOU MUST KNOW, I HAVE BEEN A LITTLE NERVOUS ABOUT SOMETHING, BUT IT'S NOT...
AMPERSAND, TURN THAT OFF!
--PORTING FROM THE WEST BANK, I'M CHRISTOPHER EMANUEL...

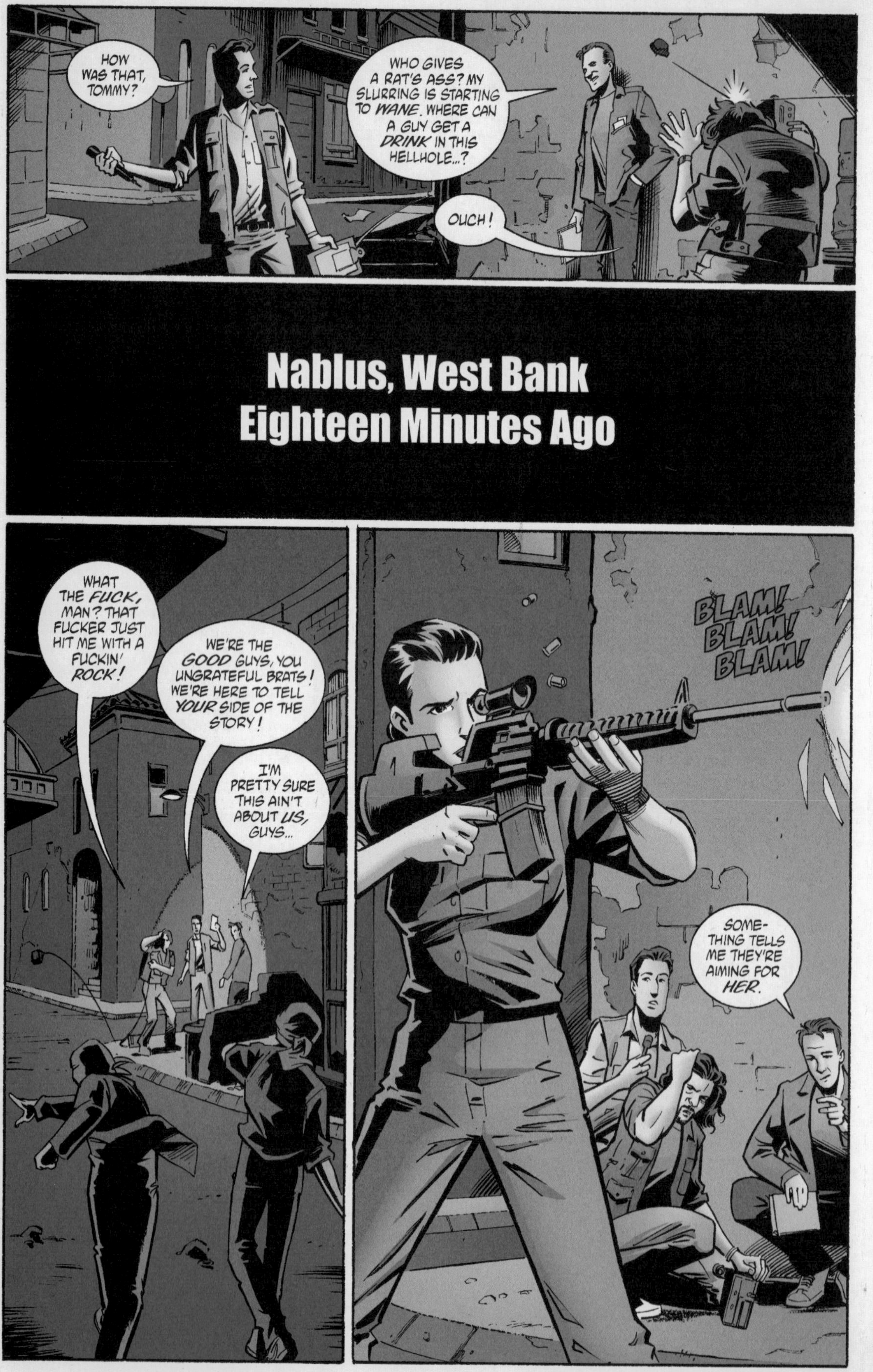
HOW WAS THAT, TOMMY?
WHO GIVES A RAT'S ASS? MY SLURRING IS STARTING TO WANE. WHERE CAN A GUY GET A DRINK IN THIS HELLHOLE...?
OUCH!
Nablus, West Bank
Eighteen Minutes Ago
WHAT THE FUCK, MAN? THAT FUCKER JUST HIT ME WITH A FUCKIN' ROCK!
WE'RE THE GOOD GUYS, YOU UNGRATEFUL BRATS! WE'RE HERE TO TELL YOUR SIDE OF THE STORY!
I'M PRETTY SURE THIS AIN'T ABOUT US, GUYS...
BLAM! BLAM! BLAM!
SOME-THING TELLS ME THEY'RE AIMING FOR HER.

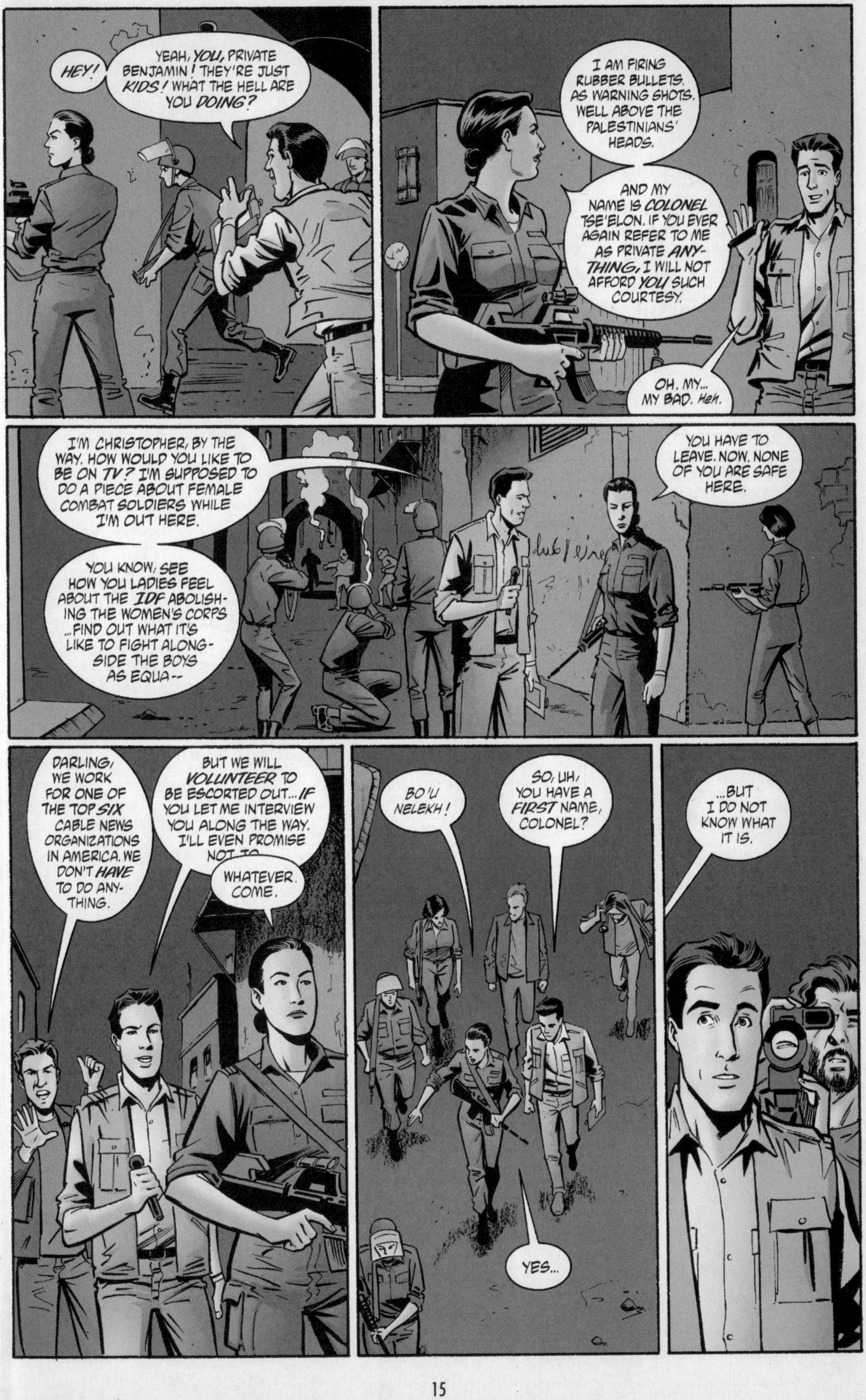
HEY!
YEAH, YOU, PRIVATE BENJAMIN! THEY'RE JUST KIDS! WHAT THE HELL ARE YOU DOING?
I AM FIRING RUBBER BULLETS. AS WARNING SHOTS. WELL ABOVE THE PALESTINIANS' HEADS.
AND MY NAME IS COLONEL TSE'ELON. IF YOU EVER AGAIN REFER TO ME AS PRIVATE ANYTHING, I WILL NOT AFFORD YOU SUCH COURTESY.
OH. MY... MY BAD. Heh.
I'M CHRISTOPHER, BY THE WAY. HOW WOULD YOU LIKE TO BE ON TV? I'M SUPPOSED TO DO A PIECE ABOUT FEMALE COMBAT SOLDIERS WHILE I'M OUT HERE.
YOU KNOW, SEE HOW YOU LADIES FEEL ABOUT THE IDF ABOLISHING THE WOMEN'S CORPS ...FIND OUT WHAT IT'S LIKE TO FIGHT ALONG-SIDE THE BOYS AS EQUA--
YOU HAVE TO LEAVE. NOW. NONE OF YOU ARE SAFE HERE.
DARLING, WE WORK FOR ONE OF THE TOP SIX CABLE NEWS ORGANIZATIONS IN AMERICA. WE DON'T HAVE TO DO ANY-THING.
BUT WE WILL VOLUNTEER TO BE ESCORTED OUT... IF YOU LET ME INTERVIEW YOU ALONG THE WAY. I'LL EVEN PROMISE NOT TO
WHATEVER. COME.
BO'U NELEKH!
SO, UH, YOU HAVE A FIRST NAME, COLONEL?
YES...
...BUT I DO NOT KNOW WHAT IT IS.

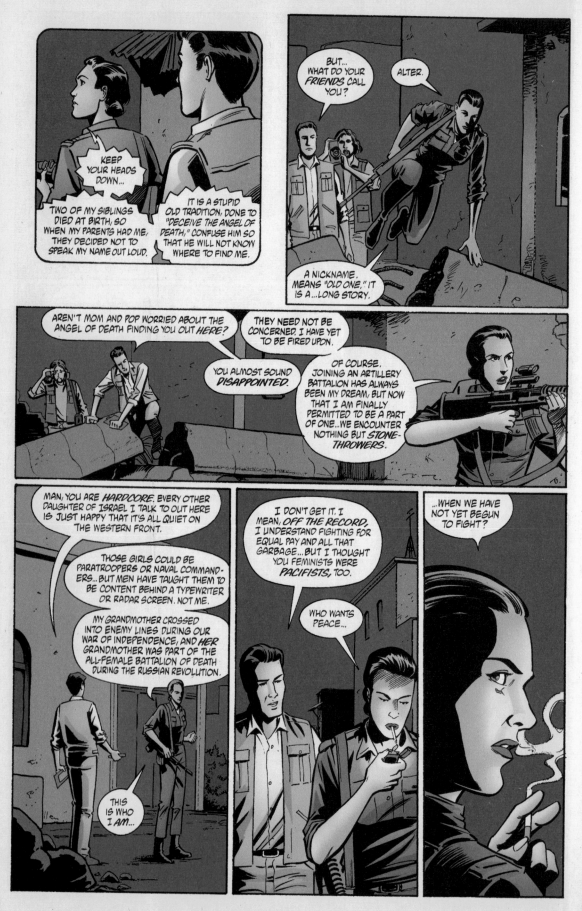

KEEP YOUR HEADS DOWN...

TWO OF MY SIBLINGS DIED AT BIRTH, SO WHEN MY PARENTS HAD ME, THEY DECIDED NOT TO SPEAK MY NAME OUT LOUD.

IT IS A STUPID OLD TRADITION, DONE TO "DECEIVE THE ANGEL OF DEATH," CONFUSE HIM SO THAT HE WILL NOT KNOW WHERE TO FIND ME.

BUT... WHAT DO YOUR FRIENDS CALL YOU?

ALTER.

A NICKNAME. MEANS "OLD ONE." IT IS A...LONG STORY.

AREN'T MOM AND POP WORRIED ABOUT THE ANGEL OF DEATH FINDING YOU OUT HERE?

THEY NEED NOT BE CONCERNED. I HAVE YET TO BE FIRED UPON.

YOU ALMOST SOUND DISAPPOINTED.

OF COURSE. JOINING AN ARTILLERY BATTALION HAS ALWAYS BEEN MY DREAM, BUT NOW THAT I AM FINALLY PERMITTED TO BE A PART OF ONE...WE ENCOUNTER NOTHING BUT STONE-THROWERS.

MAN, YOU ARE HARDCORE. EVERY OTHER DAUGHTER OF ISRAEL I TALK TO OUT HERE IS JUST HAPPY THAT IT'S ALL QUIET ON THE WESTERN FRONT.

THOSE GIRLS COULD BE PARATROOPERS OR NAVAL COMMANDERS...BUT MEN HAVE TAUGHT THEM TO BE CONTENT BEHIND A TYPEWRITER OR RADAR SCREEN. NOT ME.

MY GRANDMOTHER CROSSED INTO ENEMY LINES DURING OUR WAR OF INDEPENDENCE, AND HER GRANDMOTHER WAS PART OF THE ALL-FEMALE BATTALION OF DEATH DURING THE RUSSIAN REVOLUTION.

THIS IS WHO I AM...

I DON'T GET IT. I MEAN, OFF THE RECORD, I UNDERSTAND FIGHTING FOR EQUAL PAY AND ALL THAT GARBAGE...BUT I THOUGHT YOU FEMINISTS WERE PACIFISTS, TOO.

WHO WANTS PEACE...

...WHEN WE HAVE NOT YET BEGUN TO FIGHT?

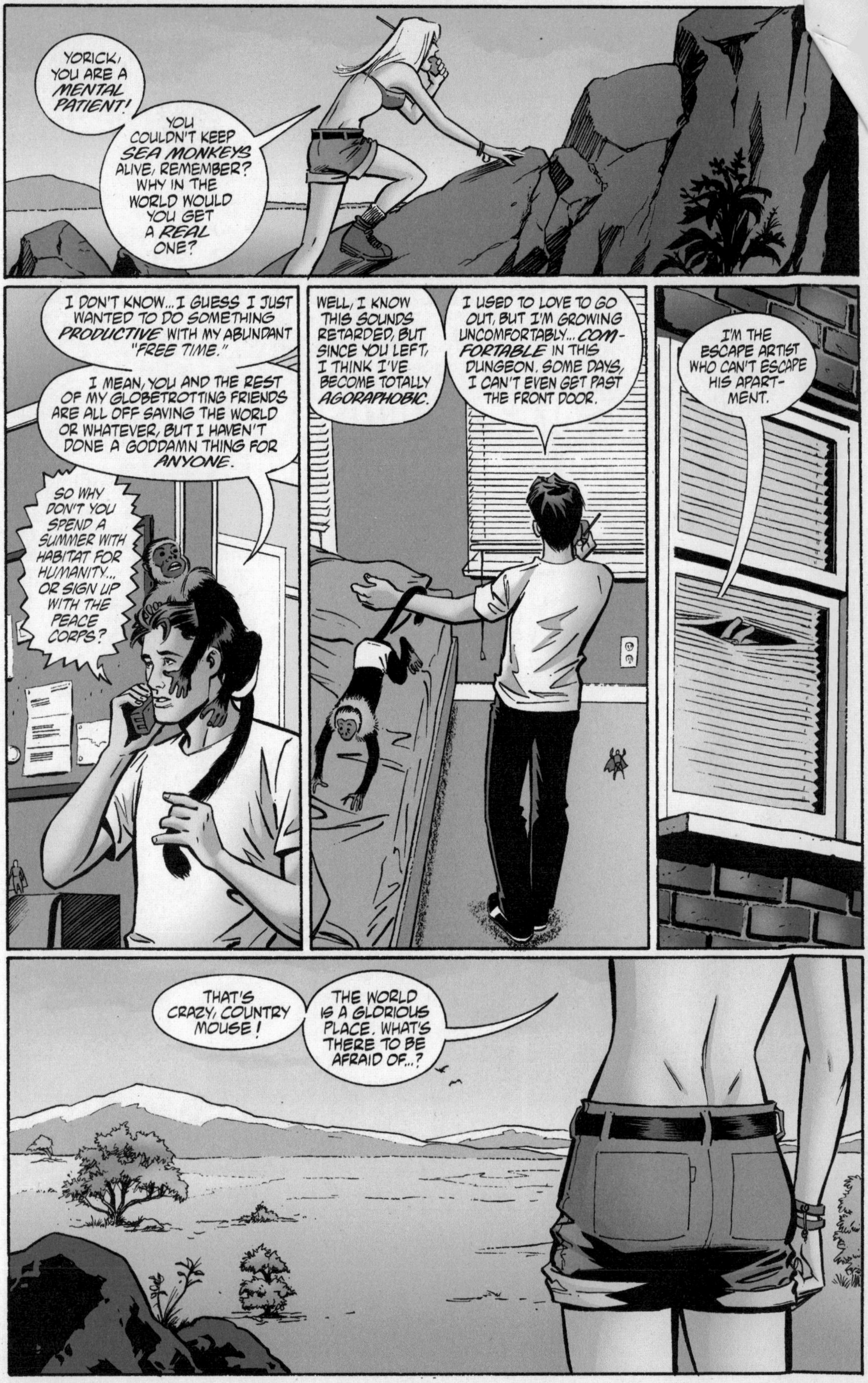
YORICK, YOU ARE A MENTAL PATIENT!
YOU COULDN'T KEEP SEA MONKEYS ALIVE, REMEMBER? WHY IN THE WORLD WOULD YOU GET A REAL ONE?
I DON'T KNOW... I GUESS I JUST WANTED TO DO SOMETHING PRODUCTIVE WITH MY ABUNDANT "FREE TIME."
I MEAN, YOU AND THE REST OF MY GLOBETROTTING FRIENDS ARE ALL OFF SAVING THE WORLD OR WHATEVER, BUT I HAVEN'T DONE A GODDAMN THING FOR ANYONE.
SO WHY DON'T YOU SPEND A SUMMER WITH HABITAT FOR HUMANITY... OR SIGN UP WITH THE PEACE CORPS?
WELL, I KNOW THIS SOUNDS RETARDED, BUT SINCE YOU LEFT, I THINK I'VE BECOME TOTALLY AGORAPHOBIC.
I USED TO LOVE TO GO OUT, BUT I'M GROWING UNCOMFORTABLY... COM-FORTABLE IN THIS DUNGEON. SOME DAYS, I CAN'T EVEN GET PAST THE FRONT DOOR.
I'M THE ESCAPE ARTIST WHO CAN'T ESCAPE HIS APART-MENT.
THAT'S CRAZY, COUNTRY MOUSE!
THE WORLD IS A GLORIOUS PLACE. WHAT'S THERE TO BE AFRAID OF...?

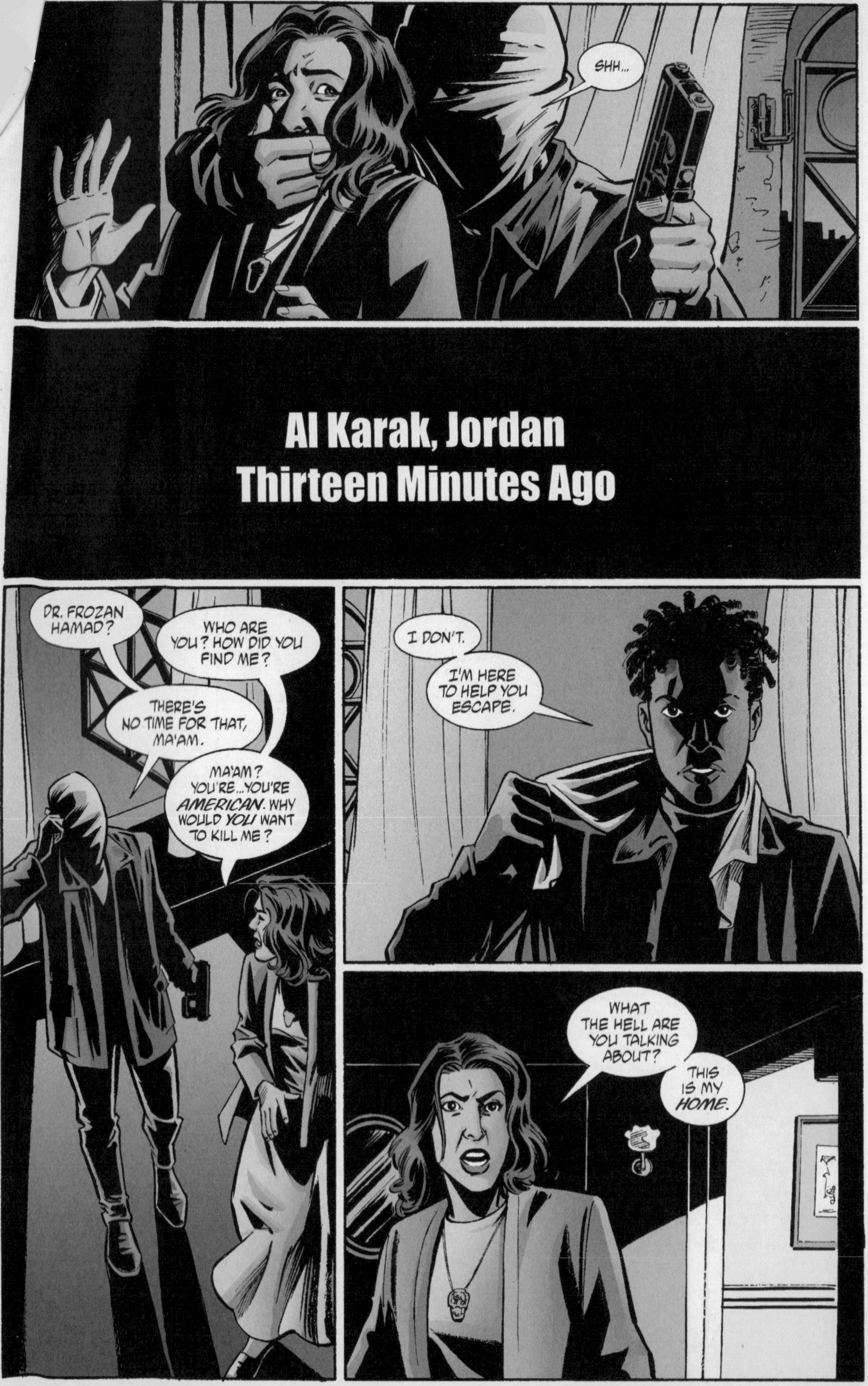
SHH...
Al Karak, Jordan
Thirteen Minutes Ago
DR. FROZAN HAMAD?
WHO ARE YOU? HOW DID YOU FIND ME?
THERE'S NO TIME FOR THAT, MA'AM.
MA'AM? YOU'RE...YOU'RE AMERICAN. WHY WOULD YOU WANT TO KILL ME?
I DON'T.
I'M HERE TO HELP YOU ESCAPE.
WHAT THE HELL ARE YOU TALKING ABOUT?
THIS IS MY HOME.

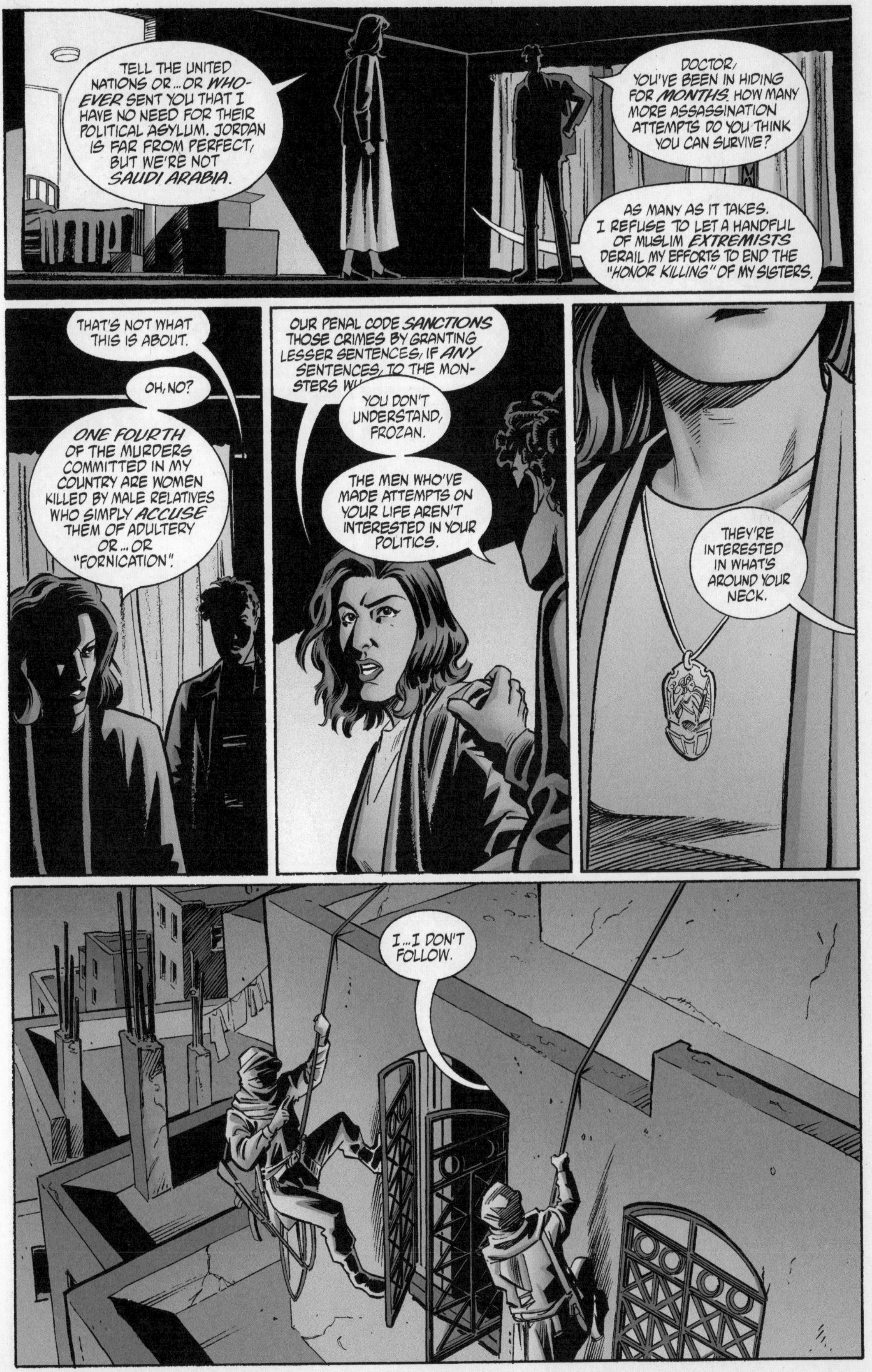
TELL THE UNITED NATIONS OR...OR WHO-EVER SENT YOU THAT I HAVE NO NEED FOR THEIR POLITICAL ASYLUM. JORDAN IS FAR FROM PERFECT, BUT WE'RE NOT SAUDI ARABIA.
DOCTOR, YOU'VE BEEN IN HIDING FOR MONTHS. HOW MANY MORE ASSASSINATION ATTEMPTS DO YOU THINK YOU CAN SURVIVE?
AS MANY AS IT TAKES. I REFUSE TO LET A HANDFUL OF MUSLIM EXTREMISTS DERAIL MY EFFORTS TO END THE "HONOR KILLING" OF MY SISTERS.
THAT'S NOT WHAT THIS IS ABOUT.
OH, NO?
ONE FOURTH OF THE MURDERS COMMITTED IN MY COUNTRY ARE WOMEN KILLED BY MALE RELATIVES WHO SIMPLY ACCUSE THEM OF ADULTERY OR...OR "FORNICATION".
OUR PENAL CODE SANCTIONS THOSE CRIMES BY GRANTING LESSER SENTENCES, IF ANY SENTENCES, TO THE MON-STERS
YOU DON'T UNDERSTAND, FROZAN.
THE MEN WHO'VE MADE ATTEMPTS ON YOUR LIFE AREN'T INTERESTED IN YOUR POLITICS.
THEY'RE INTERESTED IN WHAT'S AROUND YOUR NECK.
I...I DON'T FOLLOW.

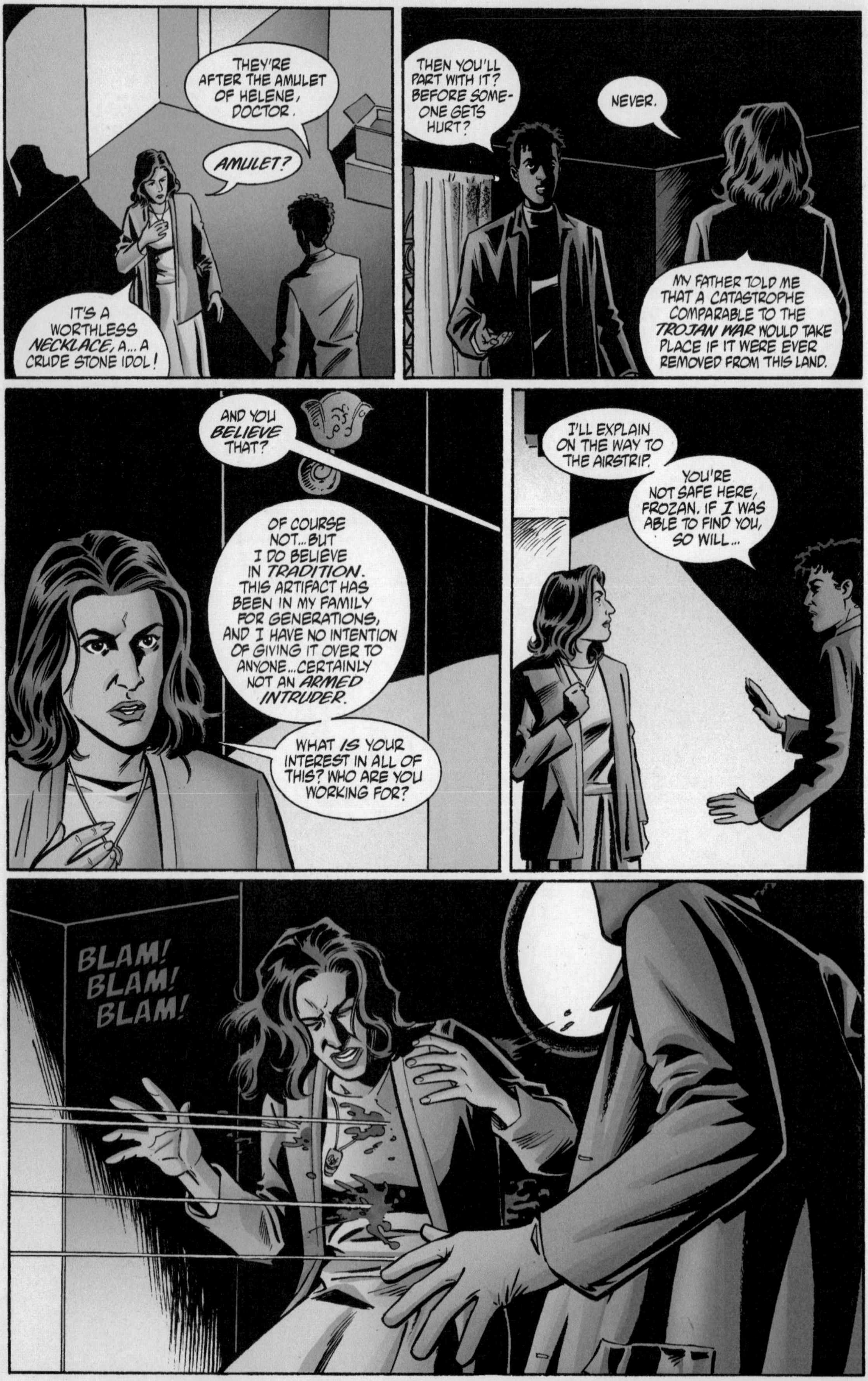
THEY'RE AFTER THE AMULET OF HELENE, DOCTOR.
AMULET?
IT'S A WORTHLESS NECKLACE, A... A CRUDE STONE IDOL!
THEN YOU'LL PART WITH IT? BEFORE SOME-ONE GETS HURT?
NEVER.
MY FATHER TOLD ME THAT A CATASTROPHE COMPARABLE TO THE TROJAN WAR WOULD TAKE PLACE IF IT WERE EVER REMOVED FROM THIS LAND.
AND YOU BELIEVE THAT?
OF COURSE NOT...BUT I DO BELIEVE IN TRADITION. THIS ARTIFACT HAS BEEN IN MY FAMILY FOR GENERATIONS, AND I HAVE NO INTENTION OF GIVING IT OVER TO ANYONE...CERTAINLY NOT AN ARMED INTRUDER.
WHAT IS YOUR INTEREST IN ALL OF THIS? WHO ARE YOU WORKING FOR?
I'LL EXPLAIN ON THE WAY TO THE AIRSTRIP.
YOU'RE NOT SAFE HERE, FROZAN. IF I WAS ABLE TO FIND YOU, SO WILL...
BLAM! BLAM! BLAM!

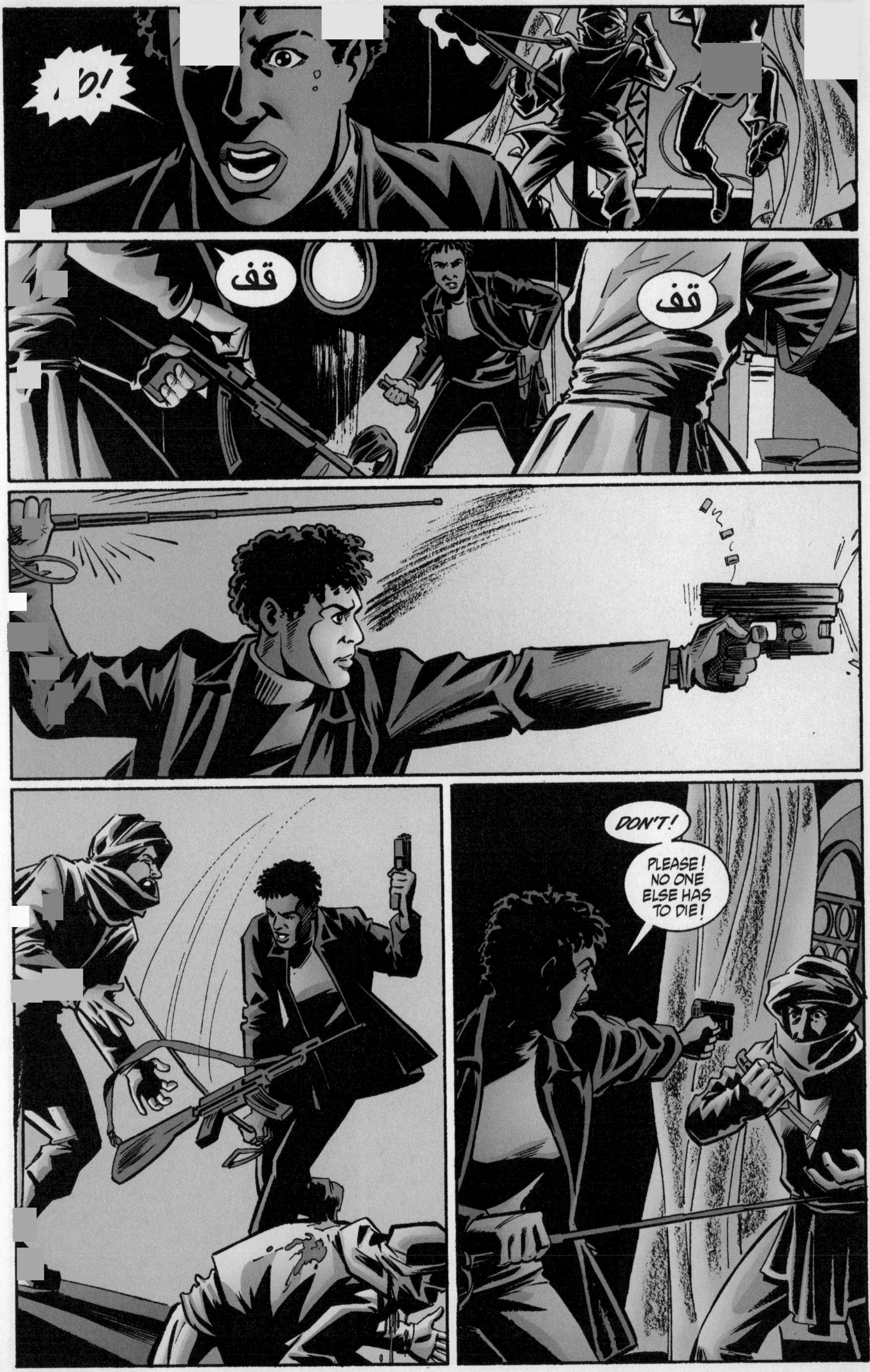
قف
قف
DON'T!
PLEASE! NO ONE ELSE HAS TO DIE!

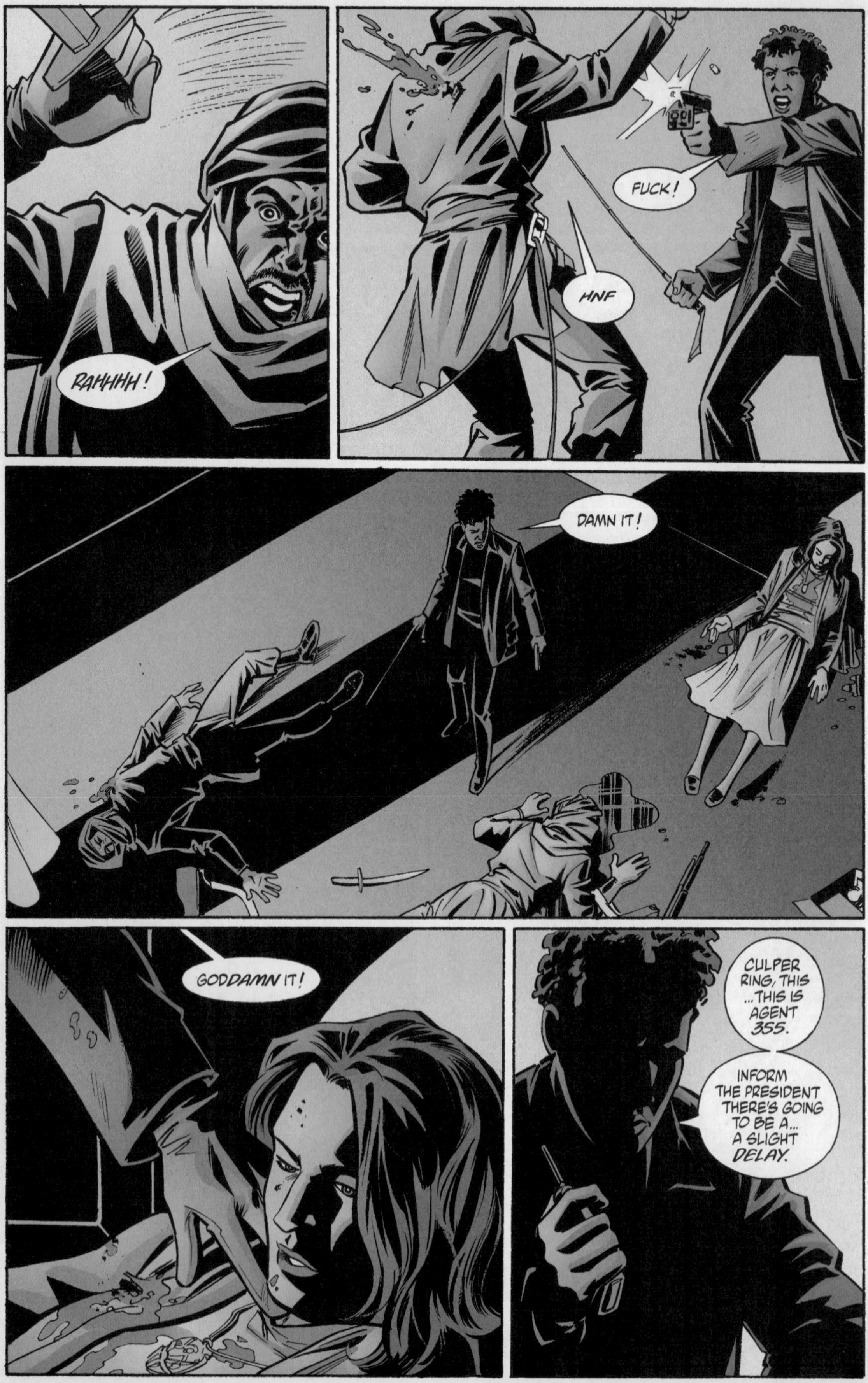
RAHHHH!
FUCK!
HNF
DAMN IT!
GODDAMN IT!
CULPER RING, THIS ...THIS IS AGENT 355.
INFORM THE PRESIDENT THERE'S GOING TO BE A... A SLIGHT DELAY.

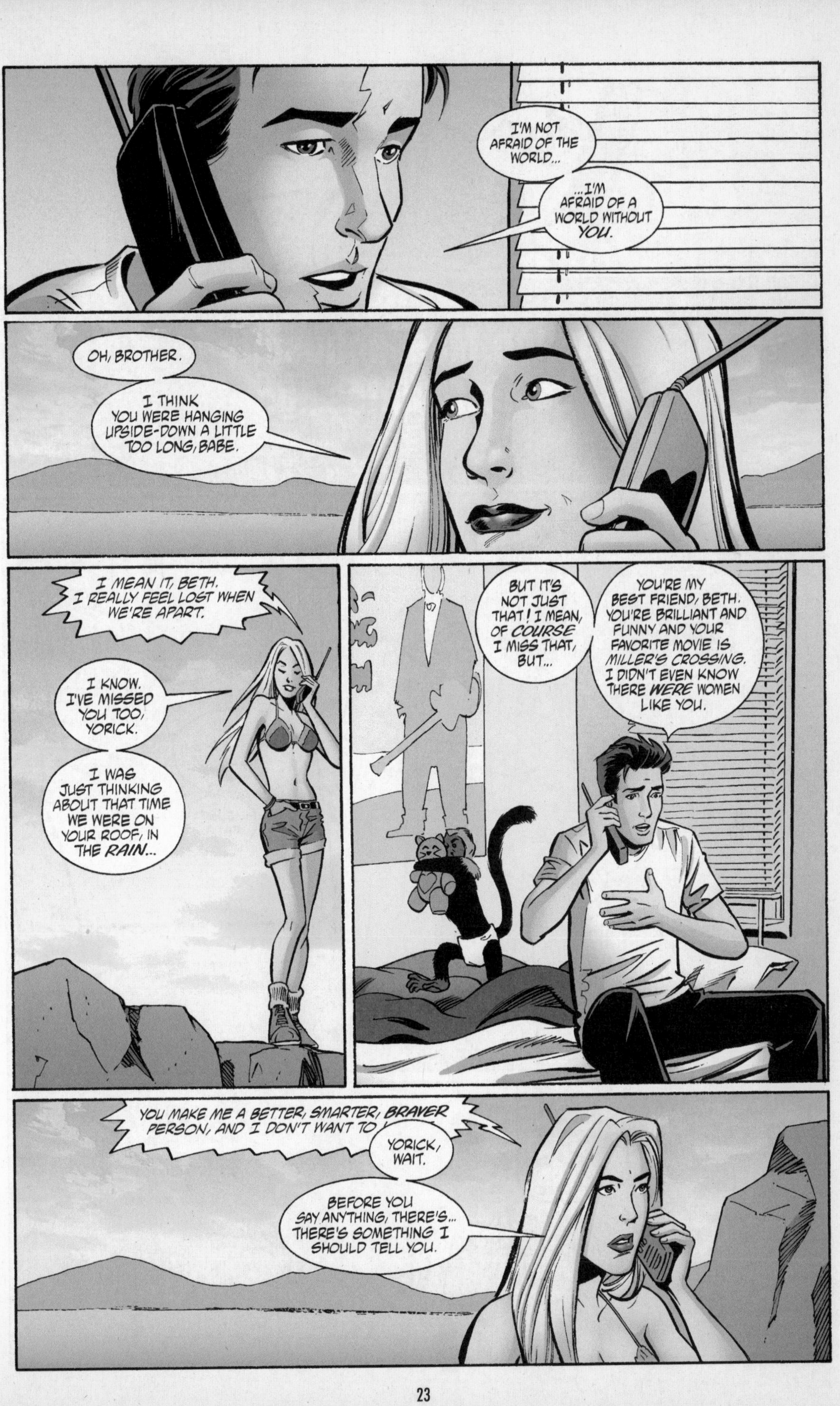
I'M NOT AFRAID OF THE WORLD...
...I'M AFRAID OF A WORLD WITHOUT YOU.
OH, BROTHER.
I THINK YOU WERE HANGING UPSIDE-DOWN A LITTLE TOO LONG, BABE.
I MEAN IT, BETH. I REALLY FEEL LOST WHEN WE'RE APART.
I KNOW. I'VE MISSED YOU TOO, YORICK.
I WAS JUST THINKING ABOUT THAT TIME WE WERE ON YOUR ROOF, IN THE RAIN...
BUT IT'S NOT JUST THAT! I MEAN, OF COURSE I MISS THAT, BUT...
YOU'RE MY BEST FRIEND, BETH. YOU'RE BRILLIANT AND FUNNY AND YOUR FAVORITE MOVIE IS MILLER'S CROSSING. I DIDN'T EVEN KNOW THERE WERE WOMEN LIKE YOU.
YOU MAKE ME A BETTER, SMARTER, BRAVER PERSON, AND I DON'T WANT TO
YORICK, WAIT.
BEFORE YOU SAY ANYTHING, THERE'S... THERE'S SOMETHING I SHOULD TELL YOU.

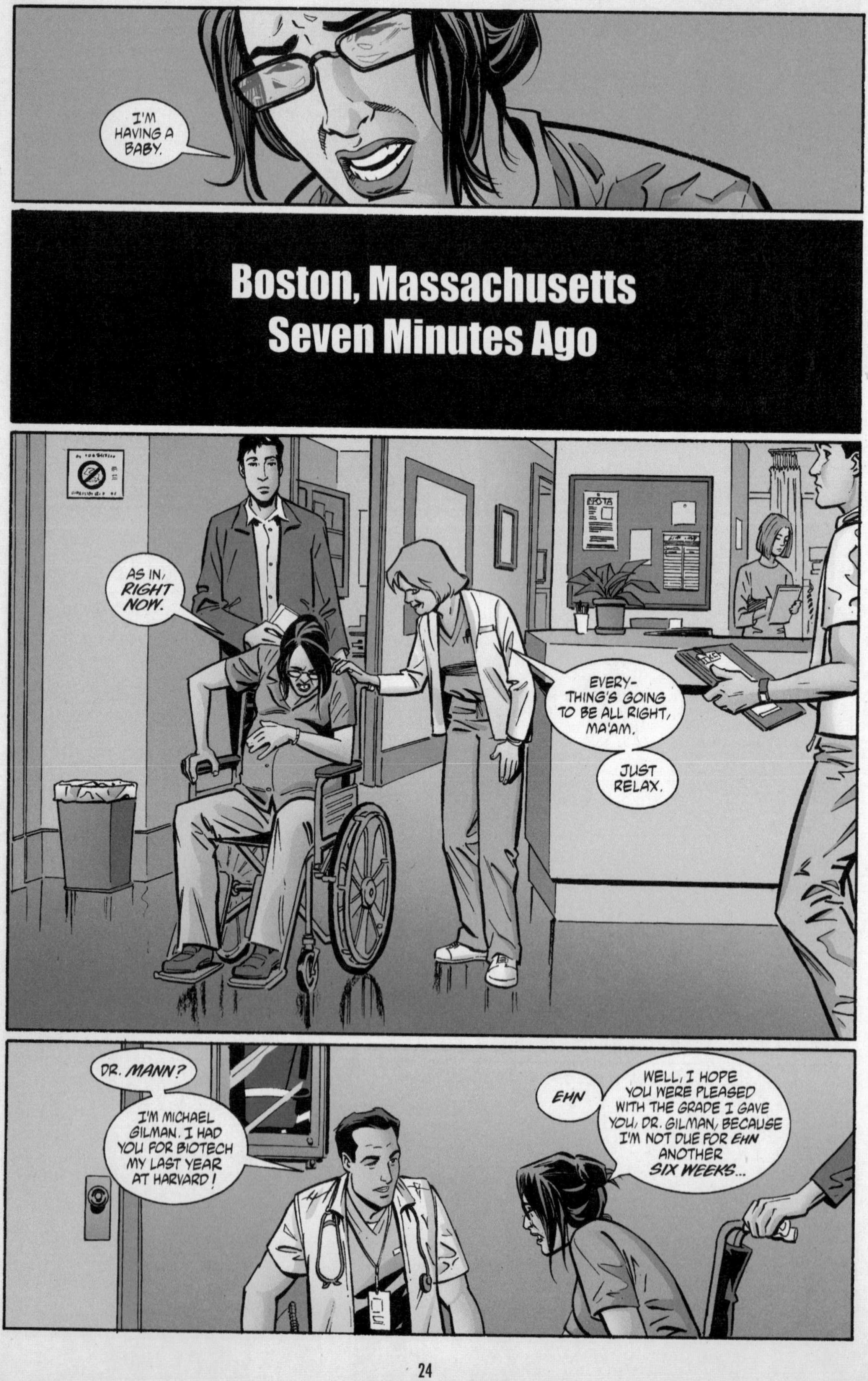
I'M HAVING A BABY.
Boston, Massachusetts
Seven Minutes Ago
AS IN, RIGHT NOW.
EVERY-THING'S GOING TO BE ALL RIGHT, MA'AM.
JUST RELAX.
DR. MANN?
I'M MICHAEL GILMAN. I HAD YOU FOR BIOTECH MY LAST YEAR AT HARVARD!
EHN
WELL, I HOPE YOU WERE PLEASED WITH THE GRADE I GAVE YOU, DR. GILMAN, BECAUSE I'M NOT DUE FOR EHN ANOTHER SIX WEEKS...

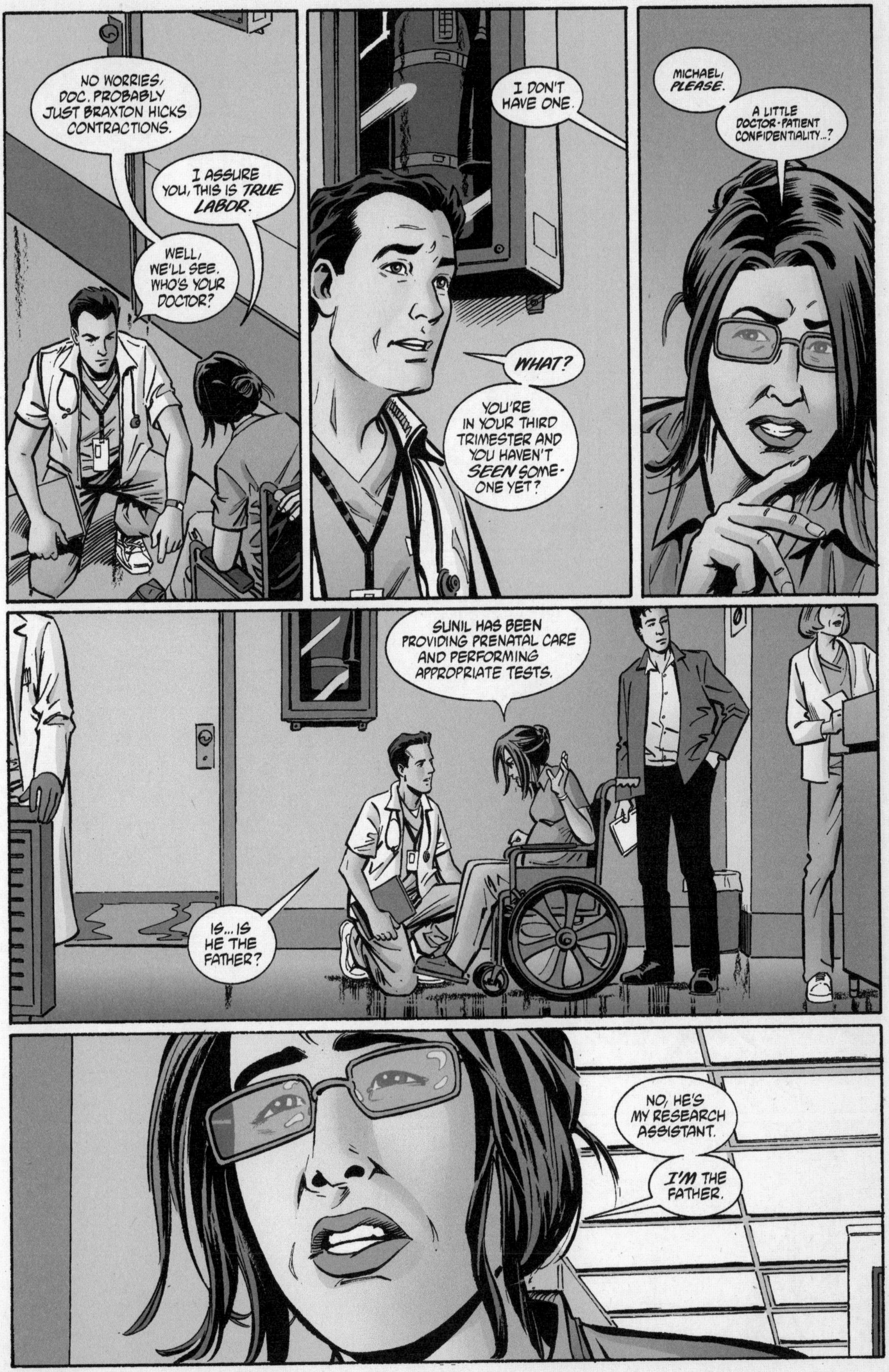

NO WORRIES, DOC. PROBABLY JUST BRAXTON HICKS CONTRACTIONS.
I ASSURE YOU, THIS IS TRUE LABOR.
WELL, WE'LL SEE. WHO'S YOUR DOCTOR?
I DON'T HAVE ONE.
WHAT?
YOU'RE IN YOUR THIRD TRIMESTER AND YOU HAVEN'T SEEN SOME-ONE YET?
MICHAEL, PLEASE.
A LITTLE DOCTOR-PATIENT CONFIDENTIALITY...?
SUNIL HAS BEEN PROVIDING PRENATAL CARE AND PERFORMING APPROPRIATE TESTS.
IS...IS HE THE FATHER?
NO, HE'S MY RESEARCH ASSISTANT.
I'M THE FATHER.

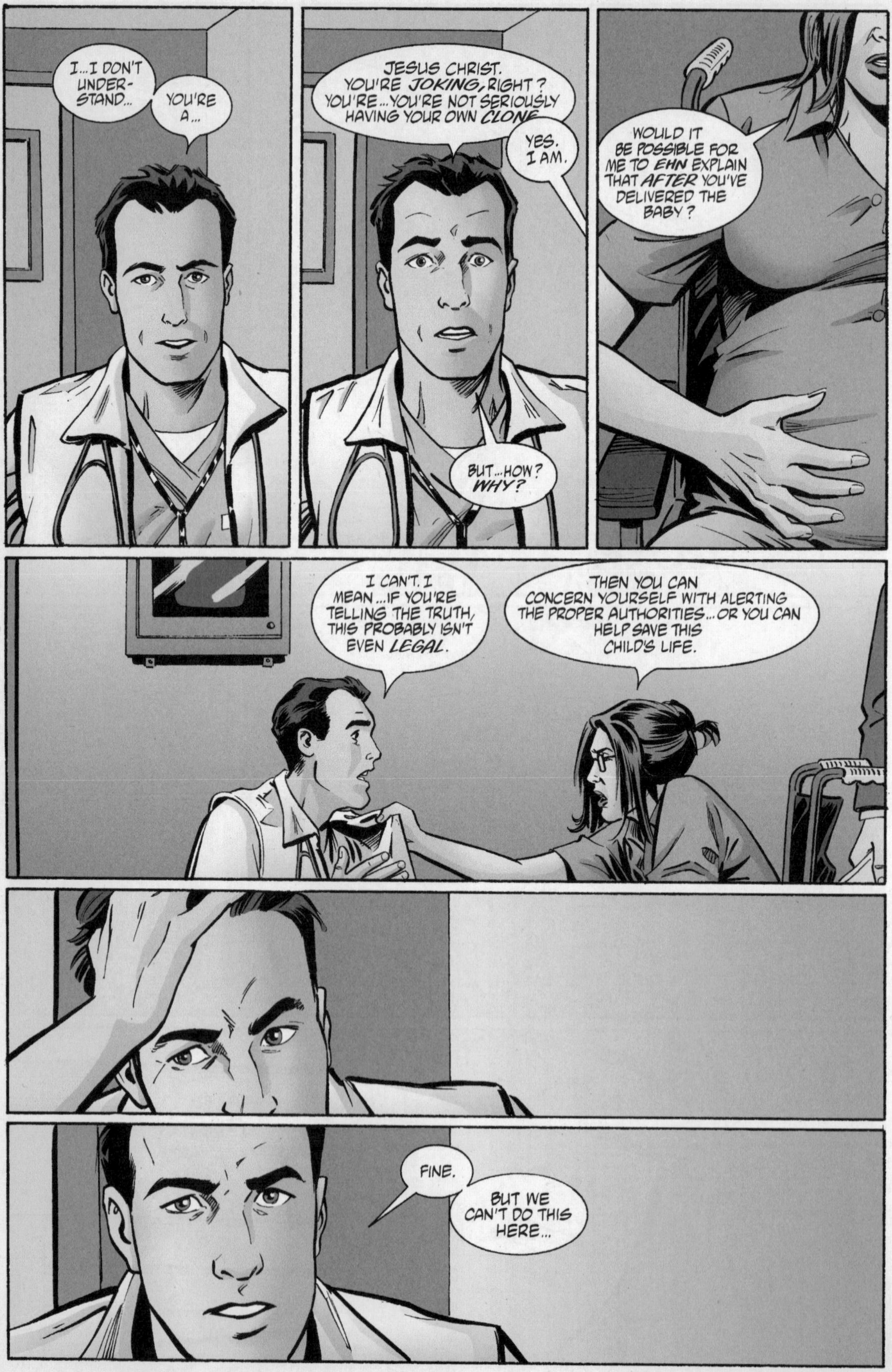
I...I DON'T UNDER-STAND...
YOU'RE A...
JESUS CHRIST. YOU'RE JOKING, RIGHT? YOU'RE...YOU'RE NOT SERIOUSLY HAVING YOUR OWN CLONE
YES. I AM.
BUT...HOW? WHY?
WOULD IT BE POSSIBLE FOR ME TO EHN EXPLAIN THAT AFTER YOU'VE DELIVERED THE BABY?
I CAN'T. I MEAN...IF YOU'RE TELLING THE TRUTH, THIS PROBABLY ISN'T EVEN LEGAL.
THEN YOU CAN CONCERN YOURSELF WITH ALERTING THE PROPER AUTHORITIES...OR YOU CAN HELP SAVE THIS CHILD'S LIFE.
FINE.
BUT WE CAN'T DO THIS HERE...

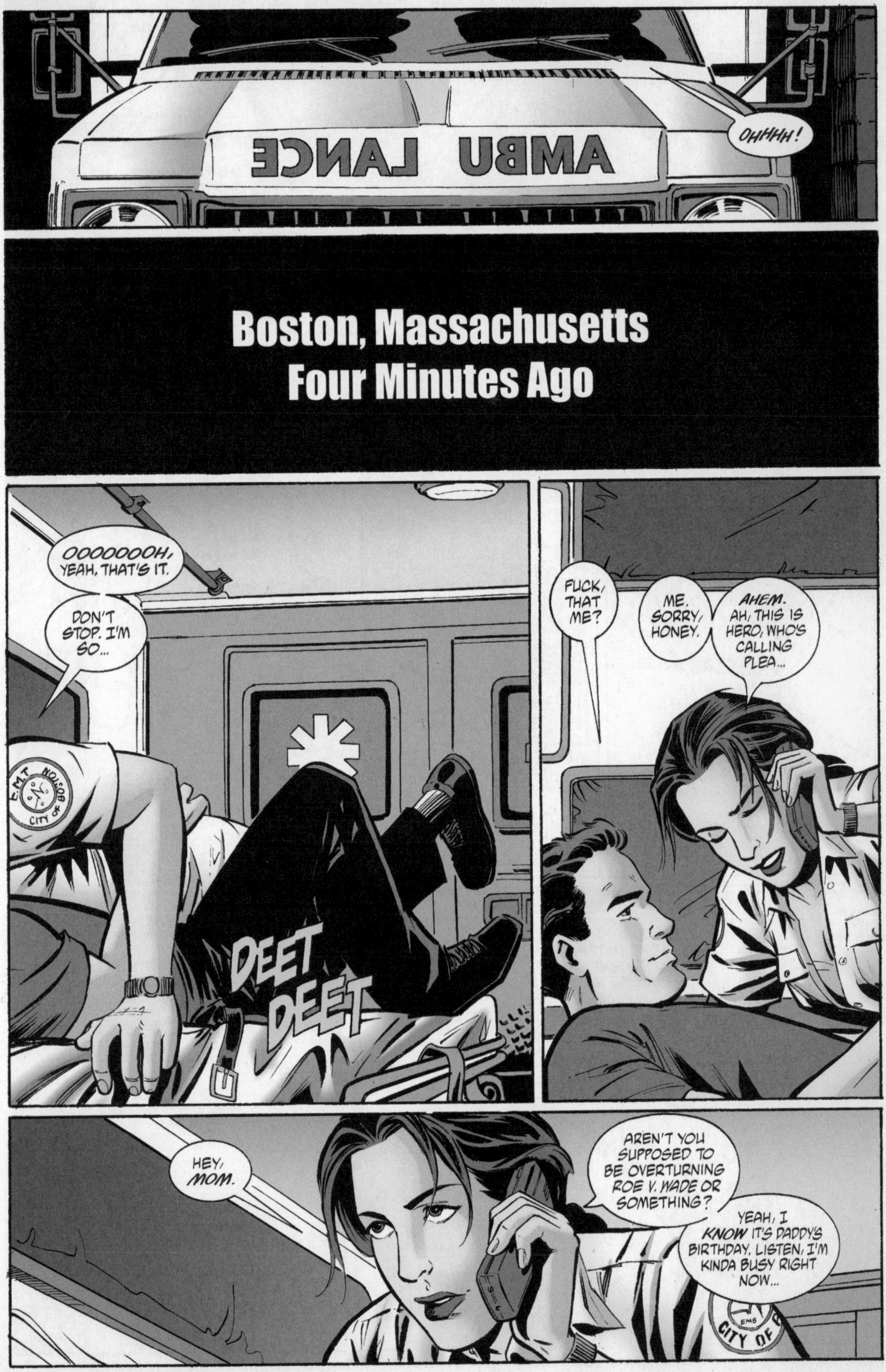
AMBU LANCE
OHHHH!
Boston, Massachusetts
Four Minutes Ago
OOOOOOOH, YEAH, THAT'S IT.
DON'T STOP. I'M SO...
DEET DEET
FUCK, THAT ME?
ME. SORRY, HONEY.
AHEM. AH, THIS IS HERO, WHO'S CALLING PLEA...
HEY, MOM.
AREN'T YOU SUPPOSED TO BE OVERTURNING ROE V. WADE OR SOMETHING?
YEAH, I KNOW IT'S DADDY'S BIRTHDAY. LISTEN, I'M KINDA BUSY RIGHT NOW...

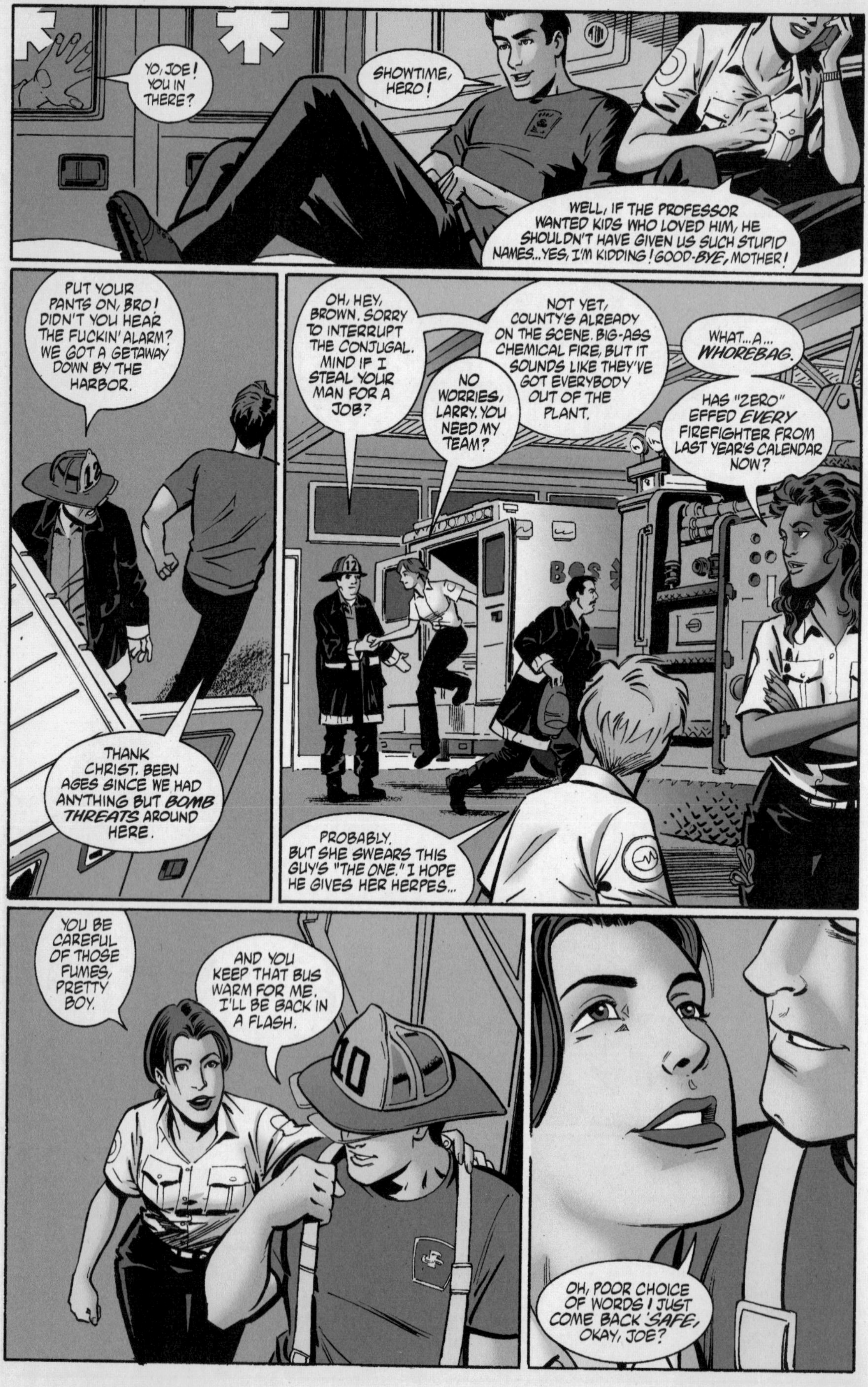
YO, JOE! YOU IN THERE?
SHOWTIME, HERO!
WELL, IF THE PROFESSOR WANTED KIDS WHO LOVED HIM, HE SHOULDN'T HAVE GIVEN US SUCH STUPID NAMES...YES, I'M KIDDING! GOOD-BYE, MOTHER!
PUT YOUR PANTS ON, BRO! DIDN'T YOU HEAR THE FUCKIN' ALARM? WE GOT A GETAWAY DOWN BY THE HARBOR.
THANK CHRIST. BEEN AGES SINCE WE HAD ANYTHING BUT BOMB THREATS AROUND HERE.
OH, HEY, BROWN. SORRY TO INTERRUPT THE CONJUGAL. MIND IF I STEAL YOUR MAN FOR A JOB?
NO WORRIES, LARRY. YOU NEED MY TEAM?
NOT YET, COUNTY'S ALREADY ON THE SCENE. BIG-ASS CHEMICAL FIRE, BUT IT SOUNDS LIKE THEY'VE GOT EVERYBODY OUT OF THE PLANT.
WHAT...A... WHOREBAG.
HAS "ZERO" EFFED EVERY FIREFIGHTER FROM LAST YEAR'S CALENDAR NOW?
PROBABLY. BUT SHE SWEARS THIS GUY'S "THE ONE." I HOPE HE GIVES HER HERPES...
YOU BE CAREFUL OF THOSE FUMES, PRETTY BOY.
AND YOU KEEP THAT BUS WARM FOR ME. I'LL BE BACK IN A FLASH.
OH, POOR CHOICE OF WORDS! JUST COME BACK SAFE, OKAY, JOE?

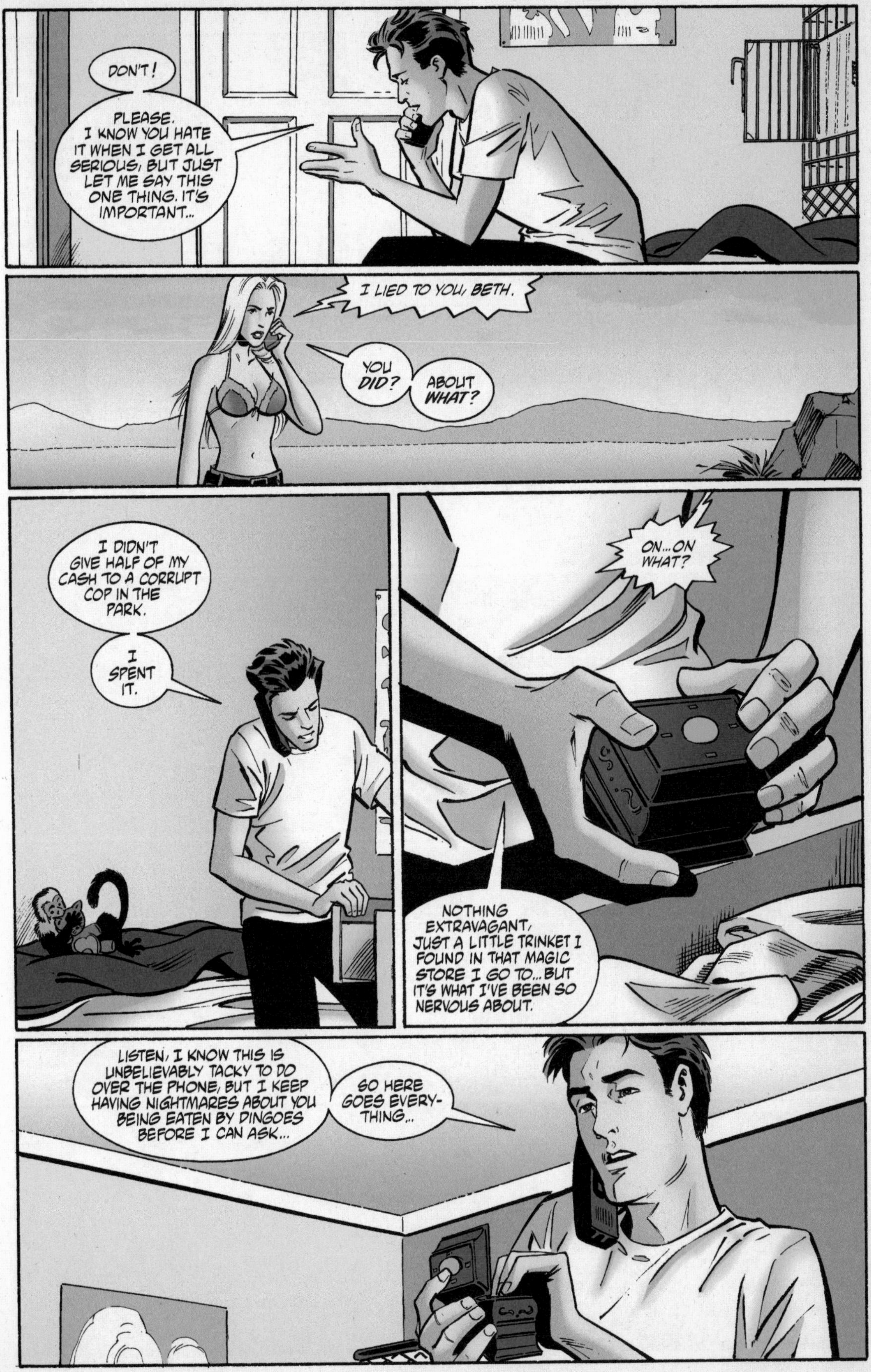
DON'T!
PLEASE. I KNOW YOU HATE IT WHEN I GET ALL SERIOUS, BUT JUST LET ME SAY THIS ONE THING. IT'S IMPORTANT...
I LIED TO YOU, BETH.
YOU *DID*?
ABOUT *WHAT*?
I DIDN'T GIVE HALF OF MY CASH TO A CORRUPT COP IN THE PARK.
I SPENT IT.
ON...ON WHAT?
NOTHING EXTRAVAGANT, JUST A LITTLE TRINKET I FOUND IN THAT MAGIC STORE I GO TO...BUT IT'S WHAT I'VE BEEN SO NERVOUS ABOUT.
LISTEN, I KNOW THIS IS UNBELIEVABLY TACKY TO DO OVER THE PHONE, BUT I KEEP HAVING NIGHTMARES ABOUT YOU BEING EATEN BY DINGOES BEFORE I CAN ASK...
SO HERE GOES EVERY-THING...

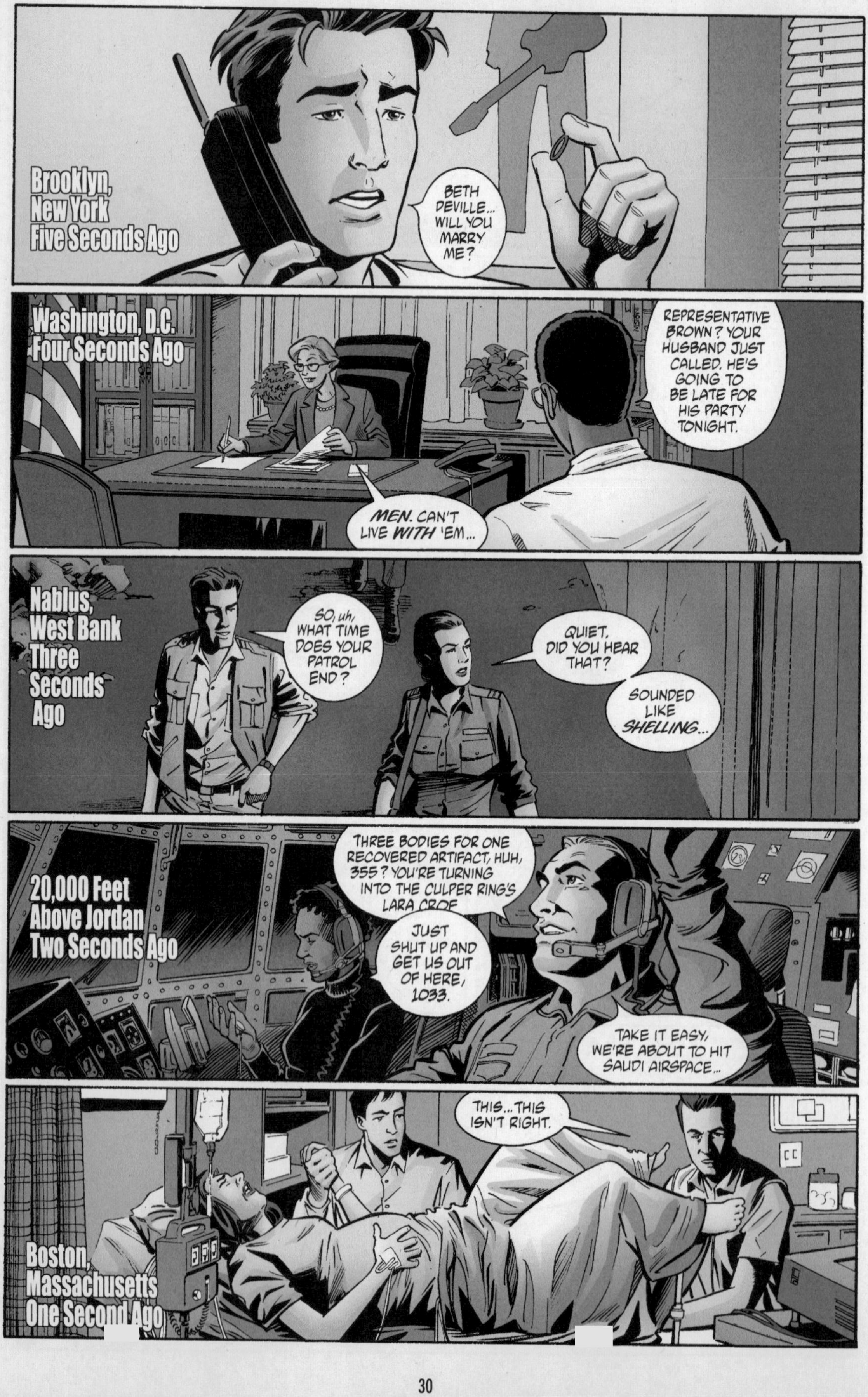
Brooklyn, New York Five Seconds Ago
BETH DEVILLE... WILL YOU MARRY ME?
Washington, D.C. Four Seconds Ago
REPRESENTATIVE BROWN? YOUR HUSBAND JUST CALLED. HE'S GOING TO BE LATE FOR HIS PARTY TONIGHT.
MEN. CAN'T LIVE WITH 'EM...
Nablus, West Bank Three Seconds Ago
SO, uh, WHAT TIME DOES YOUR PATROL END?
QUIET. DID YOU HEAR THAT?
SOUNDED LIKE SHELLING...
20,000 Feet Above Jordan Two Seconds Ago
THREE BODIES FOR ONE RECOVERED ARTIFACT, HUH, 355? YOU'RE TURNING INTO THE CULPER RING'S LARA CROF
JUST SHUT UP AND GET US OUT OF HERE, 1033.
TAKE IT EASY, WE'RE ABOUT TO HIT SAUDI AIRSPACE...
Boston, Massachusetts One Second Ago
THIS... THIS ISN'T RIGHT.

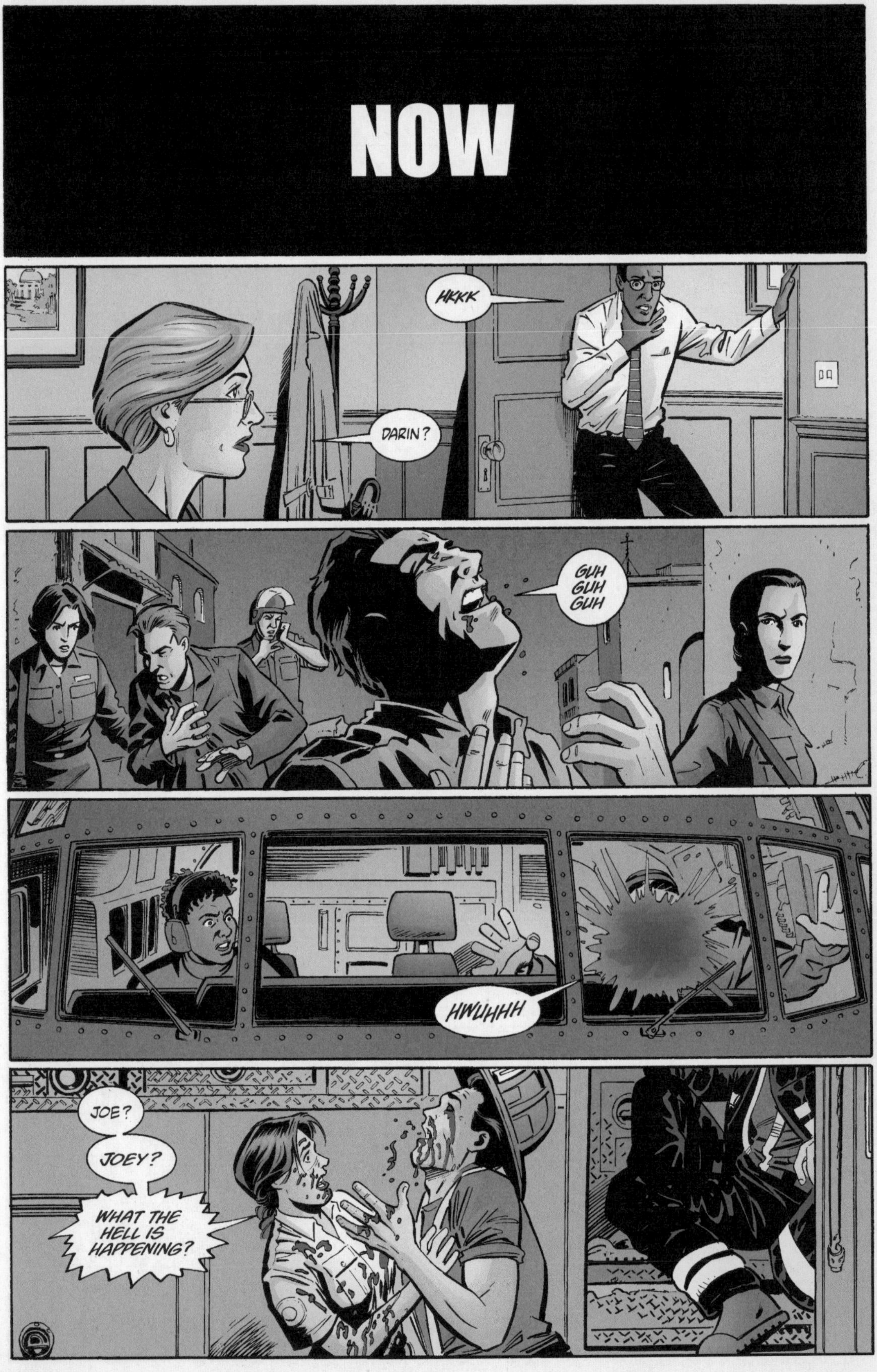
NOW
HKKK
DARIN?
GUH GUH GUH
HWUHHH
JOE?
JOEY?
WHAT THE HELL IS HAPPENING?

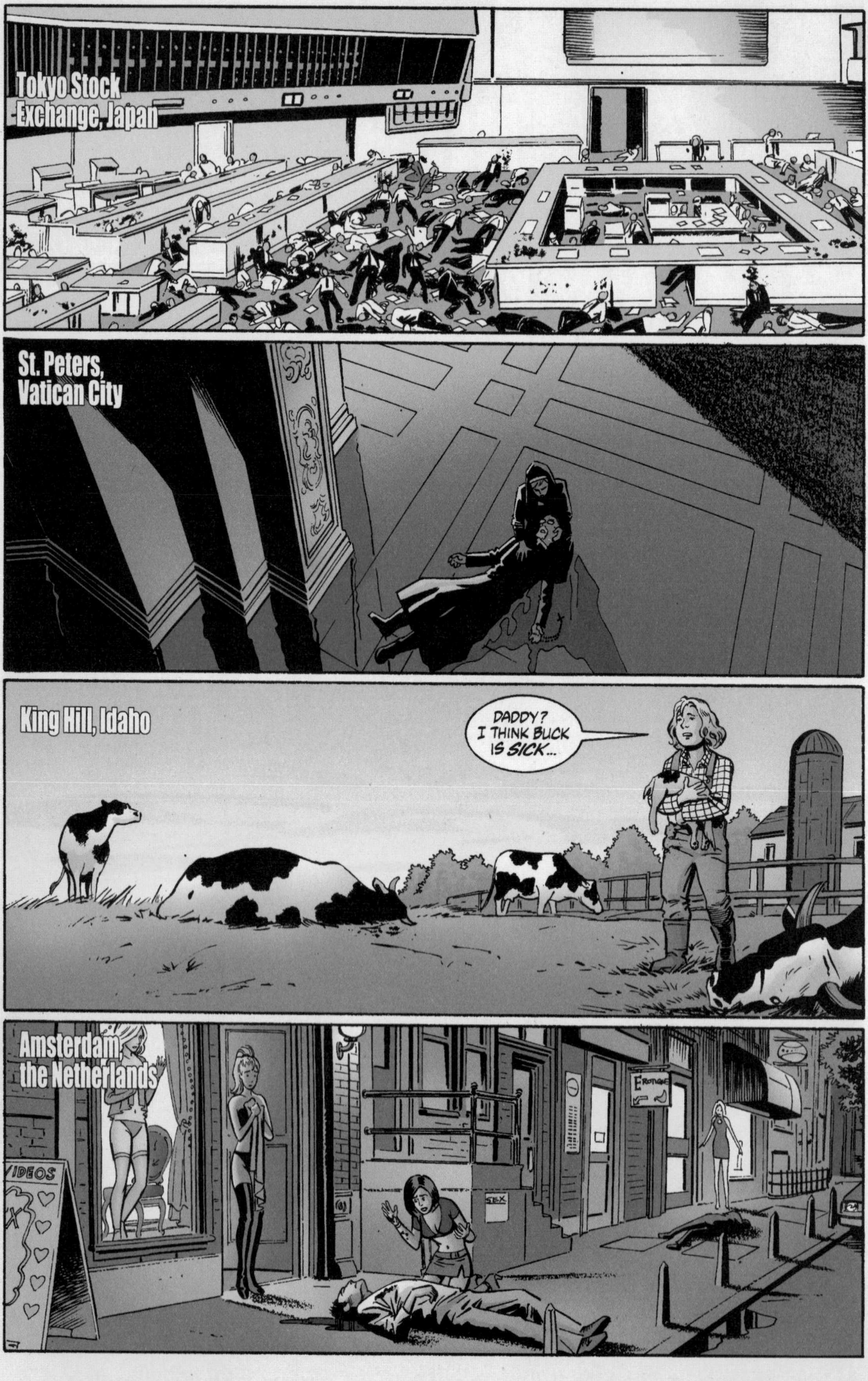
Tokyo Stock Exchange, Japan
St. Peters, Vatican City
King Hill, Idaho
DADDY? I THINK BUCK IS SICK...
Amsterdam, the Netherlands
VIDEOS

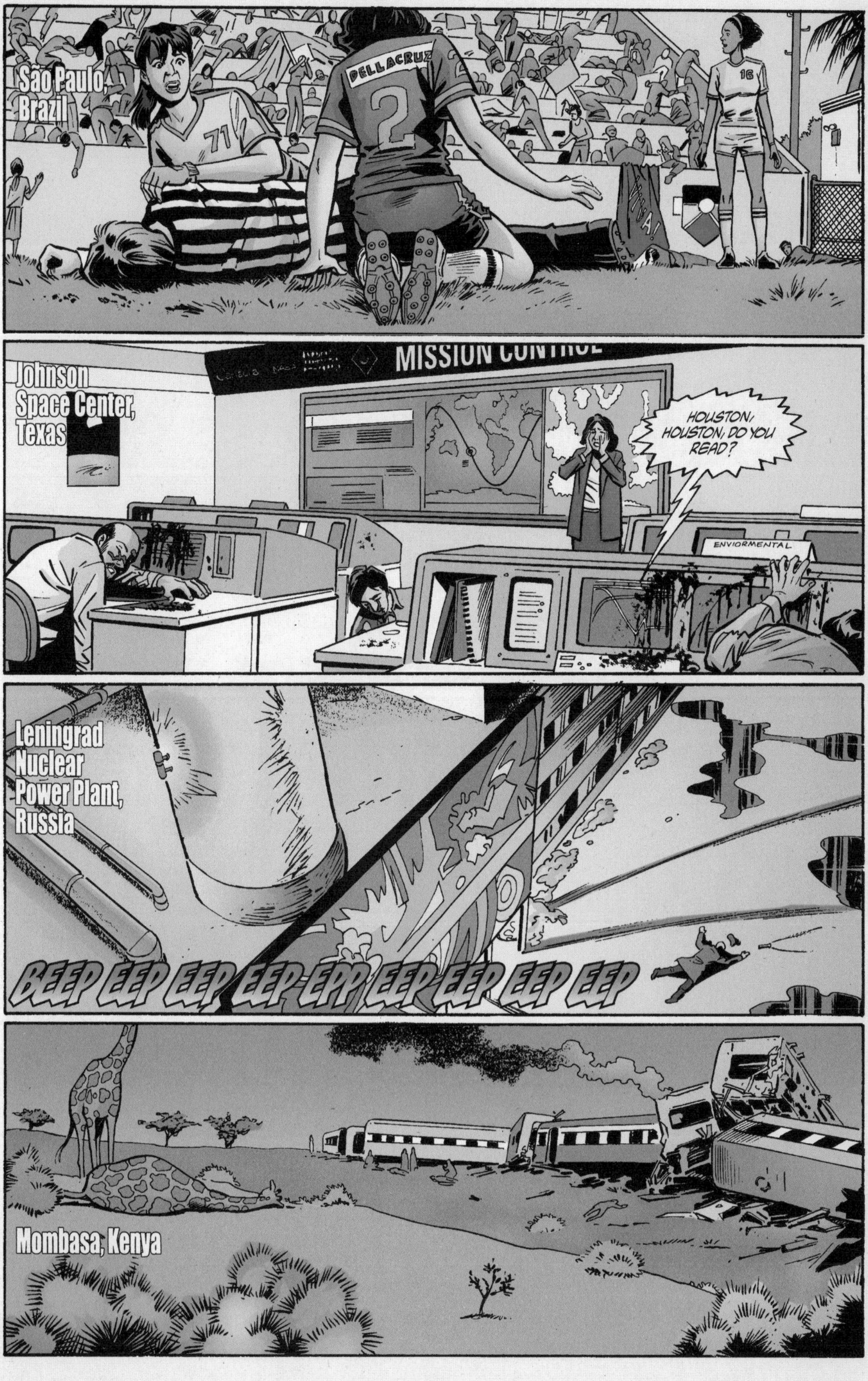
São Paulo, Brazil
PELLACRUZ
Johnson Space Center, Texas
MISSION CONTROL
HOUSTON, HOUSTON, DO YOU READ?
ENVIORMENTAL
Leningrad Nuclear Power Plant, Russia
BEEP EEP EEP EEP-EPP EEP EEP EEP EEP
Mombasa, Kenya

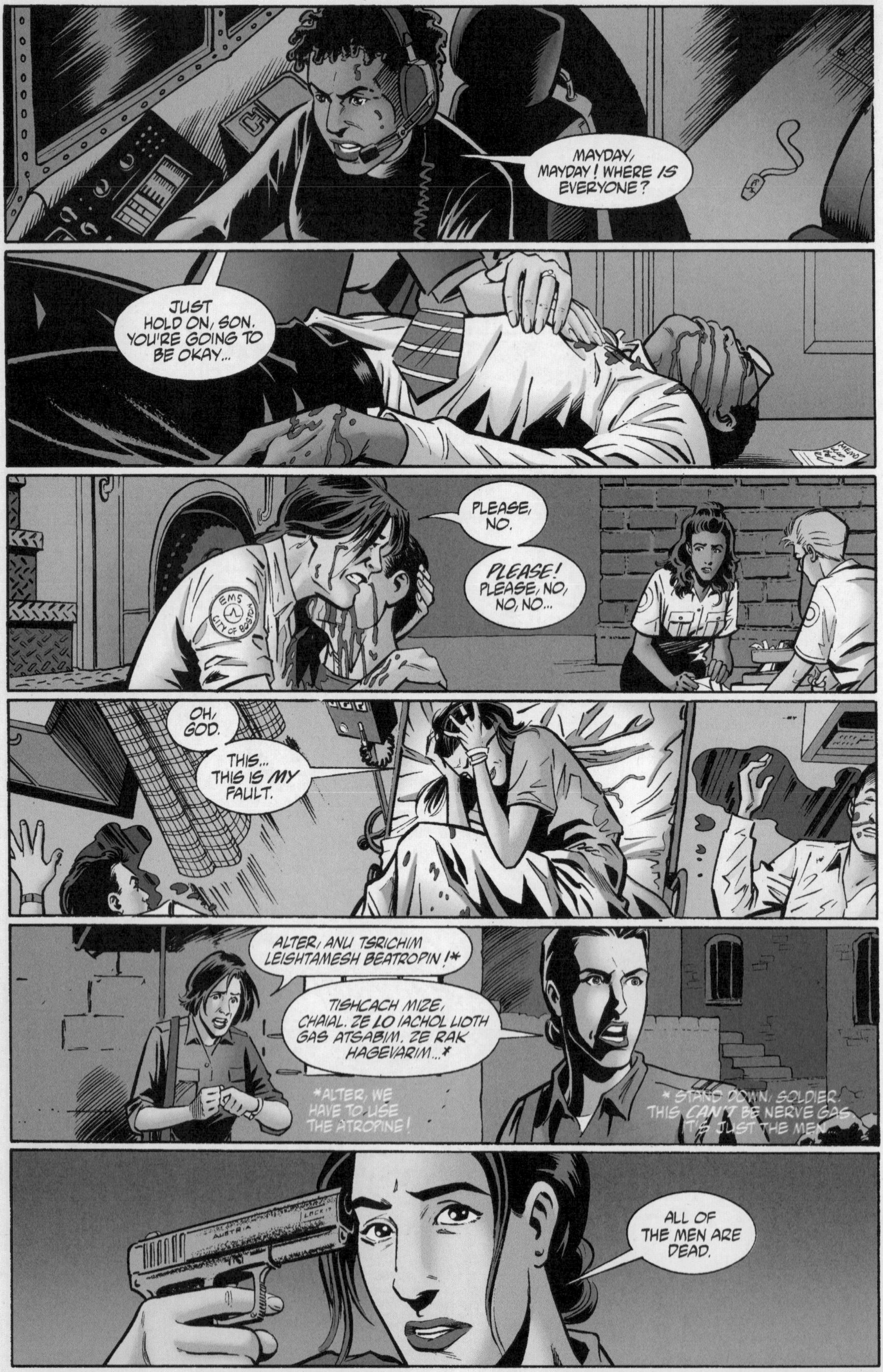
MAYDAY, MAYDAY! WHERE IS EVERYONE?
JUST HOLD ON, SON. YOU'RE GOING TO BE OKAY...
PLEASE, NO.
PLEASE! PLEASE, NO, NO, NO...
OH, GOD.
THIS... THIS IS MY FAULT.
ALTER, ANU TSRICHIM LEISHTAMESH BEATROPIN!*
TISHCACH MIZE, CHAIAL. ZE LO IACHOL LIOTH GAS ATSABIM. ZE RAK HAGEVARIM...*
*ALTER, WE HAVE TO USE THE ATROPINE!
* STAND DOWN, SOLDIER. THIS CAN'T BE NERVE GAS. IT'S JUST THE MEN...
ALL OF THE MEN ARE DEAD.

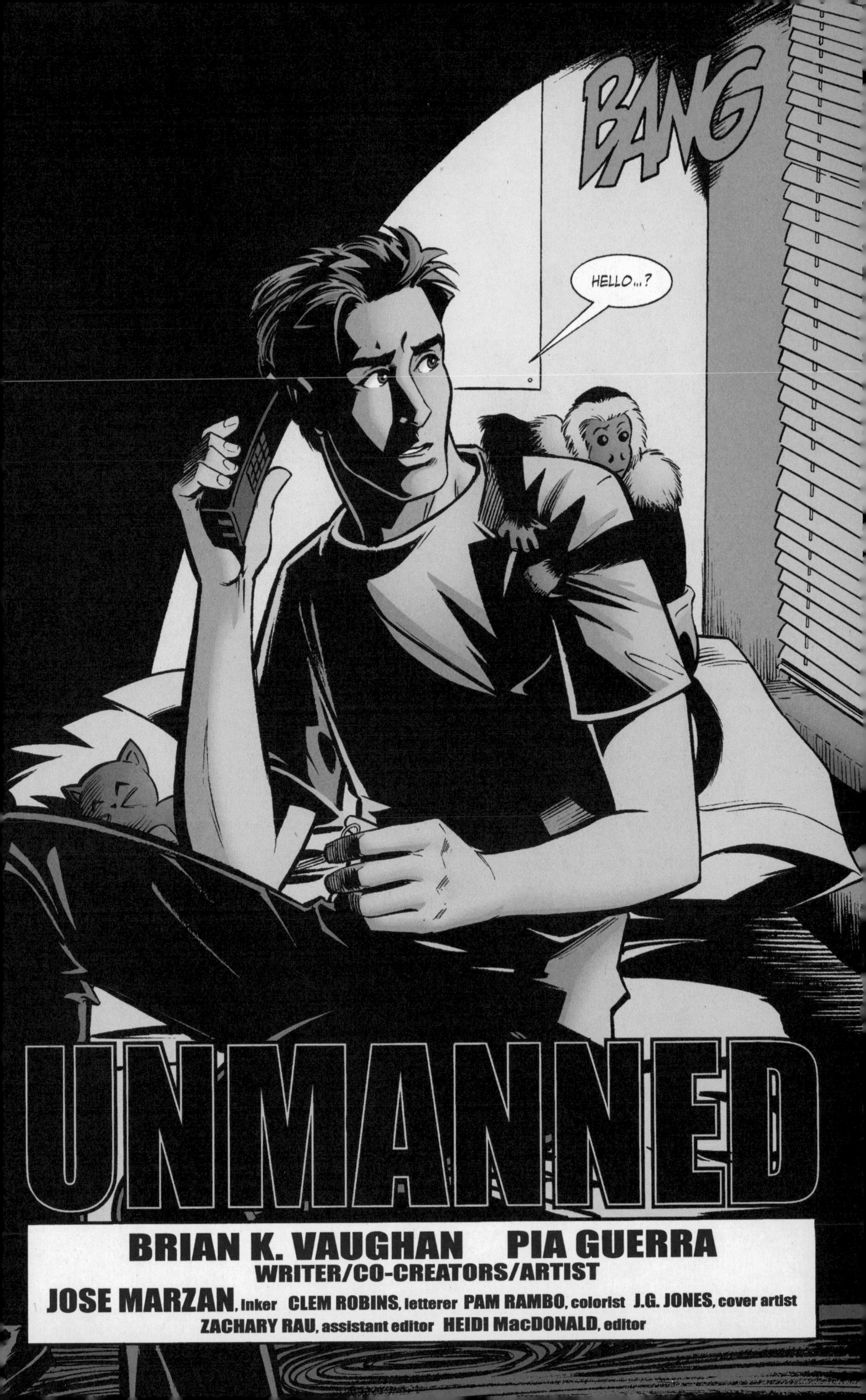
BANG
HELLO...?
UNMANNED
BRIAN K. VAUGHAN PIA GUERRA
WRITER/CO-CREATORS/ARTIST
JOSE MARZAN, inker CLEM ROBINS, letterer PAM RAMBO, colorist J.G. JONES, cover artist
ZACHARY RAU, assistant editor HEIDI MacDONALD, editor

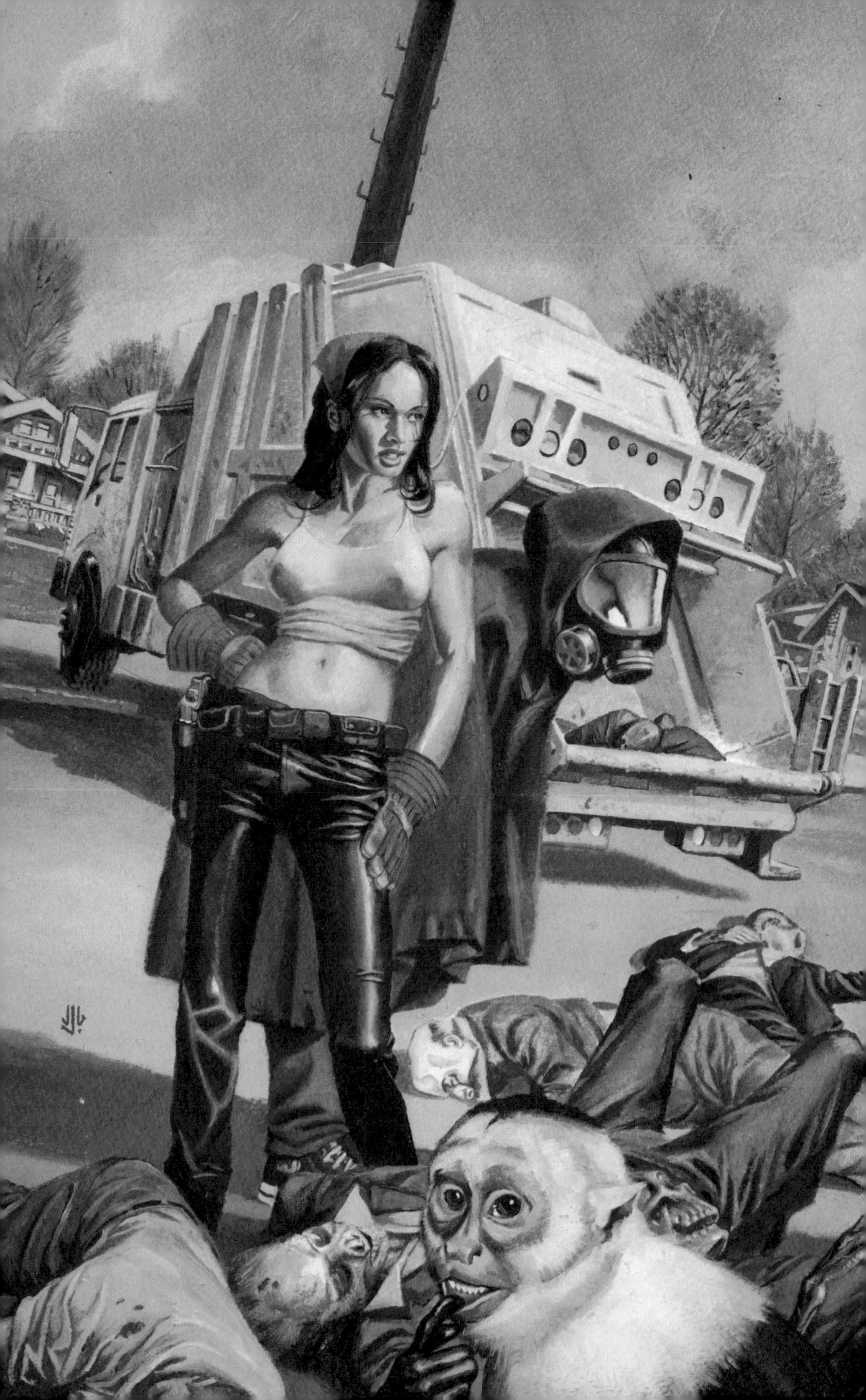

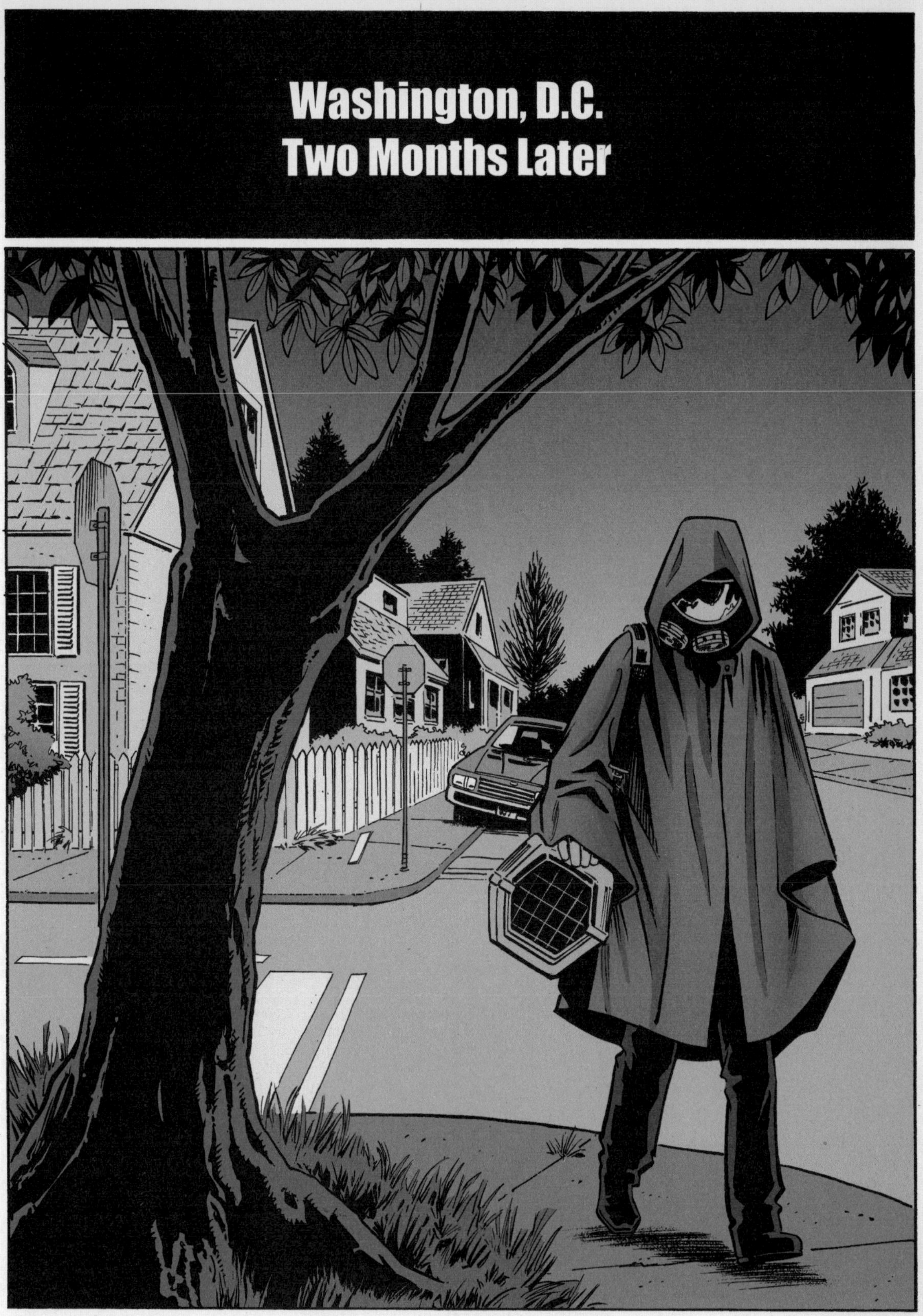
Washington, D.C.
Two Months Later

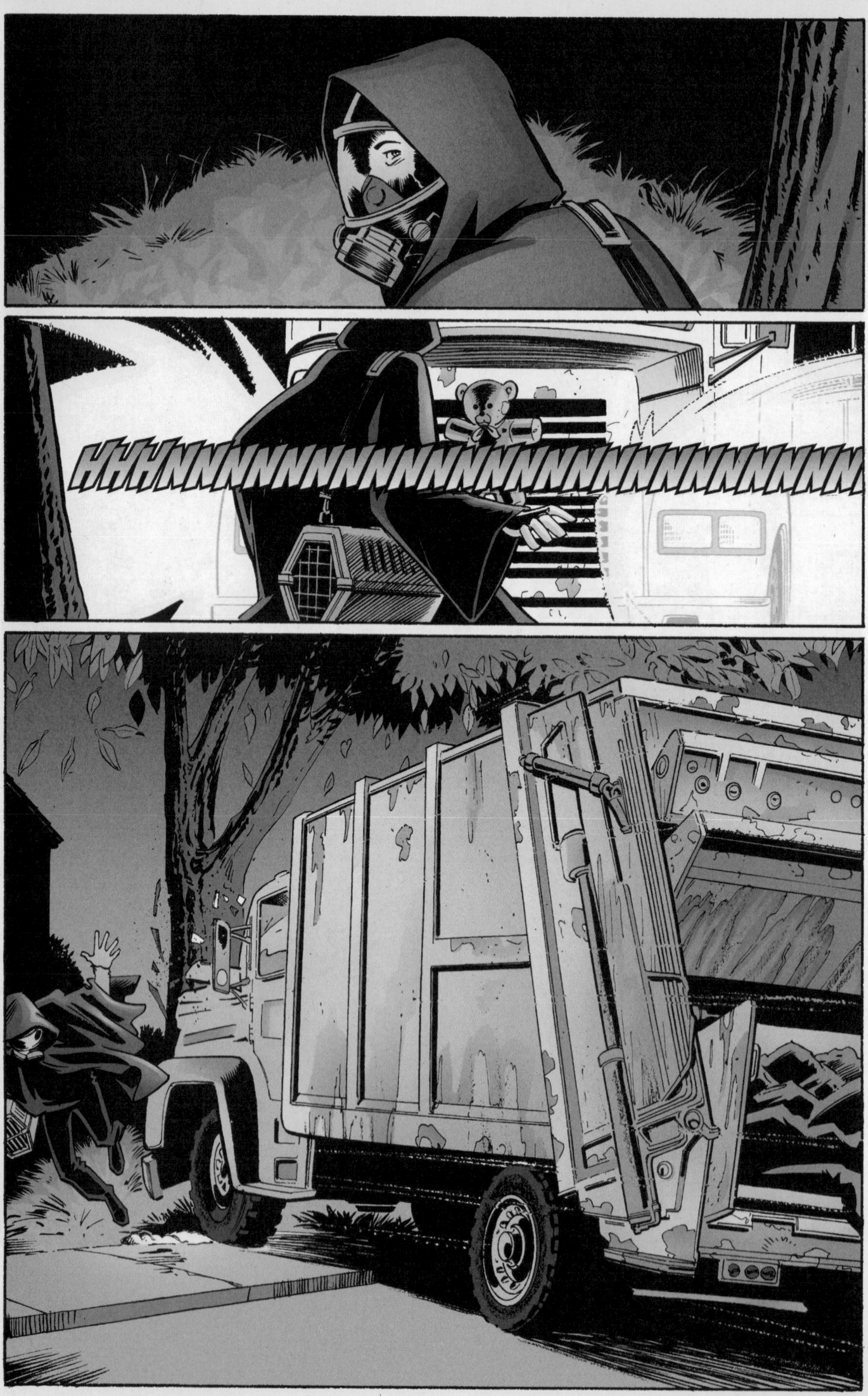
HHHNNNNNNNNNNNNNNNNNNNNNNNNNNN

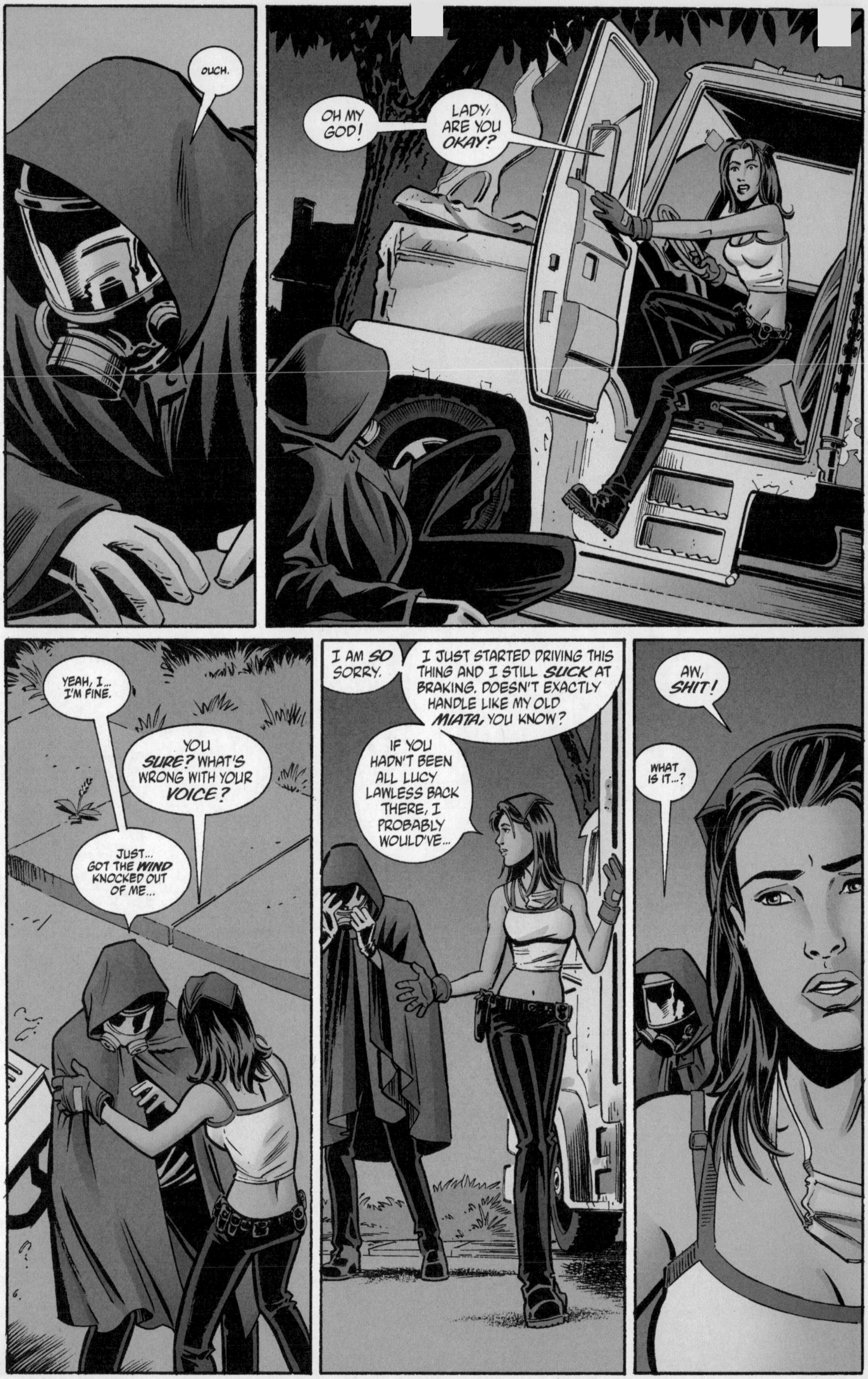
OUCH.
OH MY GOD!
LADY, ARE YOU OKAY?
YEAH, I... I'M FINE.
YOU SURE? WHAT'S WRONG WITH YOUR VOICE?
JUST... GOT THE WIND KNOCKED OUT OF ME...
I AM SO SORRY.
I JUST STARTED DRIVING THIS THING AND I STILL SUCK AT BRAKING. DOESN'T EXACTLY HANDLE LIKE MY OLD MIATA, YOU KNOW?
IF YOU HADN'T BEEN ALL LUCY LAWLESS BACK THERE, I PROBABLY WOULD'VE...
AW, SHIT!
WHAT IS IT...?

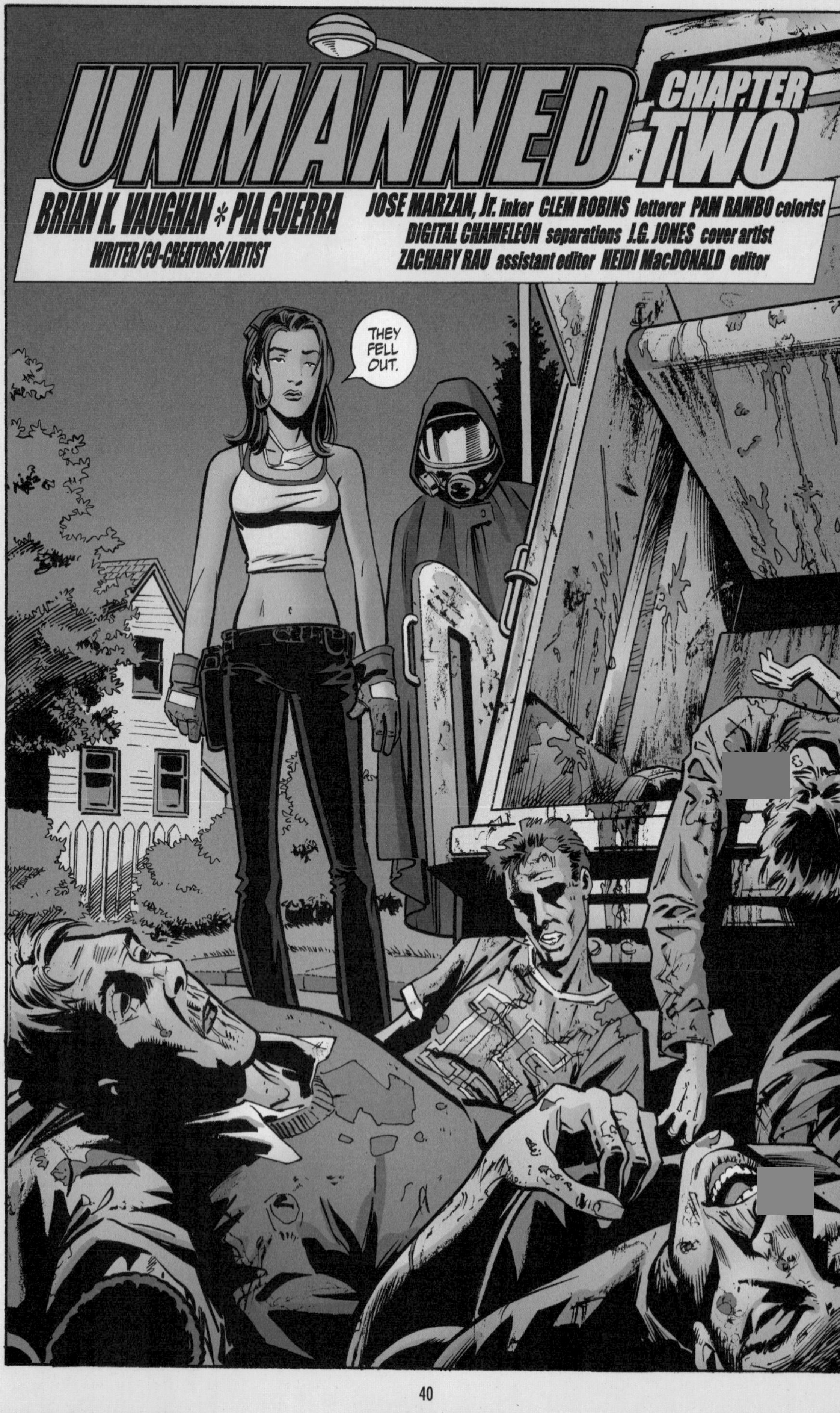
UNMANNED
CHAPTER TWO
BRIAN K. VAUGHAN * PIA GUERRA
WRITER/CO-CREATORS/ARTIST
JOSE MARZAN, Jr. inker CLEM ROBINS letterer PAM RAMBO colorist
DIGITAL CHAMELEON separations J.G. JONES cover artist
ZACHARY RAU assistant editor HEIDI MacDONALD editor
THEY FELL OUT.

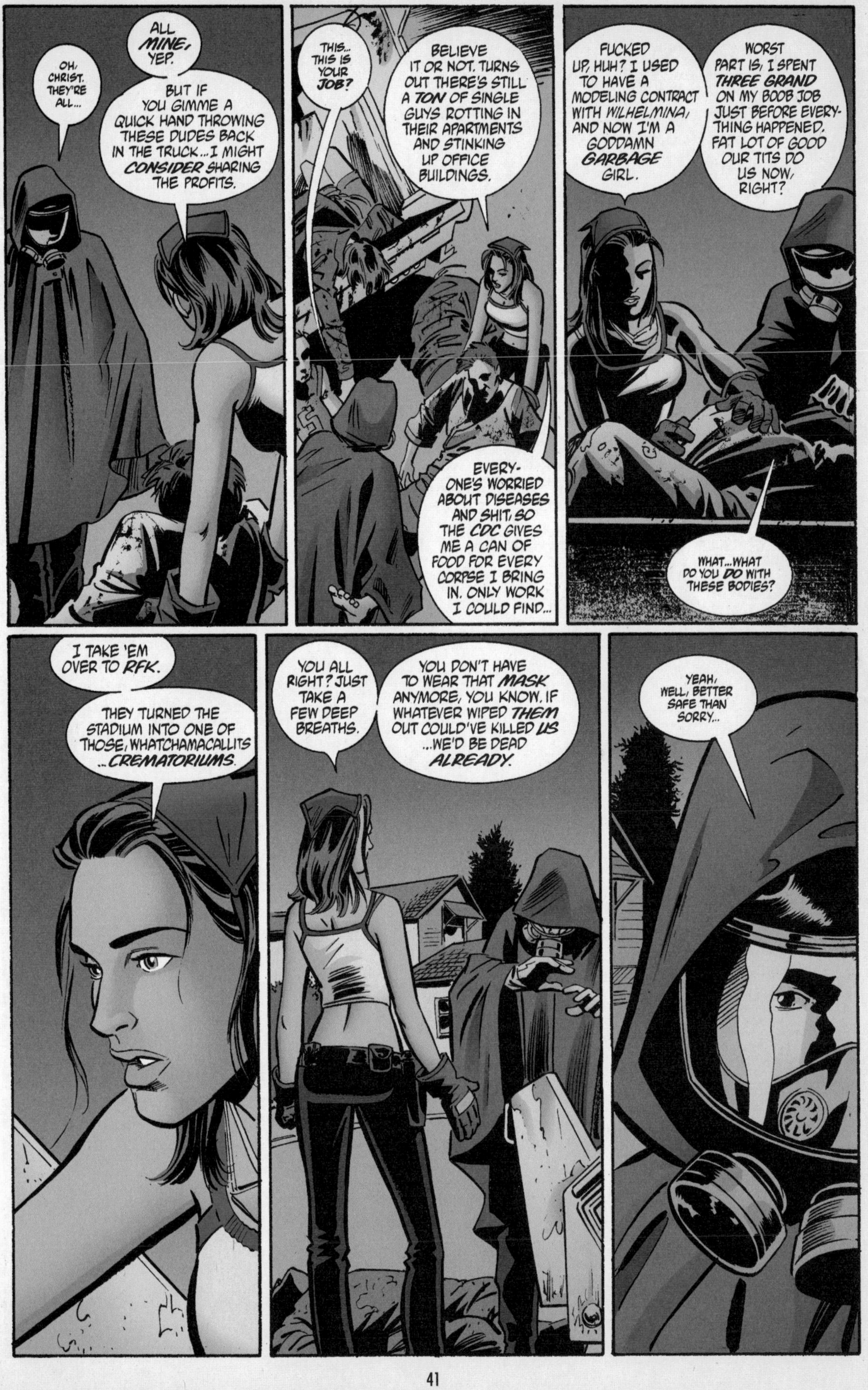
OH, CHRIST. THEY'RE ALL...
ALL MINE, YEP.
BUT IF YOU GIMME A QUICK HAND THROWING THESE DUDES BACK IN THE TRUCK... I MIGHT CONSIDER SHARING THE PROFITS.
THIS... THIS IS YOUR JOB?
BELIEVE IT OR NOT. TURNS OUT THERE'S STILL A TON OF SINGLE GUYS ROTTING IN THEIR APARTMENTS AND STINKING UP OFFICE BUILDINGS.
EVERY-ONE'S WORRIED ABOUT DISEASES AND SHIT, SO THE CDC GIVES ME A CAN OF FOOD FOR EVERY CORPSE I BRING IN. ONLY WORK I COULD FIND...
FUCKED UP, HUH? I USED TO HAVE A MODELING CONTRACT WITH WILHELMINA, AND NOW I'M A GODDAMN GARBAGE GIRL.
WORST PART IS, I SPENT THREE GRAND ON MY BOOB JOB JUST BEFORE EVERY-THING HAPPENED. FAT LOT OF GOOD OUR TITS DO US NOW, RIGHT?
WHAT... WHAT DO YOU DO WITH THESE BODIES?
I TAKE 'EM OVER TO RFK.
THEY TURNED THE STADIUM INTO ONE OF THOSE, WHATCHAMACALLITS ...CREMATORIUMS.
YOU ALL RIGHT? JUST TAKE A FEW DEEP BREATHS.
YOU DON'T HAVE TO WEAR THAT MASK ANYMORE, YOU KNOW. IF WHATEVER WIPED THEM OUT COULD'VE KILLED US ...WE'D BE DEAD ALREADY.
YEAH, WELL, BETTER SAFE THAN SORRY...

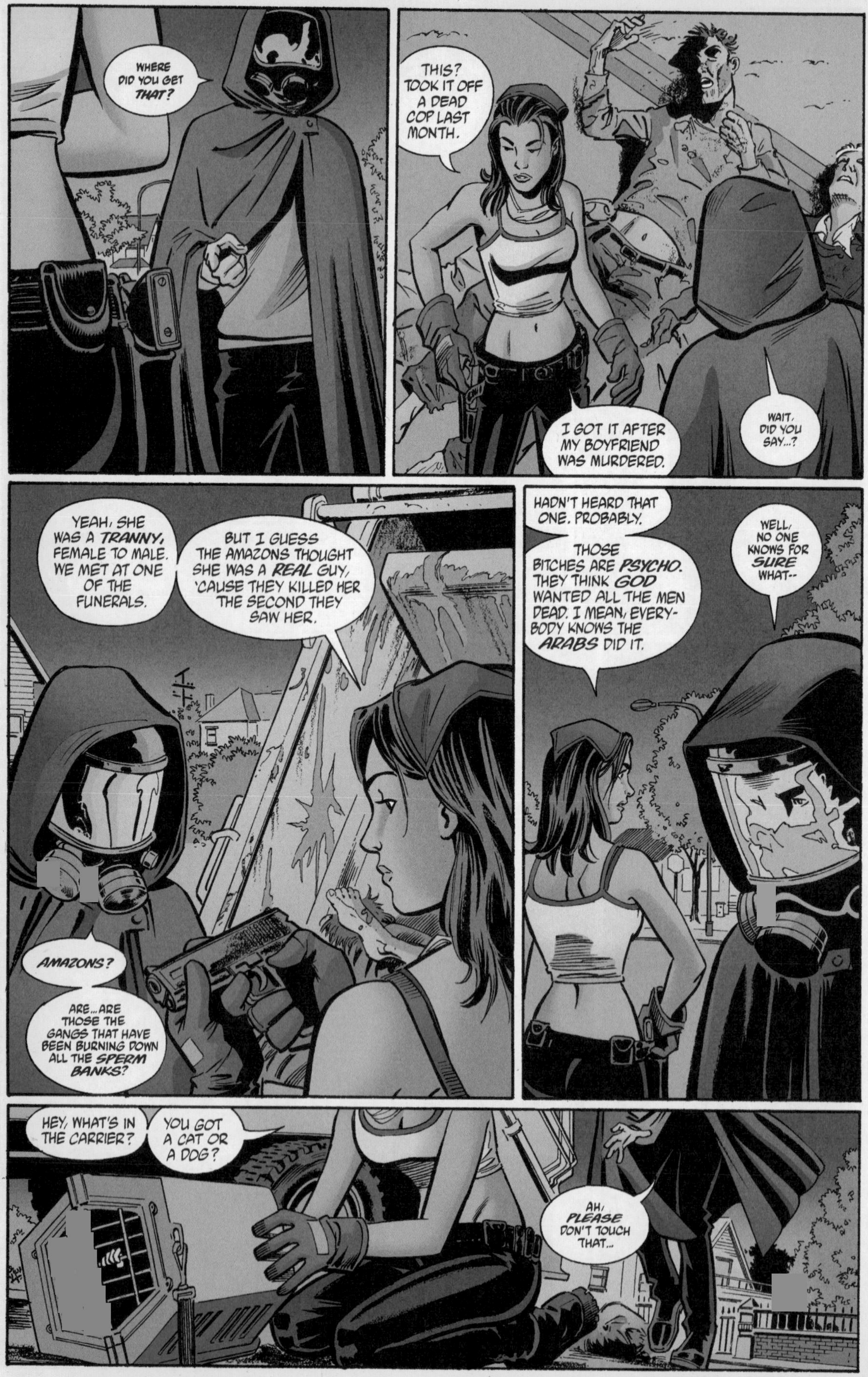
WHERE DID YOU GET THAT?
THIS? TOOK IT OFF A DEAD COP LAST MONTH.
I GOT IT AFTER MY BOYFRIEND WAS MURDERED.
WAIT. DID YOU SAY...?
YEAH, SHE WAS A TRANNY, FEMALE TO MALE. WE MET AT ONE OF THE FUNERALS.
BUT I GUESS THE AMAZONS THOUGHT SHE WAS A REAL GUY, 'CAUSE THEY KILLED HER THE SECOND THEY SAW HER.
AMAZONS?
ARE...ARE THOSE THE GANGS THAT HAVE BEEN BURNING DOWN ALL THE SPERM BANKS?
HADN'T HEARD THAT ONE. PROBABLY.
THOSE BITCHES ARE PSYCHO. THEY THINK GOD WANTED ALL THE MEN DEAD. I MEAN, EVERYBODY KNOWS THE ARABS DID IT.
WELL, NO ONE KNOWS FOR SURE WHAT--
HEY, WHAT'S IN THE CARRIER?
YOU GOT A CAT OR A DOG?
AH, PLEASE DON'T TOUCH THAT...

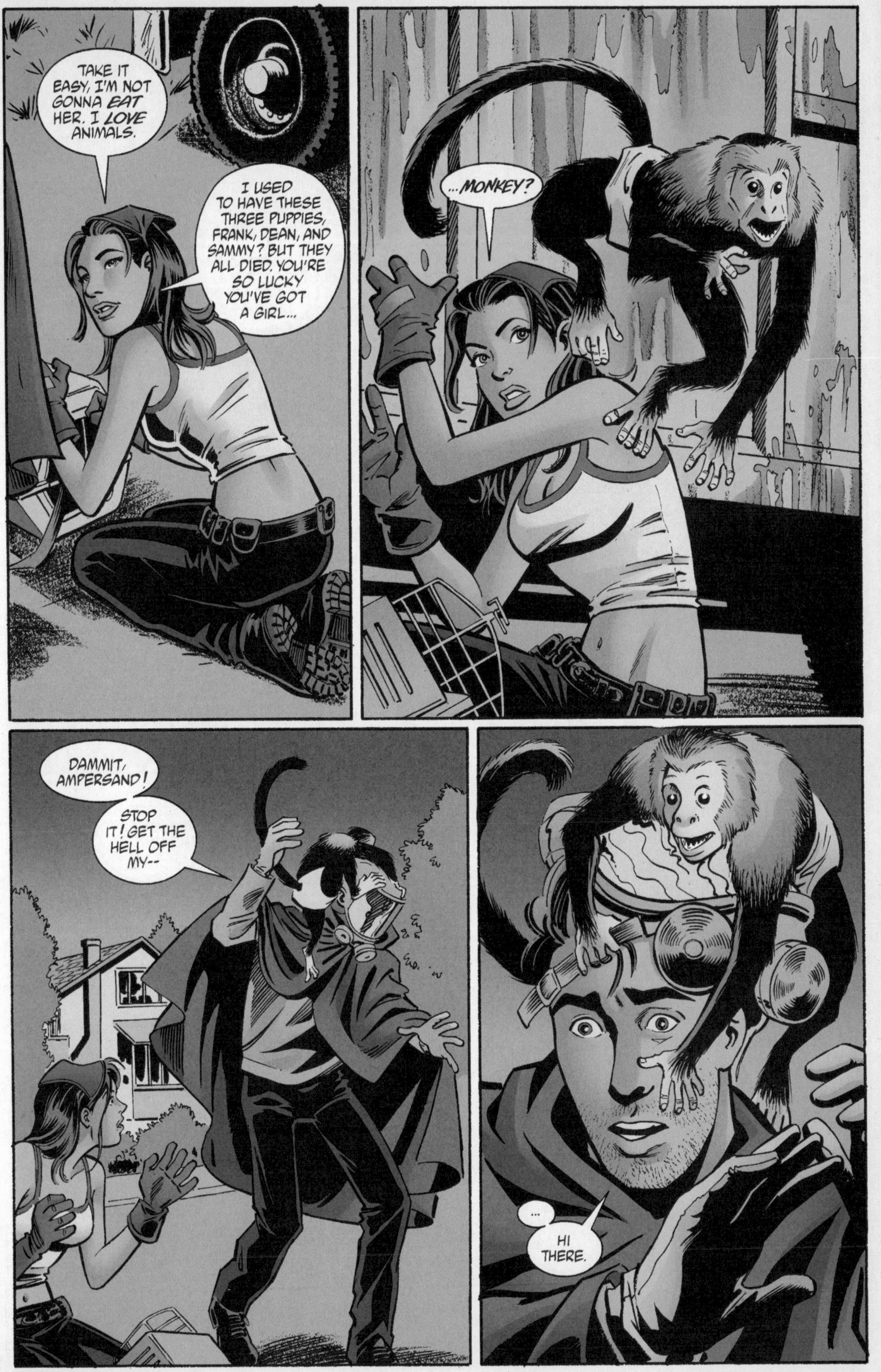
TAKE IT EASY, I'M NOT GONNA *EAT* HER. I *LOVE* ANIMALS.
I USED TO HAVE THESE THREE PUPPIES, FRANK, DEAN, AND SAMMY? BUT THEY ALL DIED. YOU'RE SO LUCKY YOU'VE GOT A GIRL...
...MONKEY?
DAMMIT, AMPERSAND!
STOP IT! GET THE HELL OFF MY--
...
HI THERE.

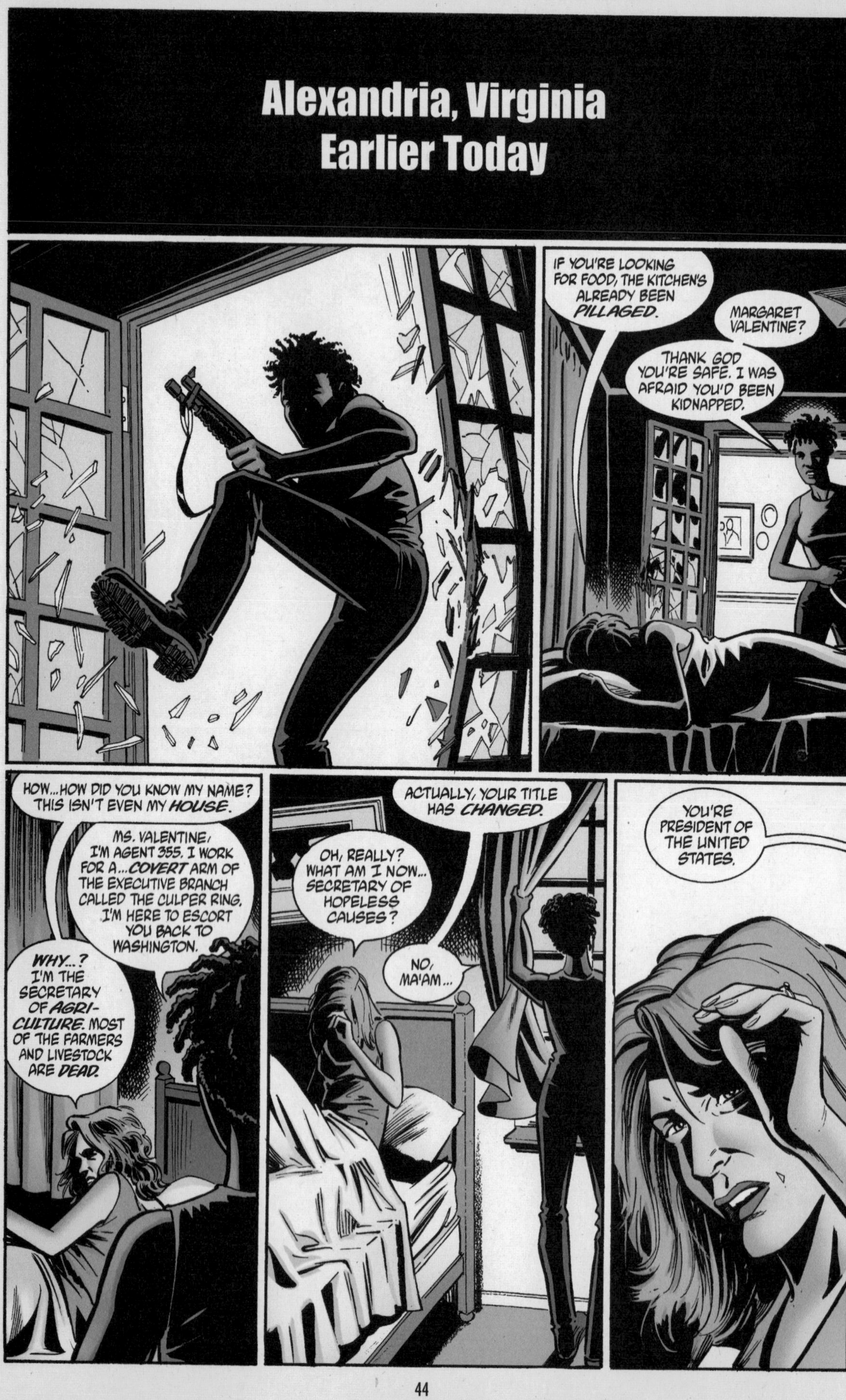
Alexandria, Virginia
Earlier Today
IF YOU'RE LOOKING FOR FOOD, THE KITCHEN'S ALREADY BEEN PILLAGED.
MARGARET VALENTINE?
THANK GOD YOU'RE SAFE. I WAS AFRAID YOU'D BEEN KIDNAPPED.
HOW...HOW DID YOU KNOW MY NAME? THIS ISN'T EVEN MY HOUSE.
MS. VALENTINE, I'M AGENT 355. I WORK FOR A...COVERT ARM OF THE EXECUTIVE BRANCH CALLED THE CULPER RING. I'M HERE TO ESCORT YOU BACK TO WASHINGTON.
WHY...? I'M THE SECRETARY OF AGRI-CULTURE. MOST OF THE FARMERS AND LIVESTOCK ARE DEAD.
ACTUALLY, YOUR TITLE HAS CHANGED.
OH, REALLY? WHAT AM I NOW... SECRETARY OF HOPELESS CAUSES?
NO, MA'AM...
YOU'RE PRESIDENT OF THE UNITED STATES.

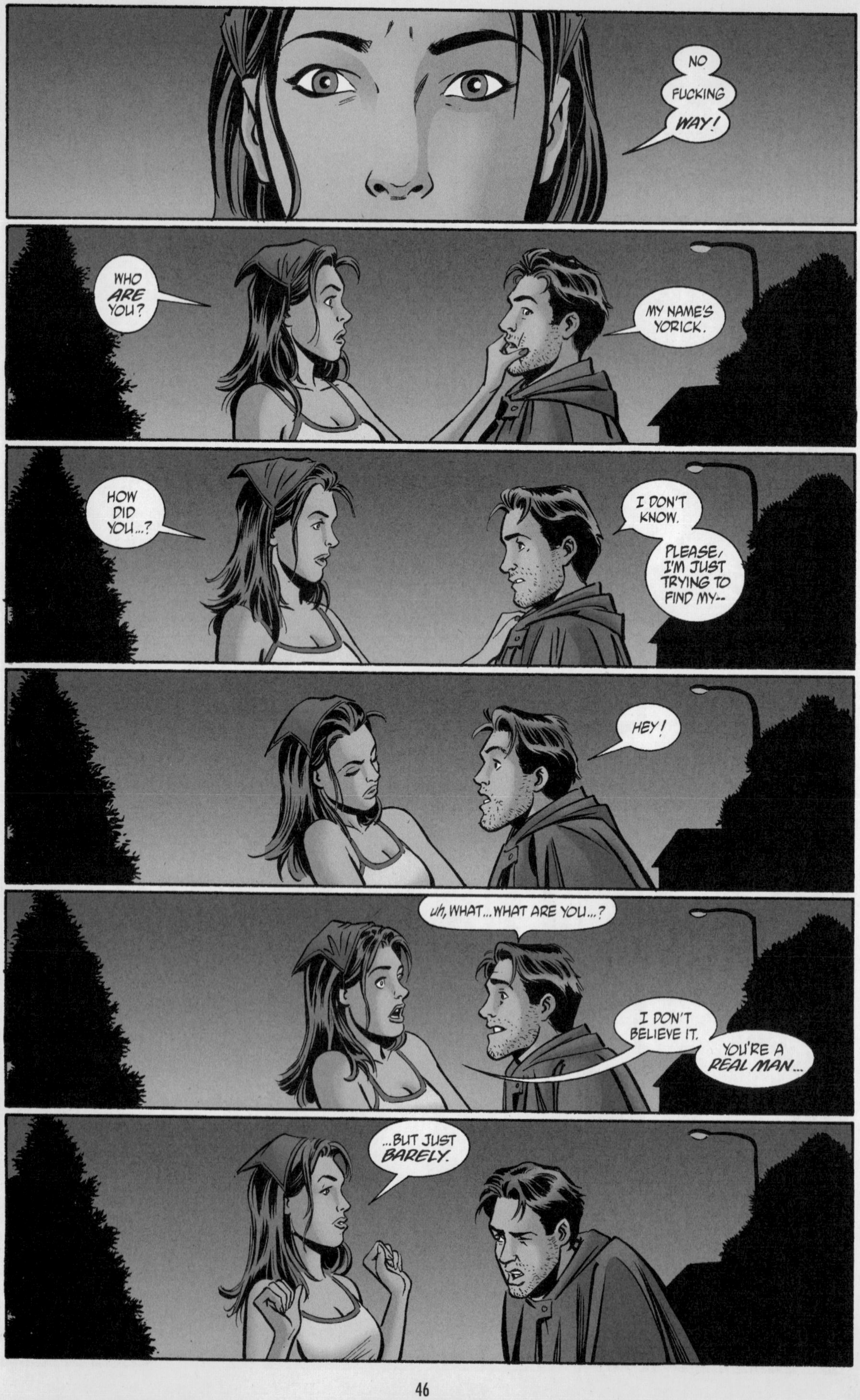
NO FUCKING WAY!
WHO ARE YOU?
MY NAME'S YORICK.
HOW DID YOU...?
I DON'T KNOW.
PLEASE, I'M JUST TRYING TO FIND MY--
HEY!
uh, WHAT... WHAT ARE YOU...?
I DON'T BELIEVE IT.
YOU'RE A REAL MAN...
...BUT JUST BARELY.

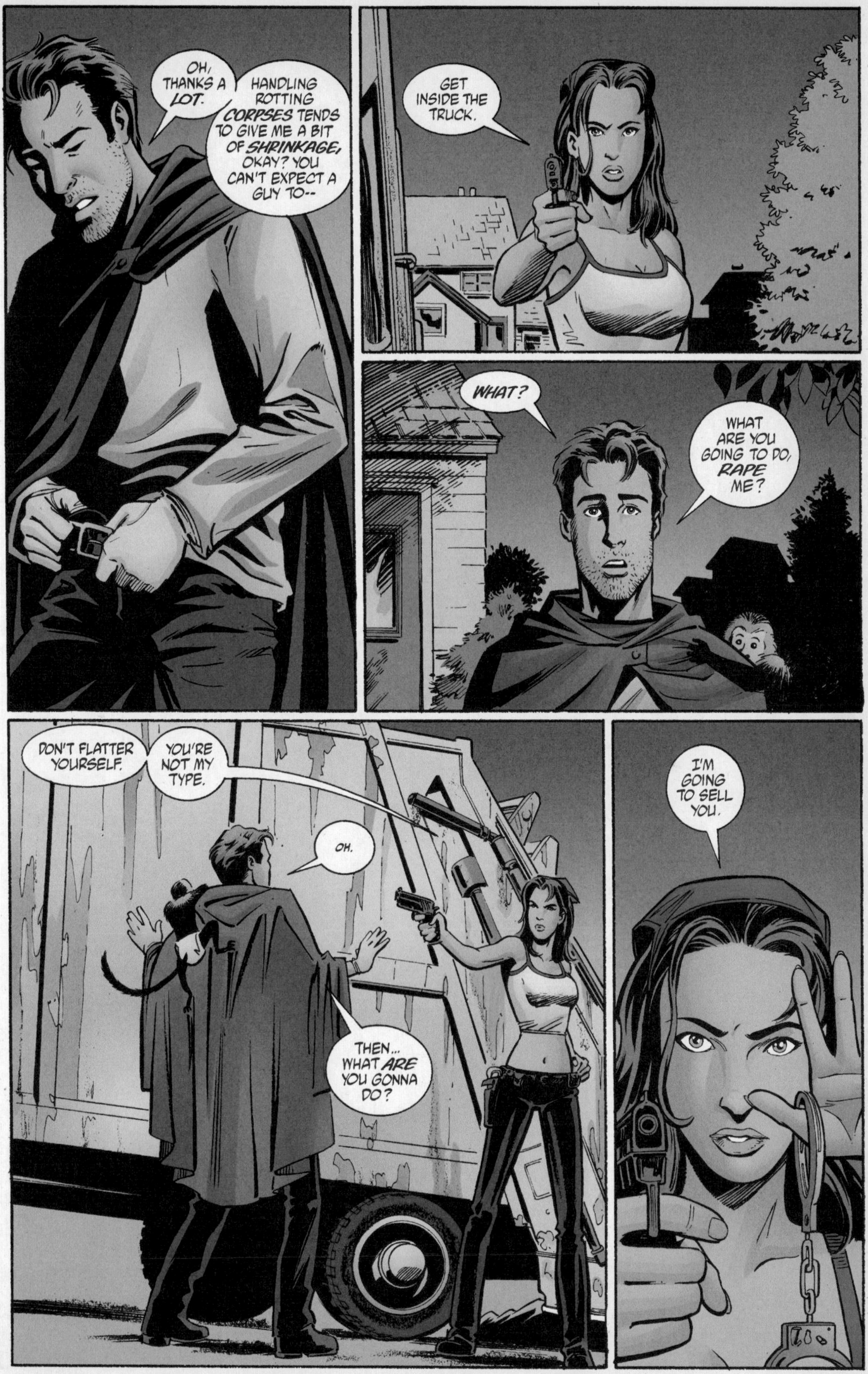
OH, THANKS A LOT.
HANDLING ROTTING CORPSES TENDS TO GIVE ME A BIT OF SHRINKAGE, OKAY? YOU CAN'T EXPECT A GUY TO--
GET INSIDE THE TRUCK.
WHAT?
WHAT ARE YOU GOING TO DO, RAPE ME?
DON'T FLATTER YOURSELF.
YOU'RE NOT MY TYPE.
OH.
THEN... WHAT ARE YOU GONNA DO?
I'M GOING TO SELL YOU.

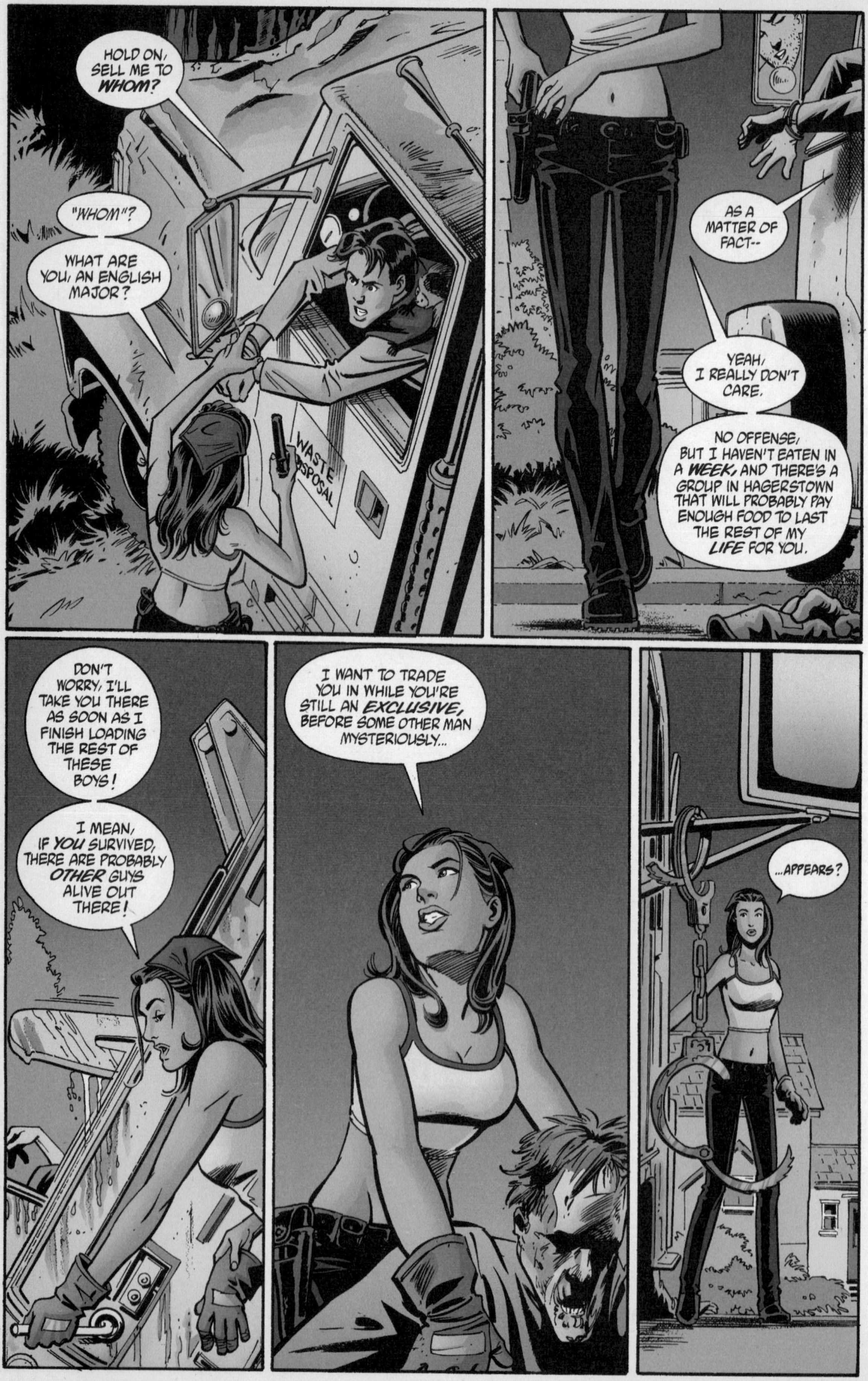
HOLD ON, SELL ME TO *WHOM*?
"WHOM"?
WHAT ARE YOU, AN ENGLISH MAJOR?
WASTE DISPOSAL
AS A MATTER OF FACT--
YEAH, I REALLY DON'T CARE.
NO OFFENSE, BUT I HAVEN'T EATEN IN A *WEEK*, AND THERE'S A GROUP IN HAGERSTOWN THAT WILL PROBABLY PAY ENOUGH FOOD TO LAST THE REST OF MY *LIFE* FOR YOU.
DON'T WORRY, I'LL TAKE YOU THERE AS SOON AS I FINISH LOADING THE REST OF THESE BOYS!
I MEAN, IF *YOU* SURVIVED, THERE ARE PROBABLY *OTHER* GUYS ALIVE OUT THERE!
I WANT TO TRADE YOU IN WHILE YOU'RE STILL AN *EXCLUSIVE*, BEFORE SOME OTHER MAN MYSTERIOUSLY...
...APPEARS?

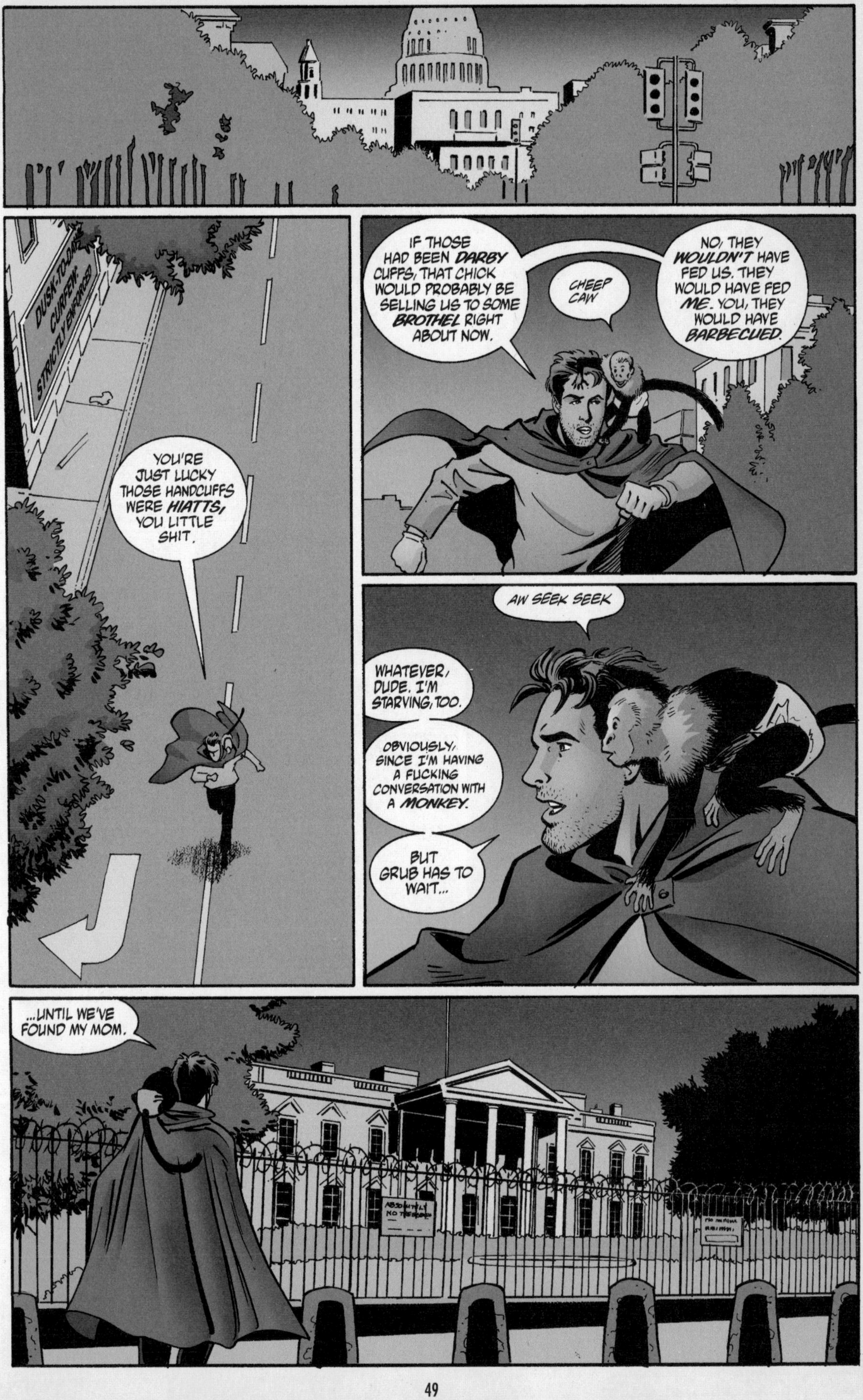
DUSK-TO-DAWN CURFEW: STRICTLY ENFORCED
YOU'RE JUST LUCKY THOSE HANDCUFFS WERE HIATTS, YOU LITTLE SHIT.
IF THOSE HAD BEEN DARBY CUFFS, THAT CHICK WOULD PROBABLY BE SELLING US TO SOME BROTHEL RIGHT ABOUT NOW.
CHEEP CAW
NO, THEY WOULDN'T HAVE FED US. THEY WOULD HAVE FED ME. YOU, THEY WOULD HAVE BARBECUED.
AW SEEK SEEK
WHATEVER, DUDE. I'M STARVING, TOO.
OBVIOUSLY, SINCE I'M HAVING A FUCKING CONVERSATION WITH A MONKEY.
BUT GRUB HAS TO WAIT...
...UNTIL WE'VE FOUND MY MOM.

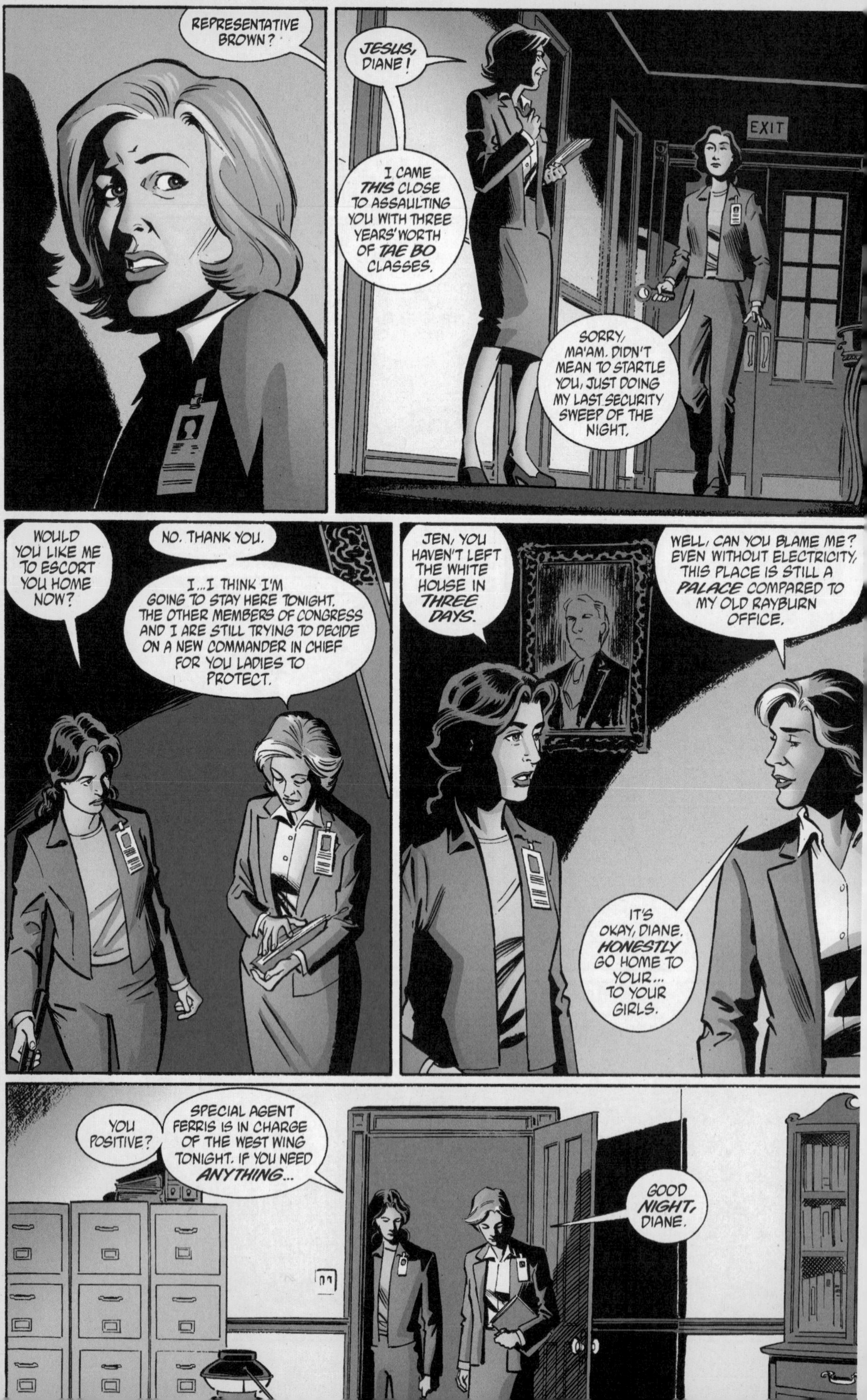

REPRESENTATIVE BROWN?
JESUS, DIANE!
I CAME THIS CLOSE TO ASSAULTING YOU WITH THREE YEARS' WORTH OF TAE BO CLASSES.
EXIT
SORRY, MA'AM. DIDN'T MEAN TO STARTLE YOU, JUST DOING MY LAST SECURITY SWEEP OF THE NIGHT.
WOULD YOU LIKE ME TO ESCORT YOU HOME NOW?
NO. THANK YOU.
I...I THINK I'M GOING TO STAY HERE TONIGHT. THE OTHER MEMBERS OF CONGRESS AND I ARE STILL TRYING TO DECIDE ON A NEW COMMANDER IN CHIEF FOR YOU LADIES TO PROTECT.
JEN, YOU HAVEN'T LEFT THE WHITE HOUSE IN THREE DAYS.
WELL, CAN YOU BLAME ME? EVEN WITHOUT ELECTRICITY, THIS PLACE IS STILL A PALACE COMPARED TO MY OLD RAYBURN OFFICE.
IT'S OKAY, DIANE. HONESTLY GO HOME TO YOUR... TO YOUR GIRLS.
YOU POSITIVE?
SPECIAL AGENT FERRIS IS IN CHARGE OF THE WEST WING TONIGHT. IF YOU NEED ANYTHING...
GOOD NIGHT, DIANE.

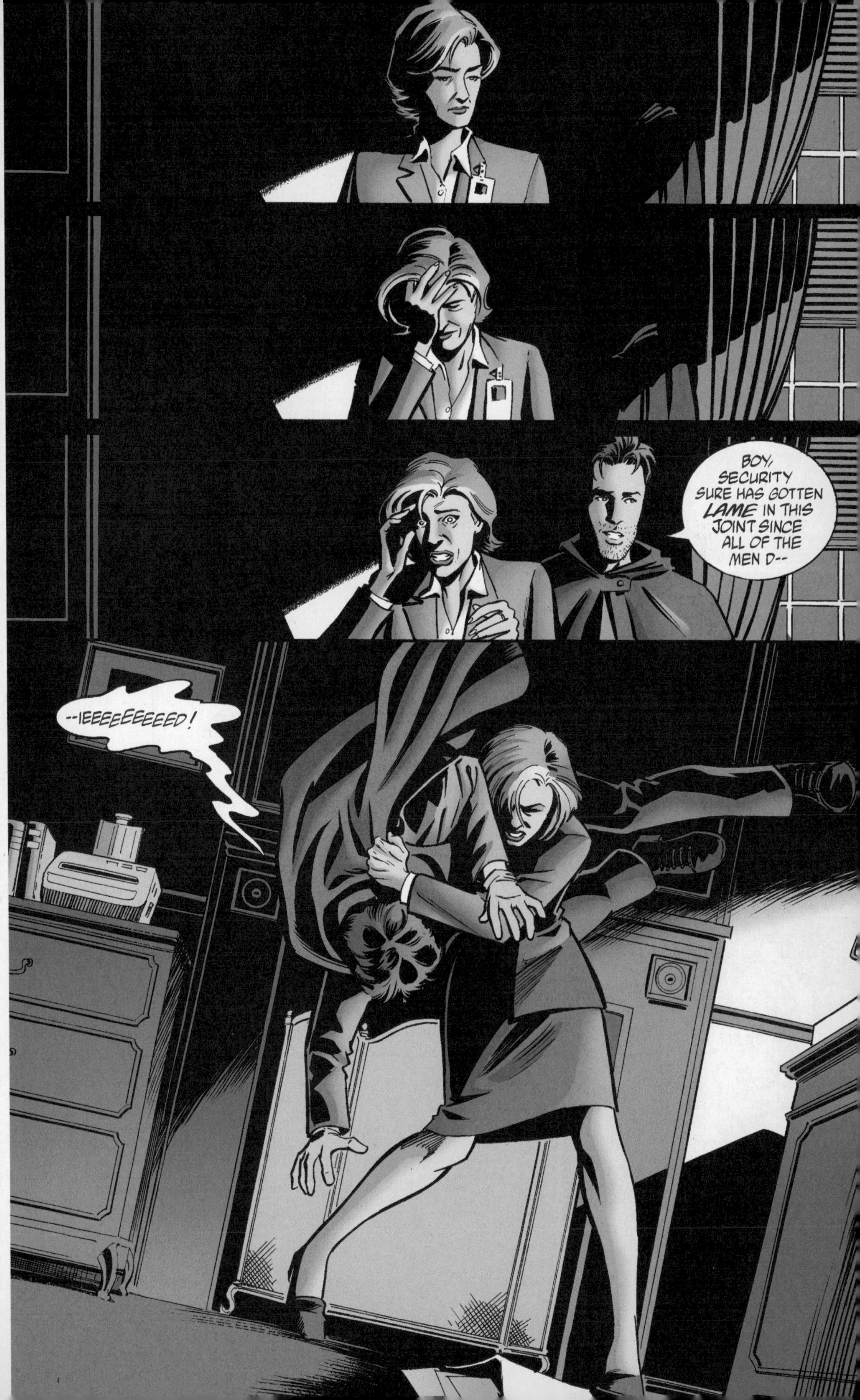
BOY, SECURITY SURE HAS GOTTEN LAME IN THIS JOINT SINCE ALL OF THE MEN D--
--IEEEEEEEEEED!

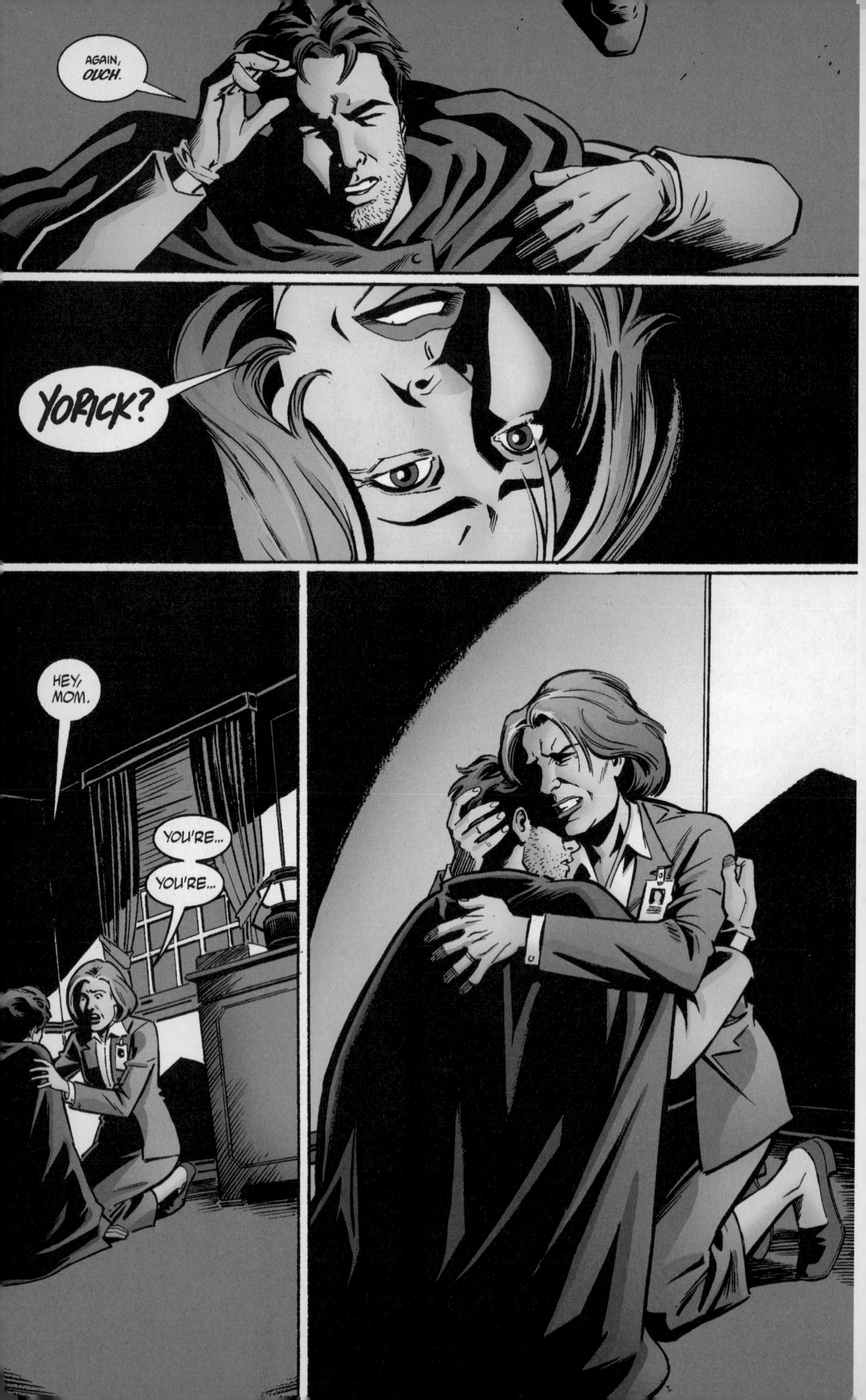

AGAIN, OUCH.
YORICK?
HEY, MOM.
YOU'RE...
YOU'RE...

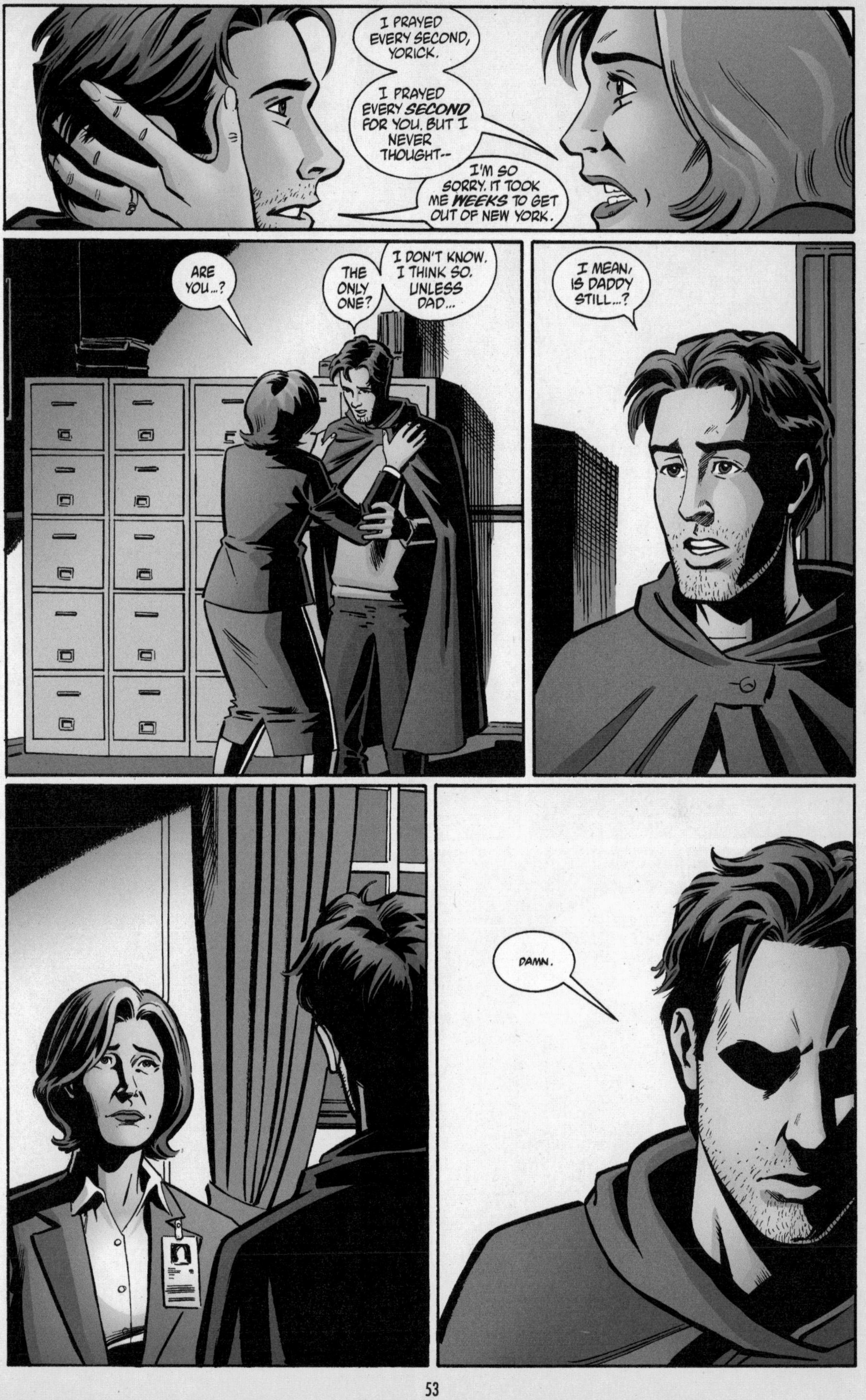
I PRAYED EVERY SECOND, YORICK.
I PRAYED EVERY SECOND FOR YOU. BUT I NEVER THOUGHT--
I'M SO SORRY. IT TOOK ME WEEKS TO GET OUT OF NEW YORK.
ARE YOU...?
THE ONLY ONE?
I DON'T KNOW. I THINK SO. UNLESS DAD...
I MEAN, IS DADDY STILL...?
DAMN.

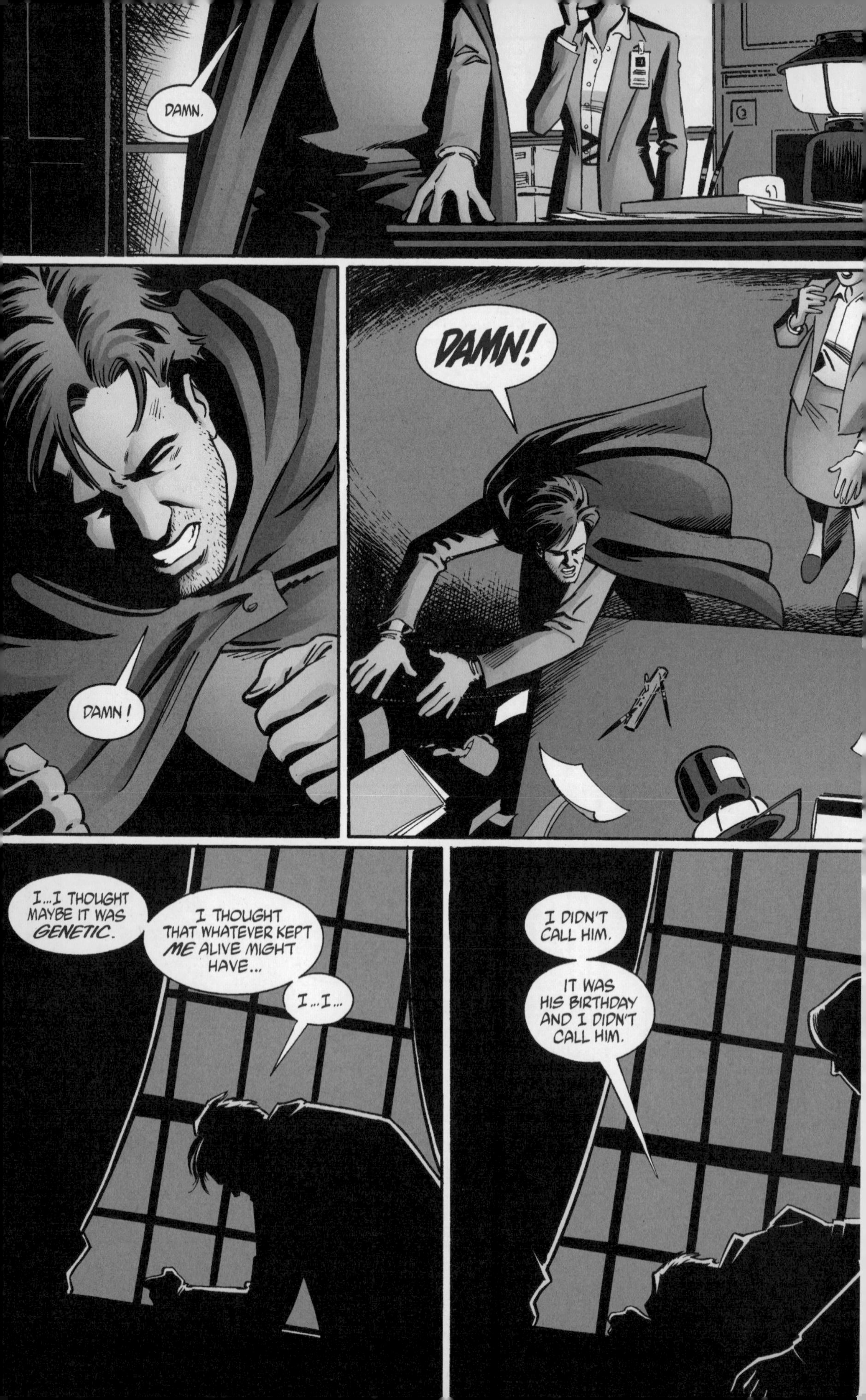
DAMN.
DAMN!
DAMN!
I...I THOUGHT MAYBE IT WAS *GENETIC*.
I THOUGHT THAT WHATEVER KEPT *ME* ALIVE MIGHT HAVE...
I...I...
I DIDN'T CALL HIM.
IT WAS HIS BIRTHDAY AND I DIDN'T CALL HIM.

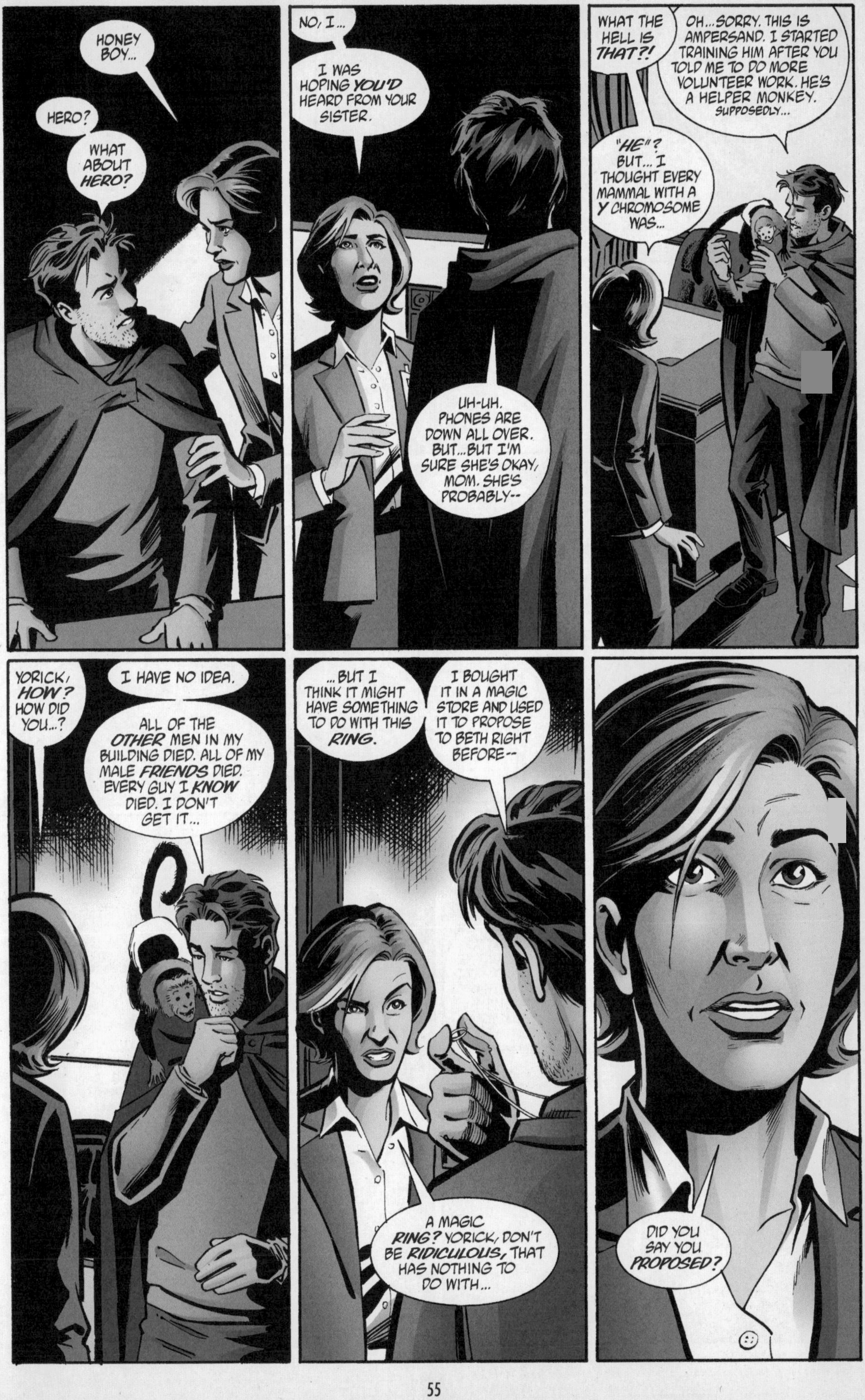
HONEY BOY...
HERO?
WHAT ABOUT HERO?
NO, I...
I WAS HOPING YOU'D HEARD FROM YOUR SISTER.
UH-UH. PHONES ARE DOWN ALL OVER. BUT...BUT I'M SURE SHE'S OKAY, MOM. SHE'S PROBABLY--
WHAT THE HELL IS THAT?!
OH...SORRY. THIS IS AMPERSAND. I STARTED TRAINING HIM AFTER YOU TOLD ME TO DO MORE VOLUNTEER WORK. HE'S A HELPER MONKEY. SUPPOSEDLY...
"HE"? BUT... I THOUGHT EVERY MAMMAL WITH A Y CHROMOSOME WAS...
YORICK, HOW? HOW DID YOU...?
I HAVE NO IDEA.
ALL OF THE OTHER MEN IN MY BUILDING DIED. ALL OF MY MALE FRIENDS DIED. EVERY GUY I KNOW DIED. I DON'T GET IT...
...BUT I THINK IT MIGHT HAVE SOMETHING TO DO WITH THIS RING.
I BOUGHT IT IN A MAGIC STORE AND USED IT TO PROPOSE TO BETH RIGHT BEFORE--
A MAGIC RING? YORICK, DON'T BE RIDICULOUS, THAT HAS NOTHING TO DO WITH...
DID YOU SAY YOU PROPOSED?

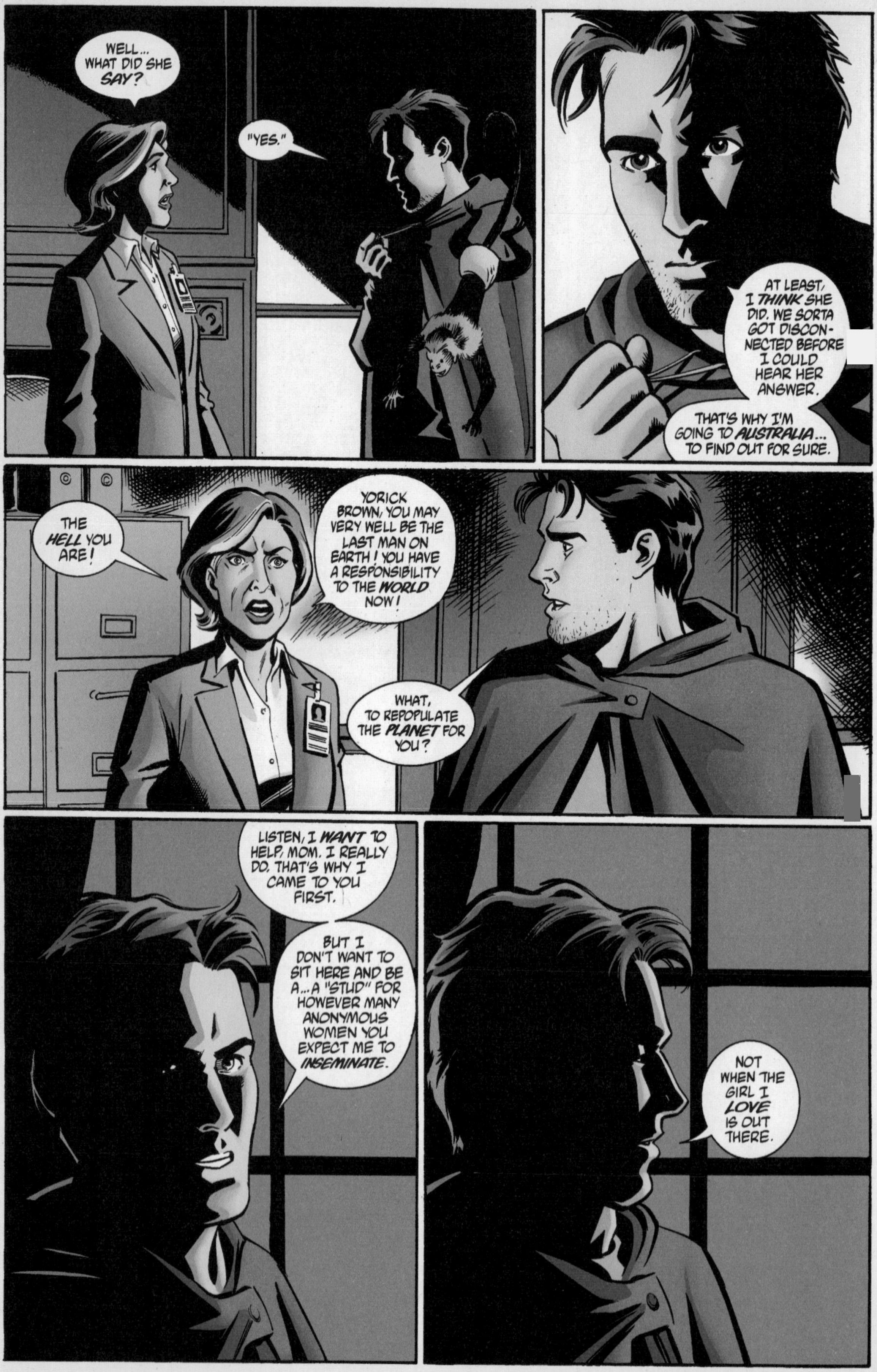
WELL... WHAT DID SHE SAY?
"YES."
AT LEAST, I THINK SHE DID. WE SORTA GOT DISCONNECTED BEFORE I COULD HEAR HER ANSWER.
THAT'S WHY I'M GOING TO AUSTRALIA... TO FIND OUT FOR SURE.
THE HELL YOU ARE!
YORICK BROWN, YOU MAY VERY WELL BE THE LAST MAN ON EARTH! YOU HAVE A RESPONSIBILITY TO THE WORLD NOW!
WHAT, TO REPOPULATE THE PLANET FOR YOU?
LISTEN, I WANT TO HELP, MOM. I REALLY DO. THAT'S WHY I CAME TO YOU FIRST.
BUT I DON'T WANT TO SIT HERE AND BE A... A "STUD" FOR HOWEVER MANY ANONYMOUS WOMEN YOU EXPECT ME TO INSEMINATE.
NOT WHEN THE GIRL I LOVE IS OUT THERE.

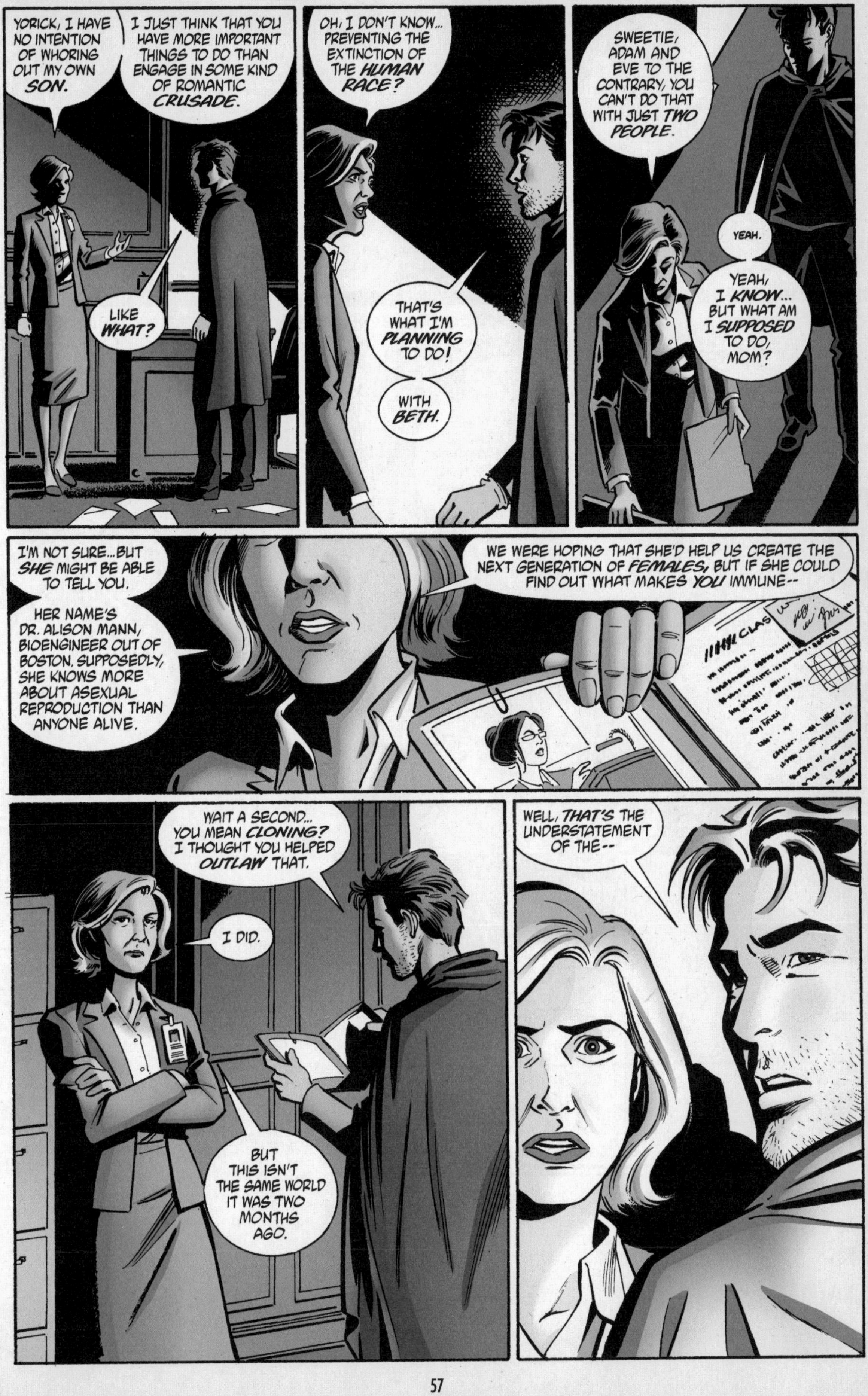
YORICK, I HAVE NO INTENTION OF WHORING OUT MY OWN SON.
I JUST THINK THAT YOU HAVE MORE IMPORTANT THINGS TO DO THAN ENGAGE IN SOME KIND OF ROMANTIC CRUSADE.
LIKE WHAT?
OH, I DON'T KNOW... PREVENTING THE EXTINCTION OF THE HUMAN RACE?
THAT'S WHAT I'M PLANNING TO DO!
WITH BETH.
SWEETIE, ADAM AND EVE TO THE CONTRARY, YOU CAN'T DO THAT WITH JUST TWO PEOPLE.
YEAH.
YEAH, I KNOW... BUT WHAT AM I SUPPOSED TO DO, MOM?
I'M NOT SURE...BUT SHE MIGHT BE ABLE TO TELL YOU.
HER NAME'S DR. ALISON MANN, BIOENGINEER OUT OF BOSTON. SUPPOSEDLY, SHE KNOWS MORE ABOUT ASEXUAL REPRODUCTION THAN ANYONE ALIVE.
WE WERE HOPING THAT SHE'D HELP US CREATE THE NEXT GENERATION OF FEMALES, BUT IF SHE COULD FIND OUT WHAT MAKES YOU IMMUNE--
WAIT A SECOND... YOU MEAN CLONING? I THOUGHT YOU HELPED OUTLAW THAT.
I DID.
BUT THIS ISN'T THE SAME WORLD IT WAS TWO MONTHS AGO.
WELL, THAT'S THE UNDERSTATEMENT OF THE--

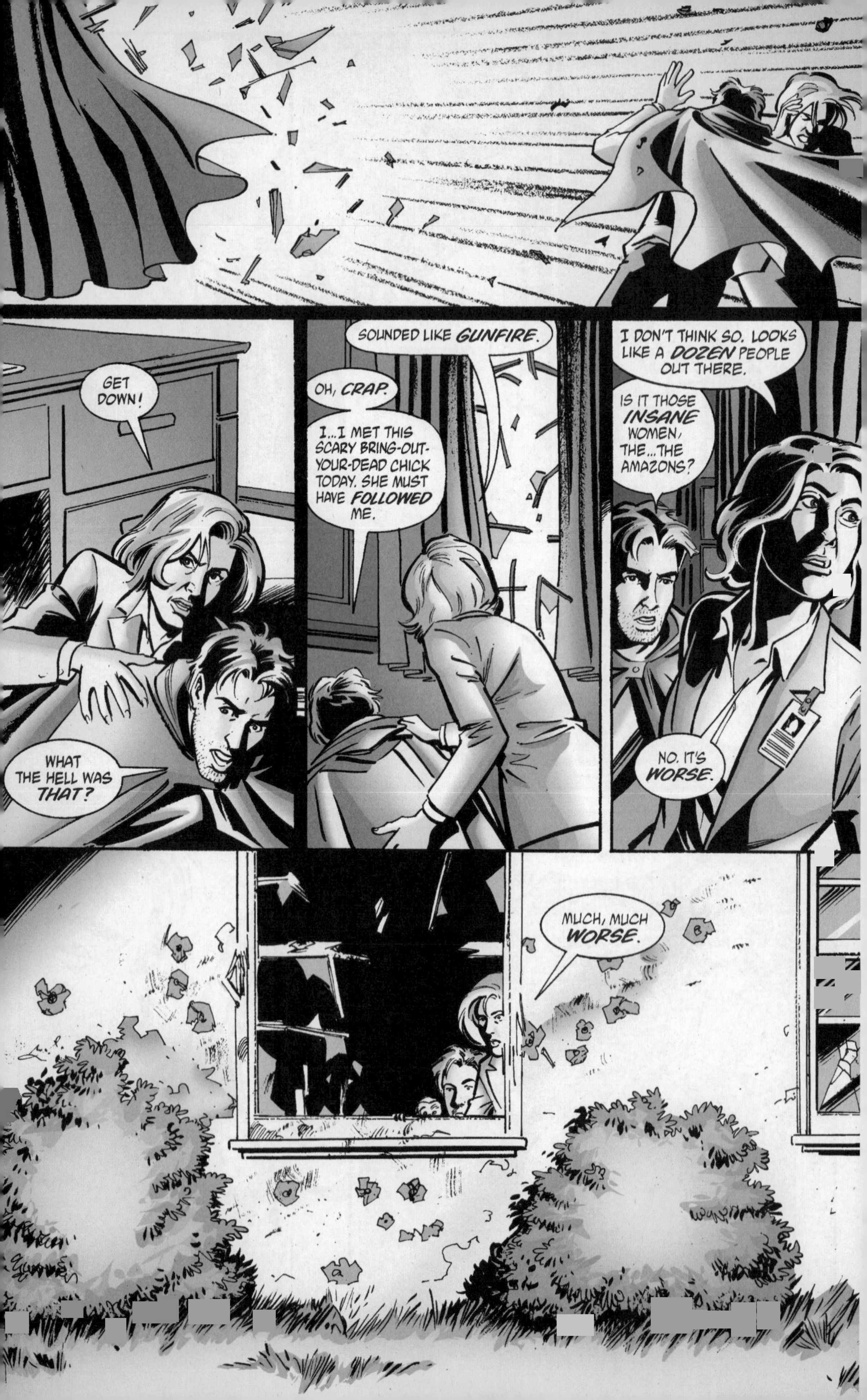
GET DOWN!
WHAT THE HELL WAS THAT?
SOUNDED LIKE GUNFIRE.
OH, CRAP.
I...I MET THIS SCARY BRING-OUT-YOUR-DEAD CHICK TODAY. SHE MUST HAVE FOLLOWED ME.
I DON'T THINK SO. LOOKS LIKE A DOZEN PEOPLE OUT THERE.
IS IT THOSE INSANE WOMEN, THE...THE AMAZONS?
NO. IT'S WORSE.
MUCH, MUCH WORSE.

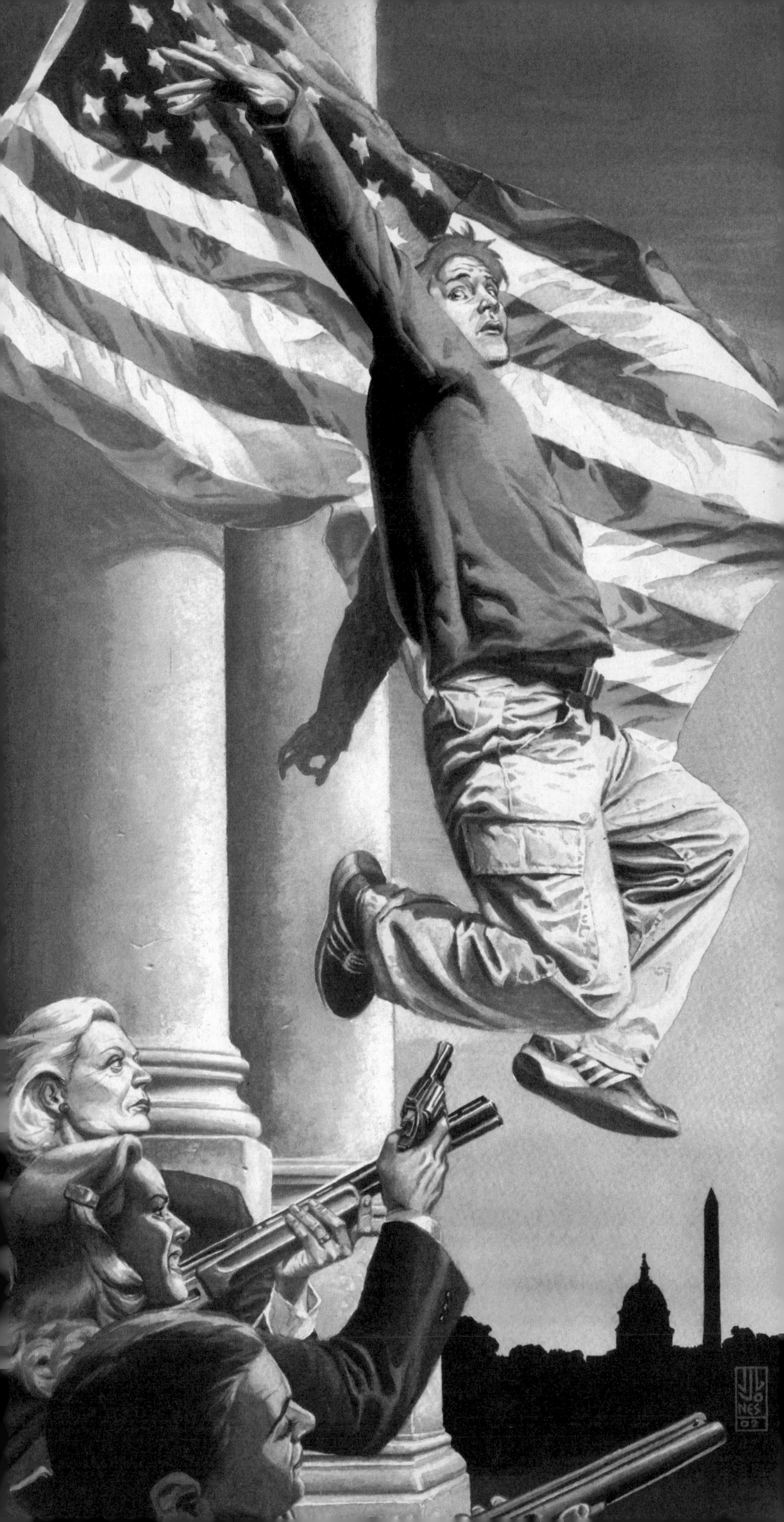

Interstate 395, Virginia
Six Hours Ago

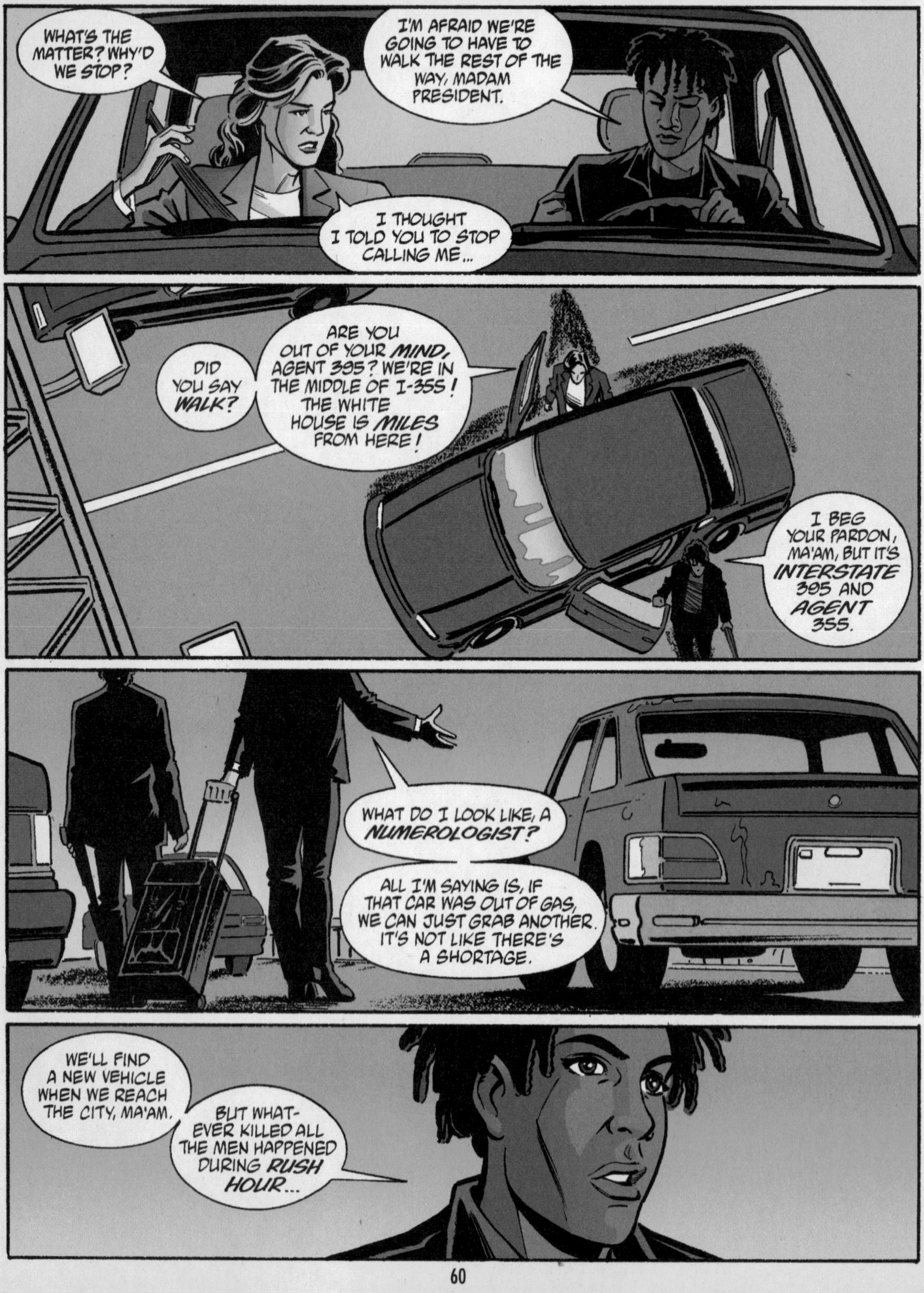
WHAT'S THE MATTER? WHY'D WE STOP?
I'M AFRAID WE'RE GOING TO HAVE TO WALK THE REST OF THE WAY, MADAM PRESIDENT.
I THOUGHT I TOLD YOU TO STOP CALLING ME...
DID YOU SAY *WALK?*
ARE YOU OUT OF YOUR *MIND,* AGENT 395? WE'RE IN THE MIDDLE OF I-355! THE WHITE HOUSE IS *MILES* FROM HERE!
I BEG YOUR PARDON, MA'AM, BUT IT'S *INTERSTATE* 395 AND *AGENT* 355.
WHAT DO I LOOK LIKE, A *NUMEROLOGIST?*
ALL I'M SAYING IS, IF THAT CAR WAS OUT OF GAS, WE CAN JUST GRAB ANOTHER. IT'S NOT LIKE THERE'S A SHORTAGE.
WE'LL FIND A NEW VEHICLE WHEN WE REACH THE CITY, MA'AM.
BUT WHATEVER KILLED ALL THE MEN HAPPENED DURING *RUSH HOUR...*

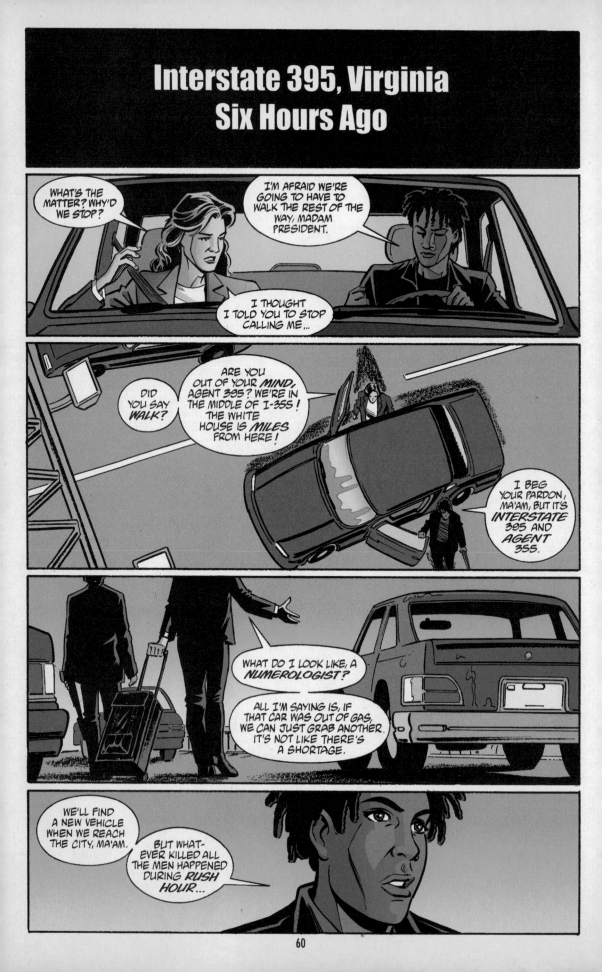

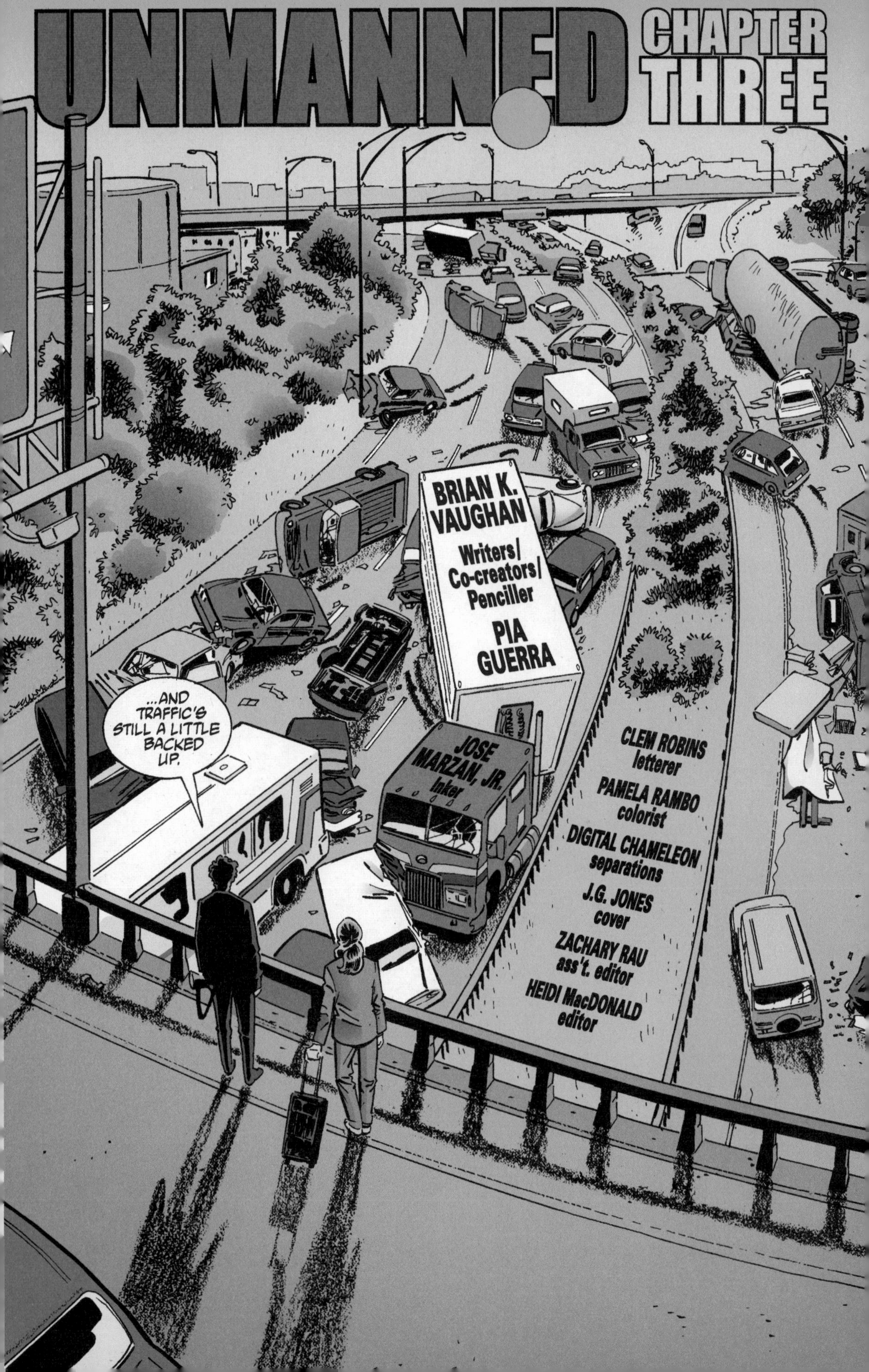
UNMANNED
CHAPTER THREE
BRIAN K. VAUGHAN
Writers/ Co-creators/ Penciller
PIA GUERRA
...AND TRAFFIC'S STILL A LITTLE BACKED UP.
JOSE MARZAN, JR. Inker
CLEM ROBINS letterer
PAMELA RAMBO colorist
DIGITAL CHAMELEON separations
J.G. JONES cover
ZACHARY RAU ass't. editor
HEIDI MacDONALD editor

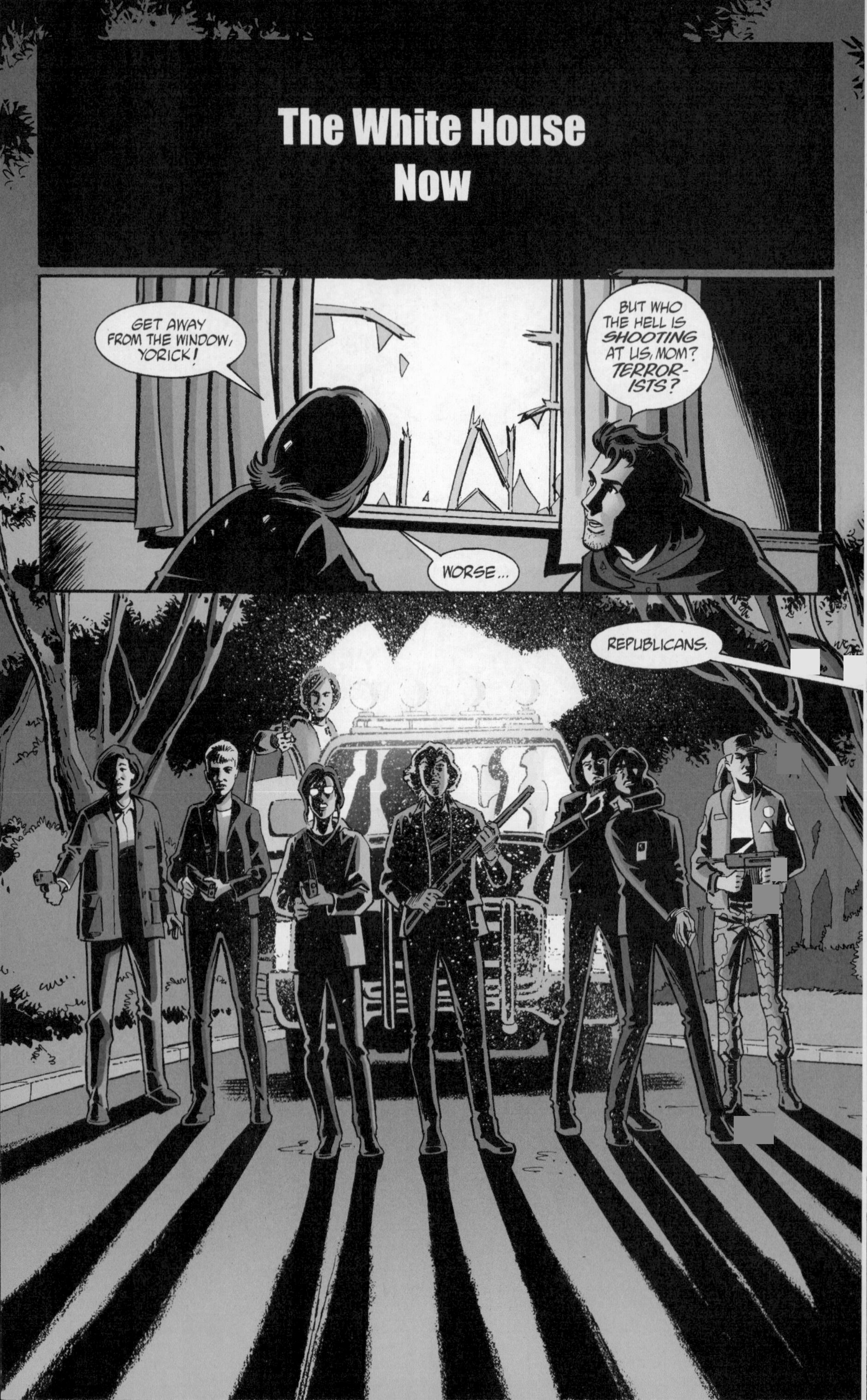
The White House
Now
GET AWAY FROM THE WINDOW, YORICK!
BUT WHO THE HELL IS SHOOTING AT US, MOM? TERRORISTS?
WORSE...
REPUBLICANS.

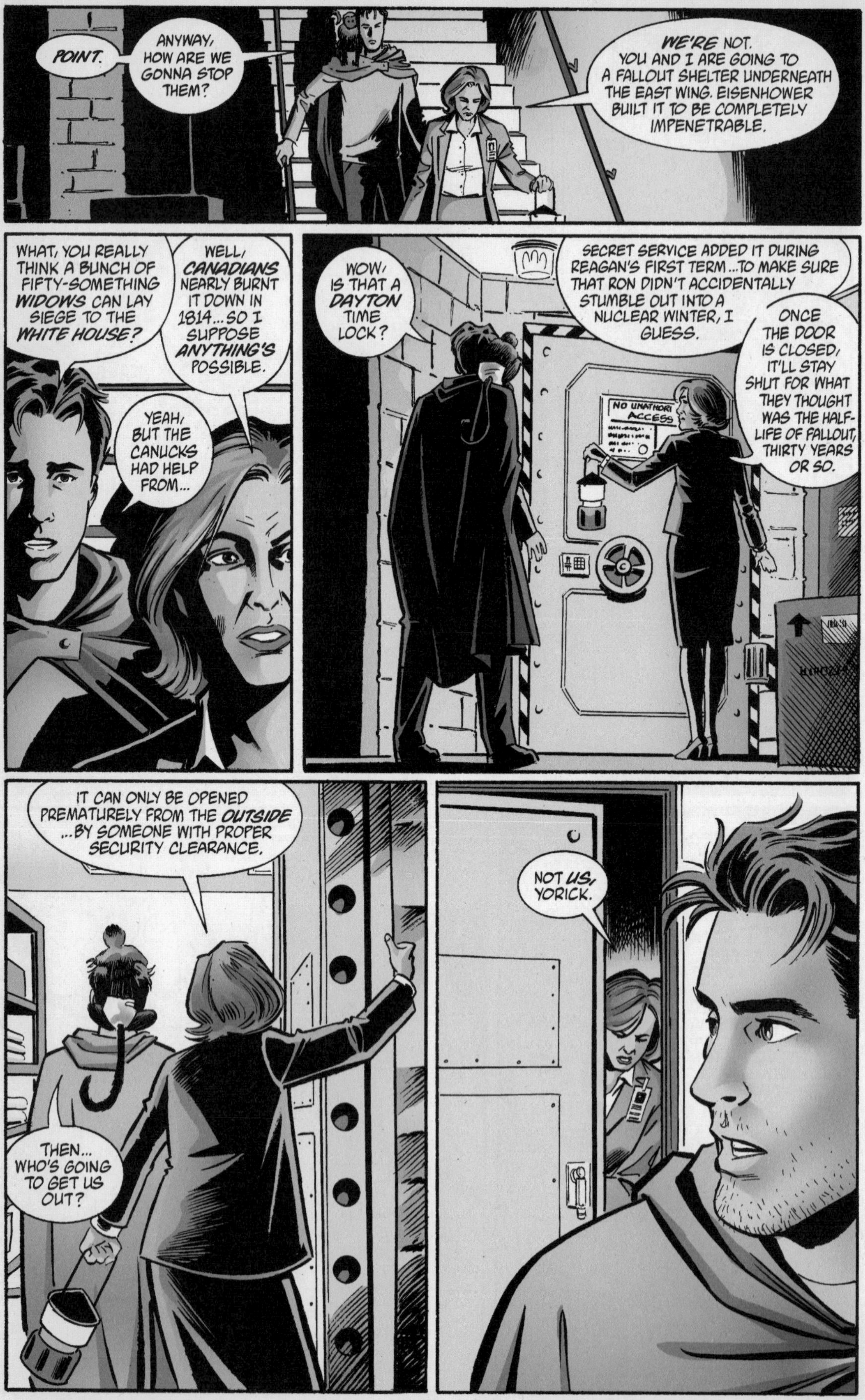
POINT.
ANYWAY, HOW ARE WE GONNA STOP THEM?
WE'RE NOT. YOU AND I ARE GOING TO A FALLOUT SHELTER UNDERNEATH THE EAST WING. EISENHOWER BUILT IT TO BE COMPLETELY IMPENETRABLE.
WHAT, YOU REALLY THINK A BUNCH OF FIFTY-SOMETHING WIDOWS CAN LAY SIEGE TO THE WHITE HOUSE?
WELL, CANADIANS NEARLY BURNT IT DOWN IN 1814... SO I SUPPOSE ANYTHING'S POSSIBLE.
YEAH, BUT THE CANUCKS HAD HELP FROM...
WOW, IS THAT A DAYTON TIME LOCK?
SECRET SERVICE ADDED IT DURING REAGAN'S FIRST TERM... TO MAKE SURE THAT RON DIDN'T ACCIDENTALLY STUMBLE OUT INTO A NUCLEAR WINTER, I GUESS.
ONCE THE DOOR IS CLOSED, IT'LL STAY SHUT FOR WHAT THEY THOUGHT WAS THE HALF-LIFE OF FALLOUT, THIRTY YEARS OR SO.
IT CAN ONLY BE OPENED PREMATURELY FROM THE OUTSIDE ...BY SOMEONE WITH PROPER SECURITY CLEARANCE.
THEN... WHO'S GOING TO GET US OUT?
NOT US, YORICK.

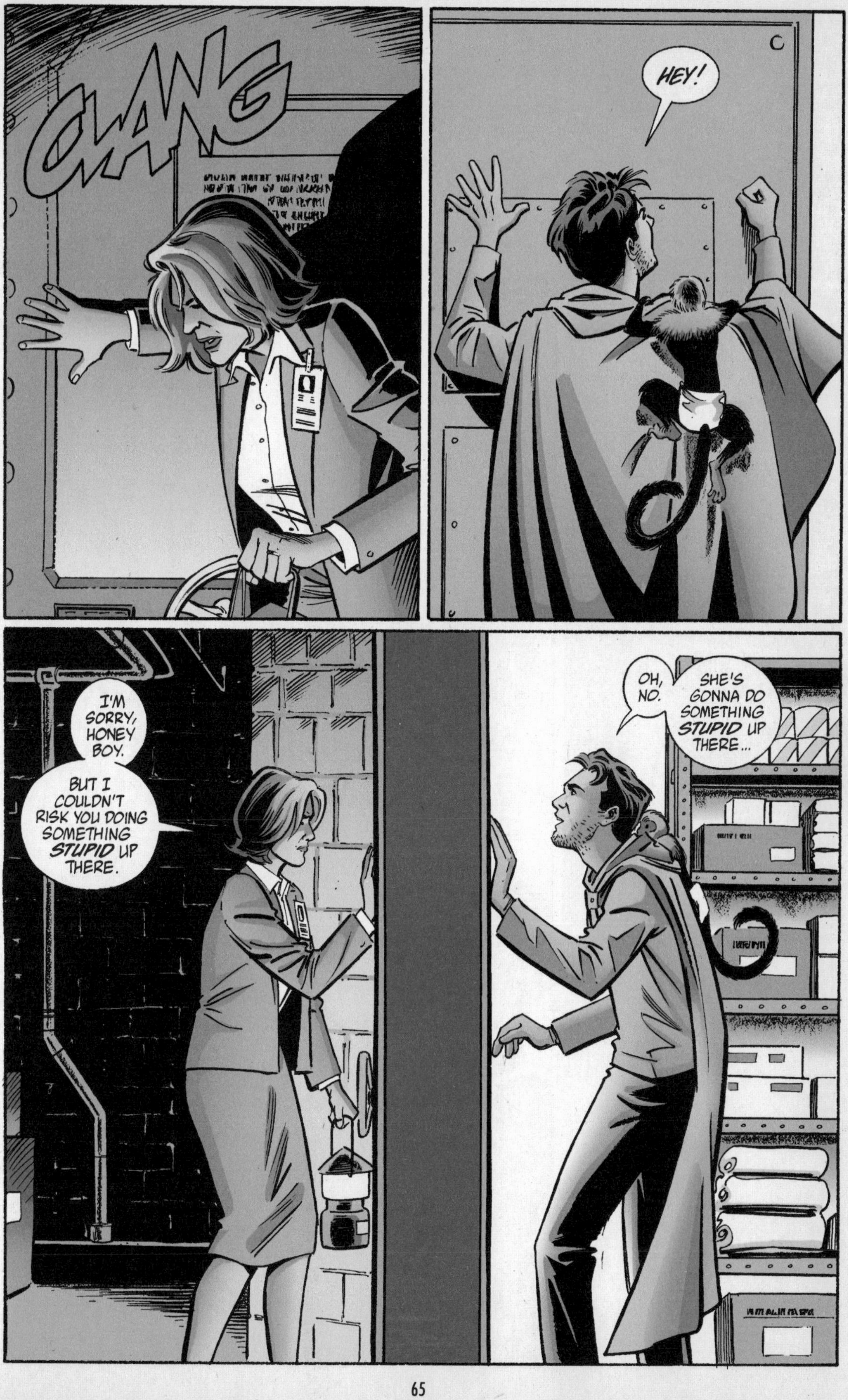
CLANG
HEY!
I'M SORRY, HONEY BOY.
BUT I COULDN'T RISK YOU DOING SOMETHING STUPID UP THERE.
OH, NO.
SHE'S GONNA DO SOMETHING STUPID UP THERE...

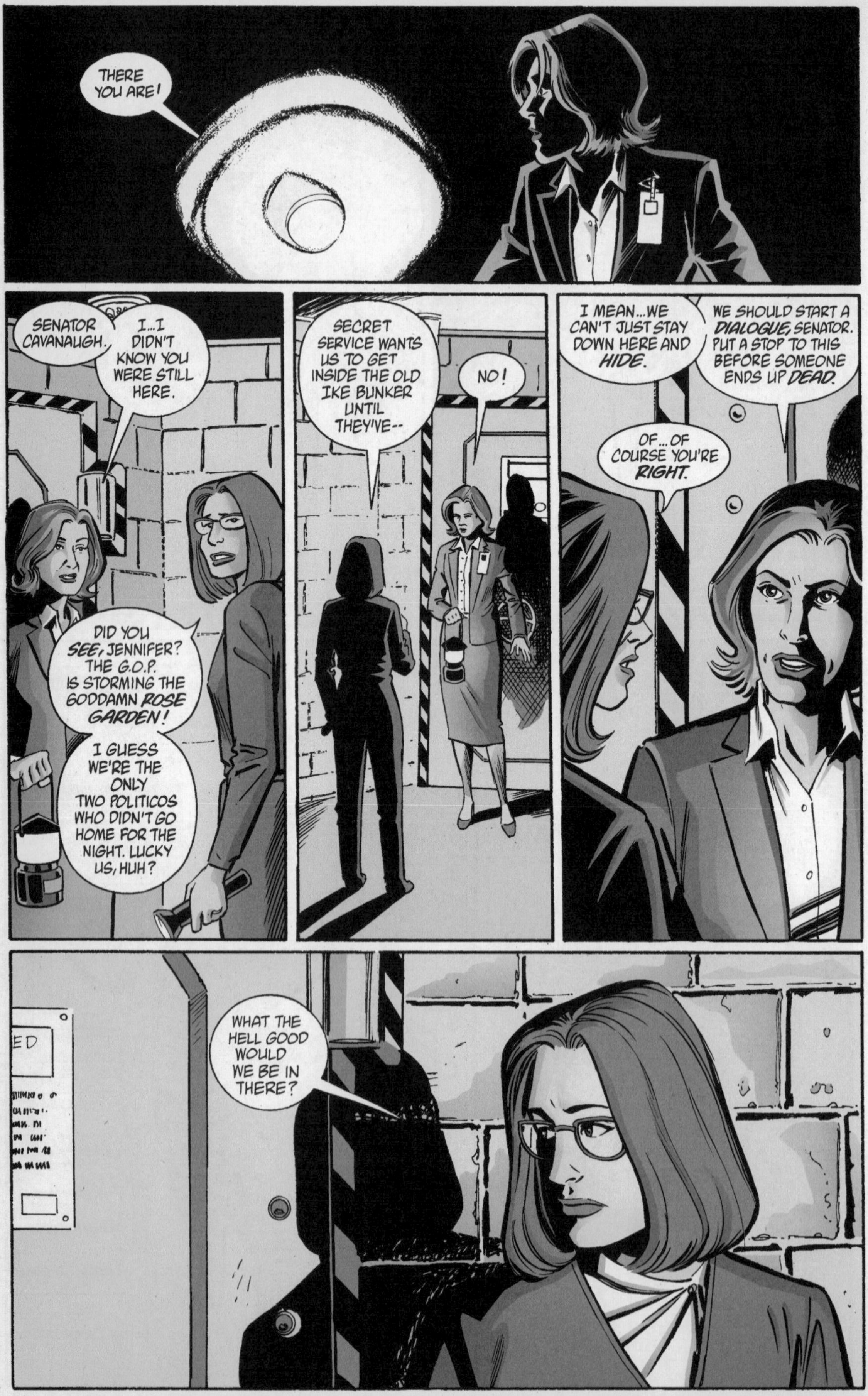
THERE YOU ARE!
SENATOR CAVANAUGH.
I...I DIDN'T KNOW YOU WERE STILL HERE.
DID YOU SEE, JENNIFER? THE G.O.P. IS STORMING THE GODDAMN ROSE GARDEN!
I GUESS WE'RE THE ONLY TWO POLITICOS WHO DIDN'T GO HOME FOR THE NIGHT. LUCKY US, HUH?
SECRET SERVICE WANTS US TO GET INSIDE THE OLD IKE BUNKER UNTIL THEY'VE--
NO!
I MEAN...WE CAN'T JUST STAY DOWN HERE AND HIDE.
WE SHOULD START A DIALOGUE, SENATOR. PUT A STOP TO THIS BEFORE SOMEONE ENDS UP DEAD.
OF...OF COURSE YOU'RE RIGHT.
WHAT THE HELL GOOD WOULD WE BE IN THERE?

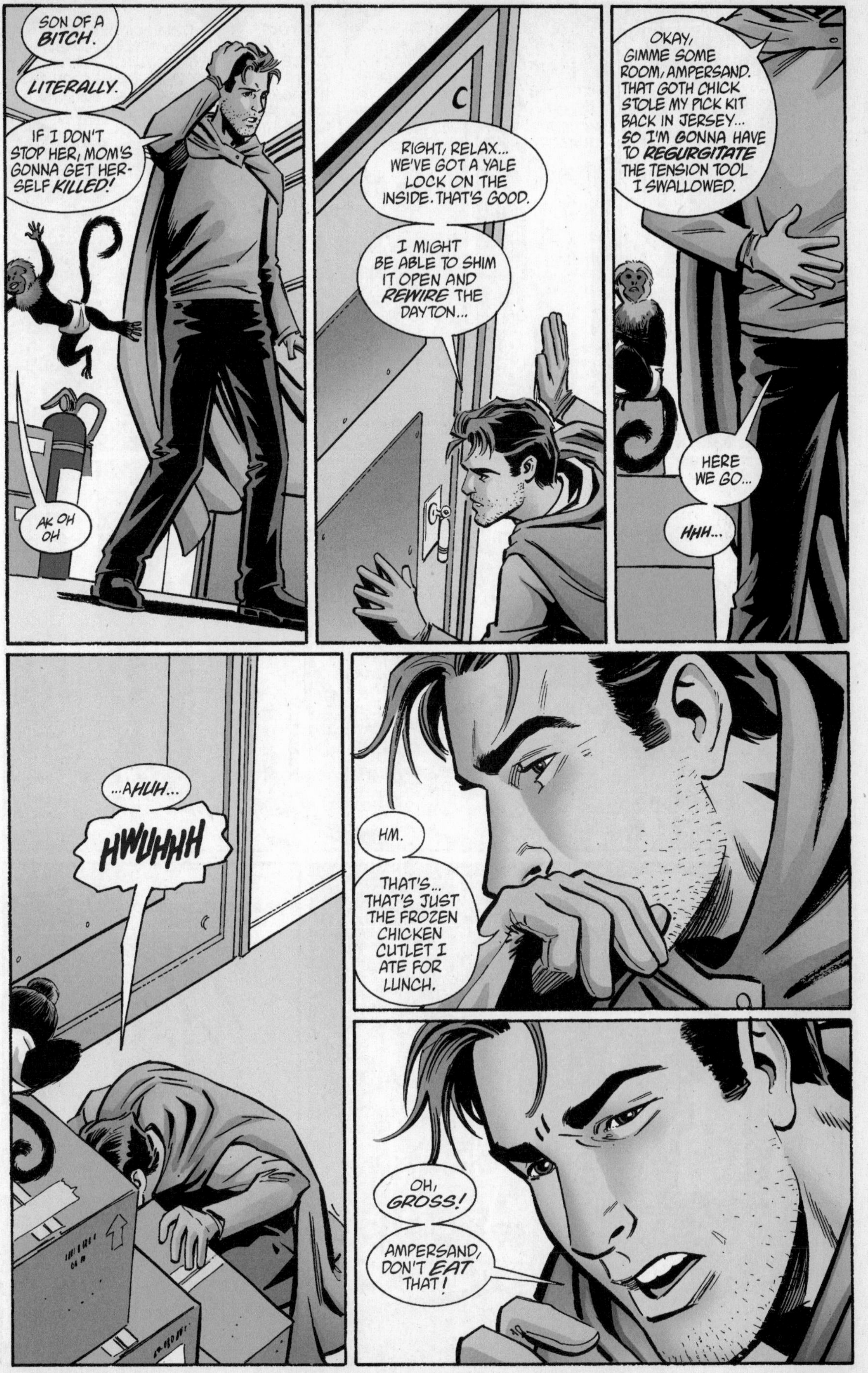
SON OF A BITCH.
LITERALLY.
IF I DON'T STOP HER, MOM'S GONNA GET HERSELF KILLED!
AK OH OH
RIGHT, RELAX... WE'VE GOT A YALE LOCK ON THE INSIDE. THAT'S GOOD.
I MIGHT BE ABLE TO SHIM IT OPEN AND REWIRE THE DAYTON...
OKAY, GIMME SOME ROOM, AMPERSAND. THAT GOTH CHICK STOLE MY PICK KIT BACK IN JERSEY... SO I'M GONNA HAVE TO REGURGITATE THE TENSION TOOL I SWALLOWED.
HERE WE GO...
HHH...
...AHUH...
HWUHHH
HM.
THAT'S... THAT'S JUST THE FROZEN CHICKEN CUTLET I ATE FOR LUNCH.
OH, GROSS!
AMPERSAND, DON'T EAT THAT!

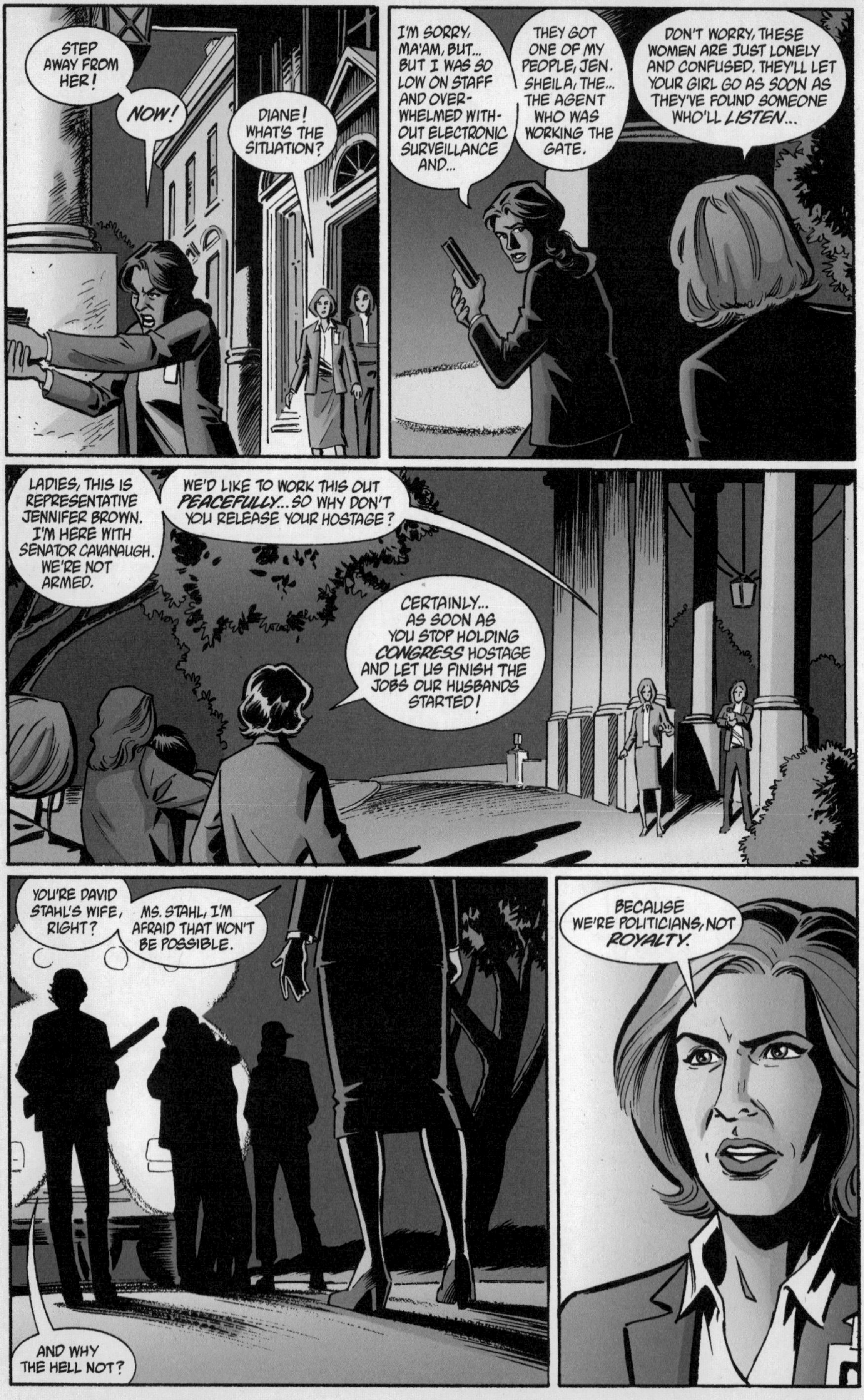
STEP AWAY FROM HER!
NOW!
DIANE! WHAT'S THE SITUATION?
I'M SORRY, MA'AM, BUT... BUT I WAS SO LOW ON STAFF AND OVER-WHELMED WITH-OUT ELECTRONIC SURVEILLANCE AND...
THEY GOT ONE OF MY PEOPLE, JEN. SHEILA, THE... THE AGENT WHO WAS WORKING THE GATE.
DON'T WORRY, THESE WOMEN ARE JUST LONELY AND CONFUSED. THEY'LL LET YOUR GIRL GO AS SOON AS THEY'VE FOUND SOMEONE WHO'LL LISTEN...
LADIES, THIS IS REPRESENTATIVE JENNIFER BROWN. I'M HERE WITH SENATOR CAVANAUGH. WE'RE NOT ARMED.
WE'D LIKE TO WORK THIS OUT PEACEFULLY... SO WHY DON'T YOU RELEASE YOUR HOSTAGE?
CERTAINLY... AS SOON AS YOU STOP HOLDING CONGRESS HOSTAGE AND LET US FINISH THE JOBS OUR HUSBANDS STARTED!
YOU'RE DAVID STAHL'S WIFE, RIGHT?
MS. STAHL, I'M AFRAID THAT WON'T BE POSSIBLE.
AND WHY THE HELL NOT?
BECAUSE WE'RE POLITICIANS, NOT ROYALTY.

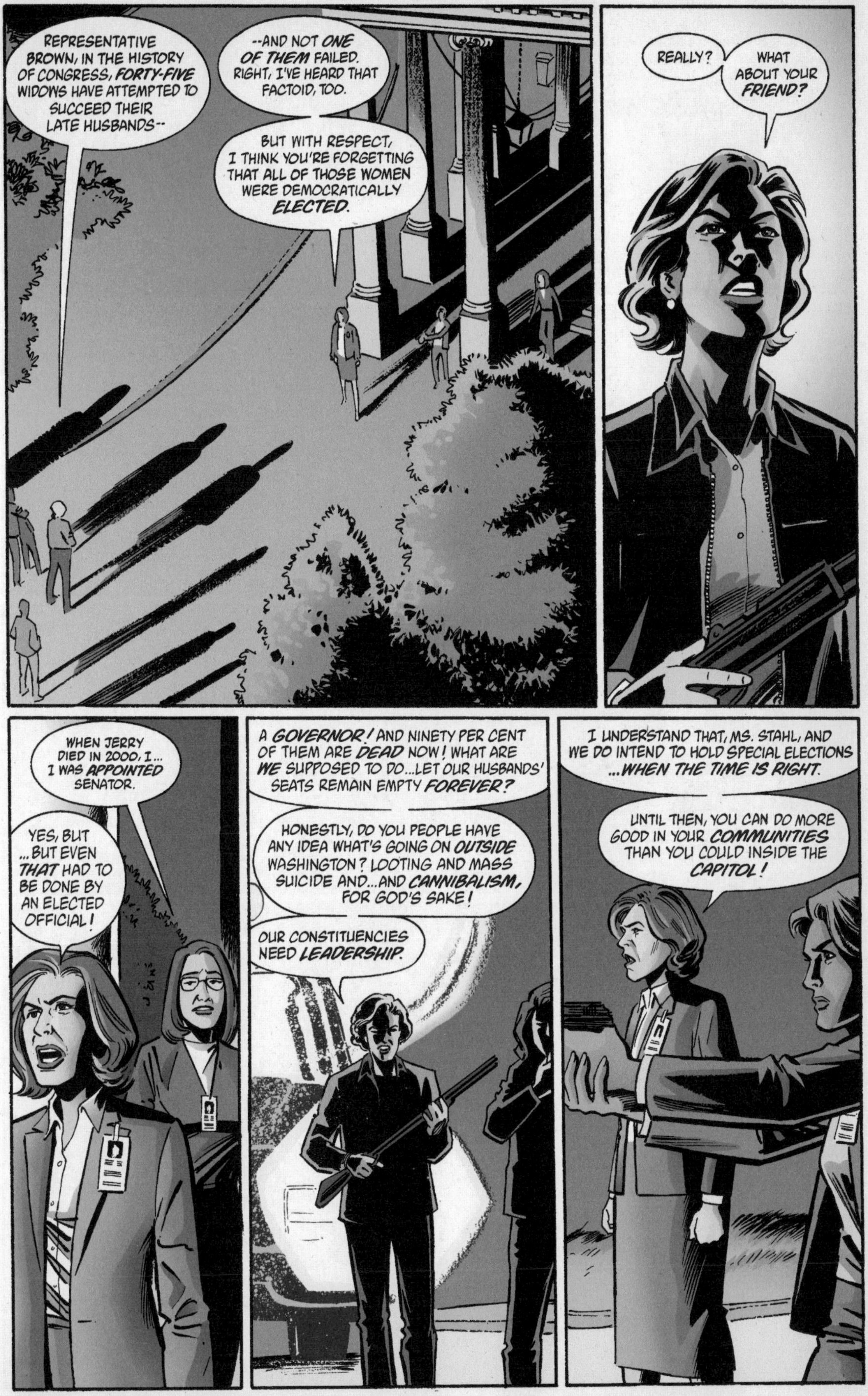
REPRESENTATIVE BROWN, IN THE HISTORY OF CONGRESS, FORTY-FIVE WIDOWS HAVE ATTEMPTED TO SUCCEED THEIR LATE HUSBANDS--
--AND NOT ONE OF THEM FAILED. RIGHT, I'VE HEARD THAT FACTOID, TOO.
BUT WITH RESPECT, I THINK YOU'RE FORGETTING THAT ALL OF THOSE WOMEN WERE DEMOCRATICALLY ELECTED.
REALLY?
WHAT ABOUT YOUR FRIEND?
WHEN JERRY DIED IN 2000, I... I WAS APPOINTED SENATOR.
YES, BUT ...BUT EVEN THAT HAD TO BE DONE BY AN ELECTED OFFICIAL!
A GOVERNOR! AND NINETY PER CENT OF THEM ARE DEAD NOW! WHAT ARE WE SUPPOSED TO DO...LET OUR HUSBANDS' SEATS REMAIN EMPTY FOREVER?
HONESTLY, DO YOU PEOPLE HAVE ANY IDEA WHAT'S GOING ON OUTSIDE WASHINGTON? LOOTING AND MASS SUICIDE AND...AND CANNIBALISM, FOR GOD'S SAKE!
OUR CONSTITUENCIES NEED LEADERSHIP.
I UNDERSTAND THAT, MS. STAHL, AND WE DO INTEND TO HOLD SPECIAL ELECTIONS ...WHEN THE TIME IS RIGHT.
UNTIL THEN, YOU CAN DO MORE GOOD IN YOUR COMMUNITIES THAN YOU COULD INSIDE THE CAPITOL!

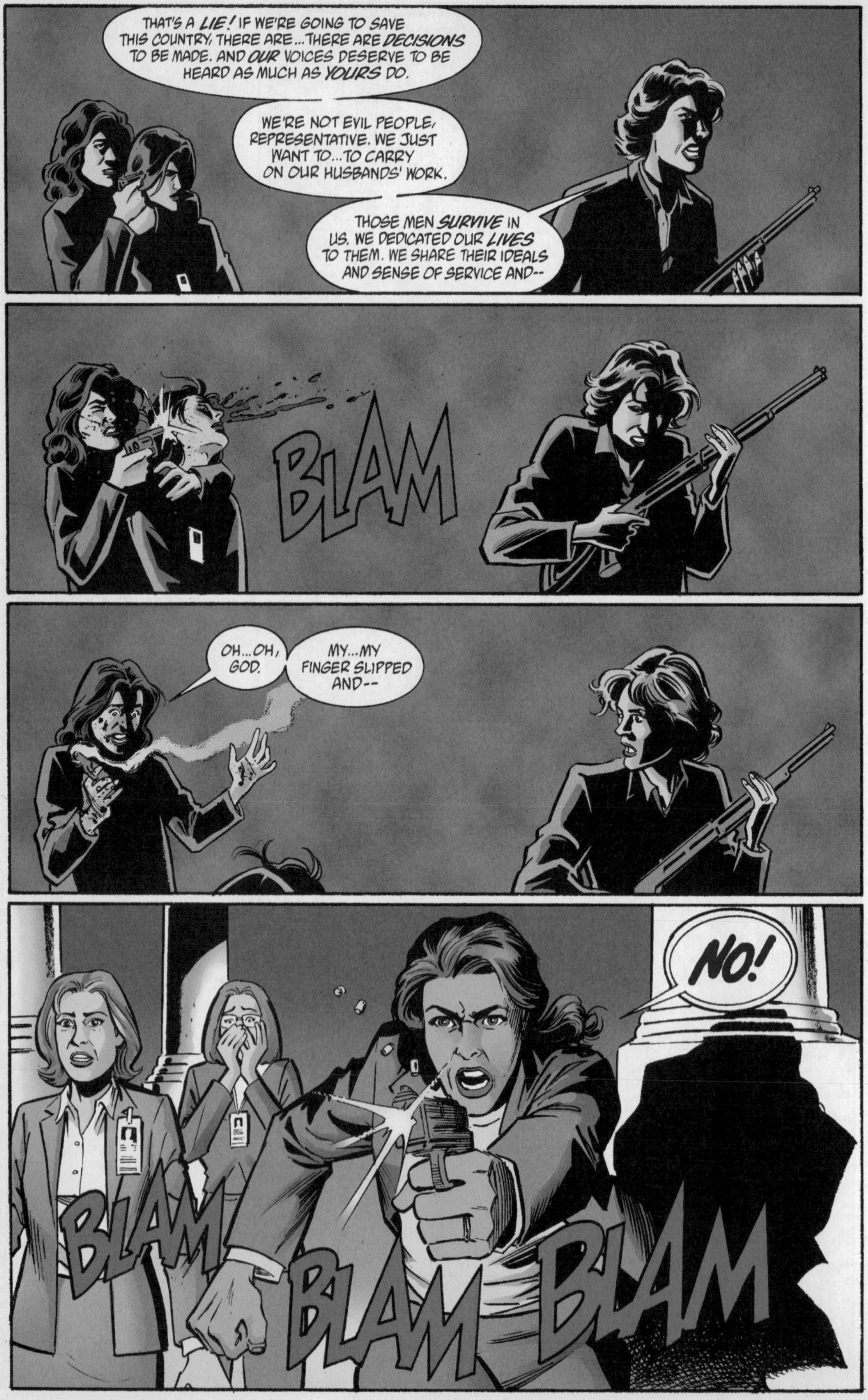
THAT'S A LIE! IF WE'RE GOING TO SAVE THIS COUNTRY, THERE ARE...THERE ARE DECISIONS TO BE MADE. AND OUR VOICES DESERVE TO BE HEARD AS MUCH AS YOURS DO.
WE'RE NOT EVIL PEOPLE, REPRESENTATIVE. WE JUST WANT TO...TO CARRY ON OUR HUSBANDS' WORK.
THOSE MEN SURVIVE IN US. WE DEDICATED OUR LIVES TO THEM. WE SHARE THEIR IDEALS AND SENSE OF SERVICE AND--
BLAM
OH...OH, GOD.
MY...MY FINGER SLIPPED AND--
NO!
BLAM
BLAM
BLAM

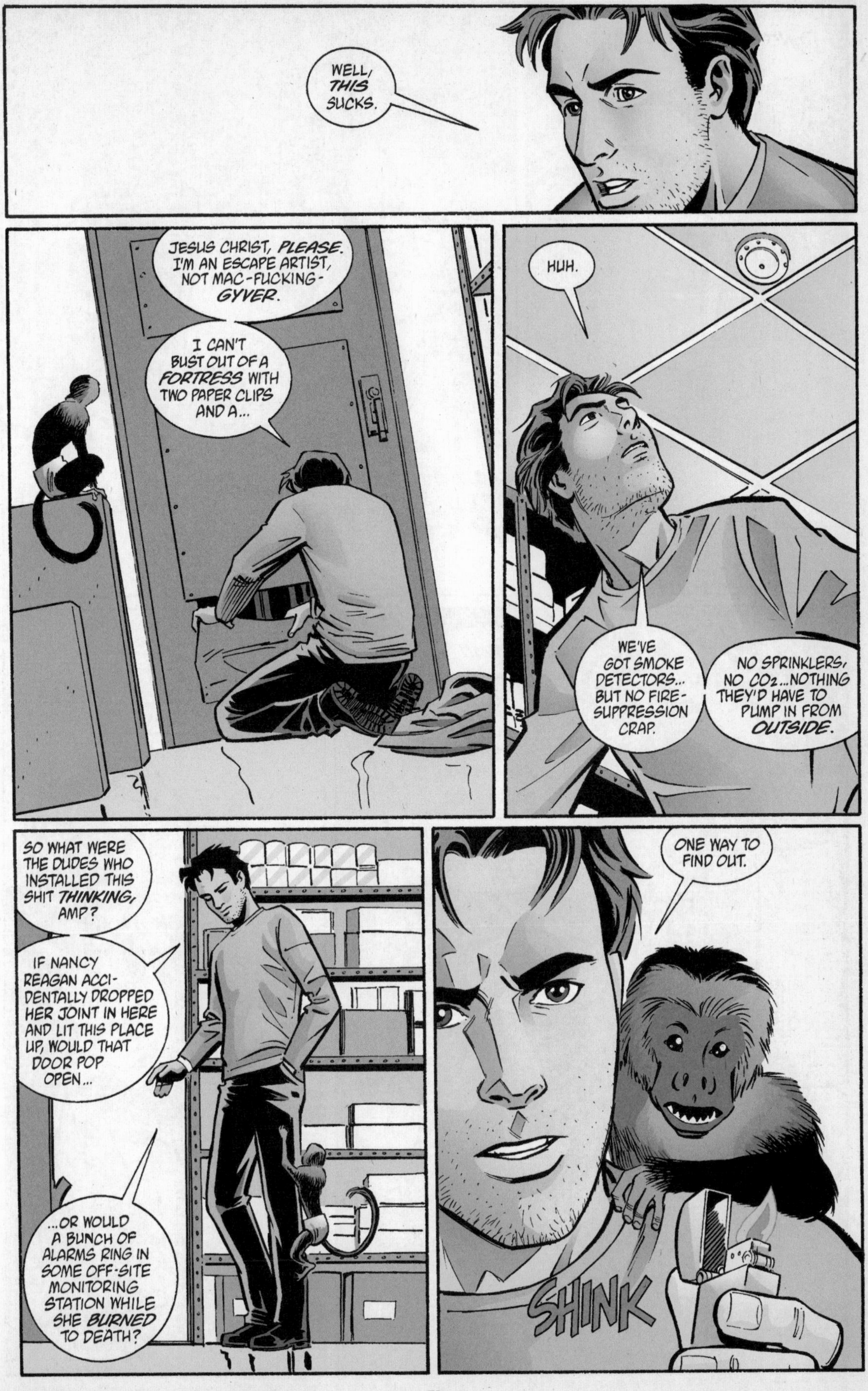
WELL, THIS SUCKS.
JESUS CHRIST, PLEASE. I'M AN ESCAPE ARTIST, NOT MAC-FUCKING-GYVER.
I CAN'T BUST OUT OF A FORTRESS WITH TWO PAPER CLIPS AND A...
HUH.
WE'VE GOT SMOKE DETECTORS... BUT NO FIRE-SUPPRESSION CRAP.
NO SPRINKLERS, NO CO2...NOTHING THEY'D HAVE TO PUMP IN FROM OUTSIDE.
SO WHAT WERE THE DUDES WHO INSTALLED THIS SHIT THINKING, AMP?
IF NANCY REAGAN ACCIDENTALLY DROPPED HER JOINT IN HERE AND LIT THIS PLACE UP, WOULD THAT DOOR POP OPEN...
...OR WOULD A BUNCH OF ALARMS RING IN SOME OFF-SITE MONITORING STATION WHILE SHE BURNED TO DEATH?
ONE WAY TO FIND OUT.
SHINK

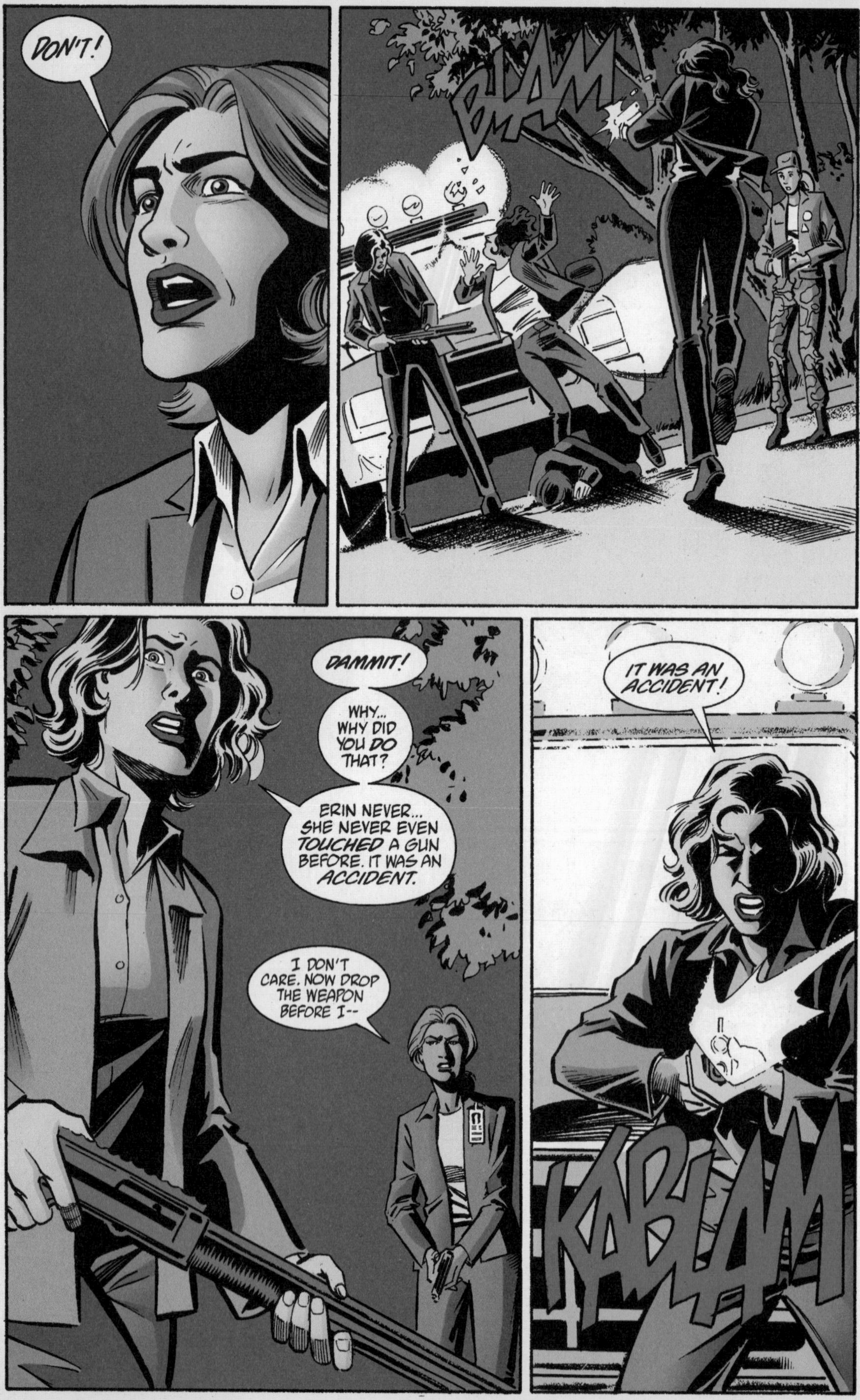
DON'T!
BLAM
DAMMIT!
WHY... WHY DID YOU DO THAT?
ERIN NEVER... SHE NEVER EVEN TOUCHED A GUN BEFORE. IT WAS AN ACCIDENT.
I DON'T CARE. NOW DROP THE WEAPON BEFORE I--
IT WAS AN ACCIDENT!
KABLAM

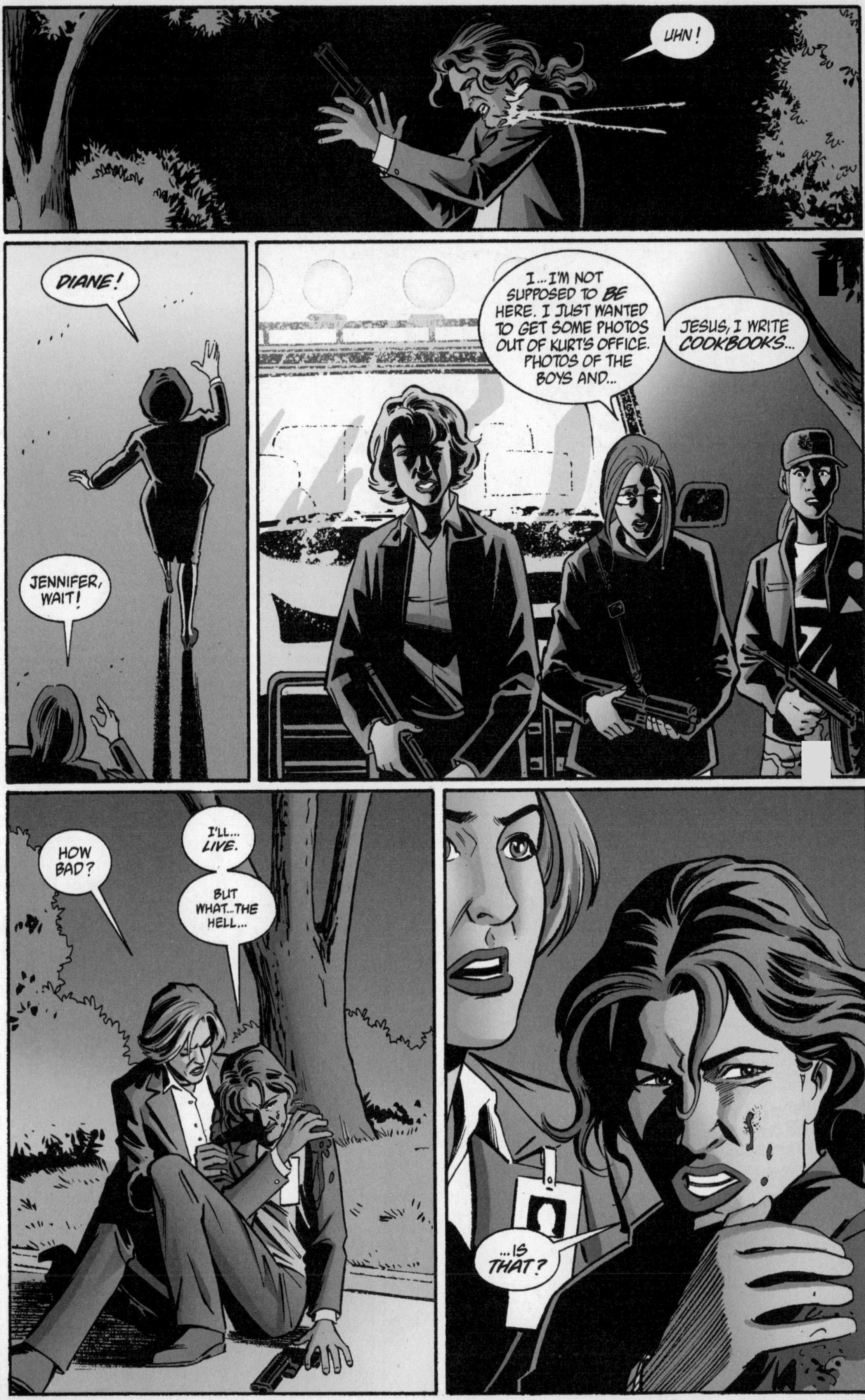
UHN!
DIANE!
JENNIFER, WAIT!
I... I'M NOT SUPPOSED TO BE HERE. I JUST WANTED TO GET SOME PHOTOS OUT OF KURT'S OFFICE. PHOTOS OF THE BOYS AND...
JESUS, I WRITE COOKBOOKS...
HOW BAD?
I'LL... LIVE.
BUT WHAT...THE HELL...
...IS THAT?

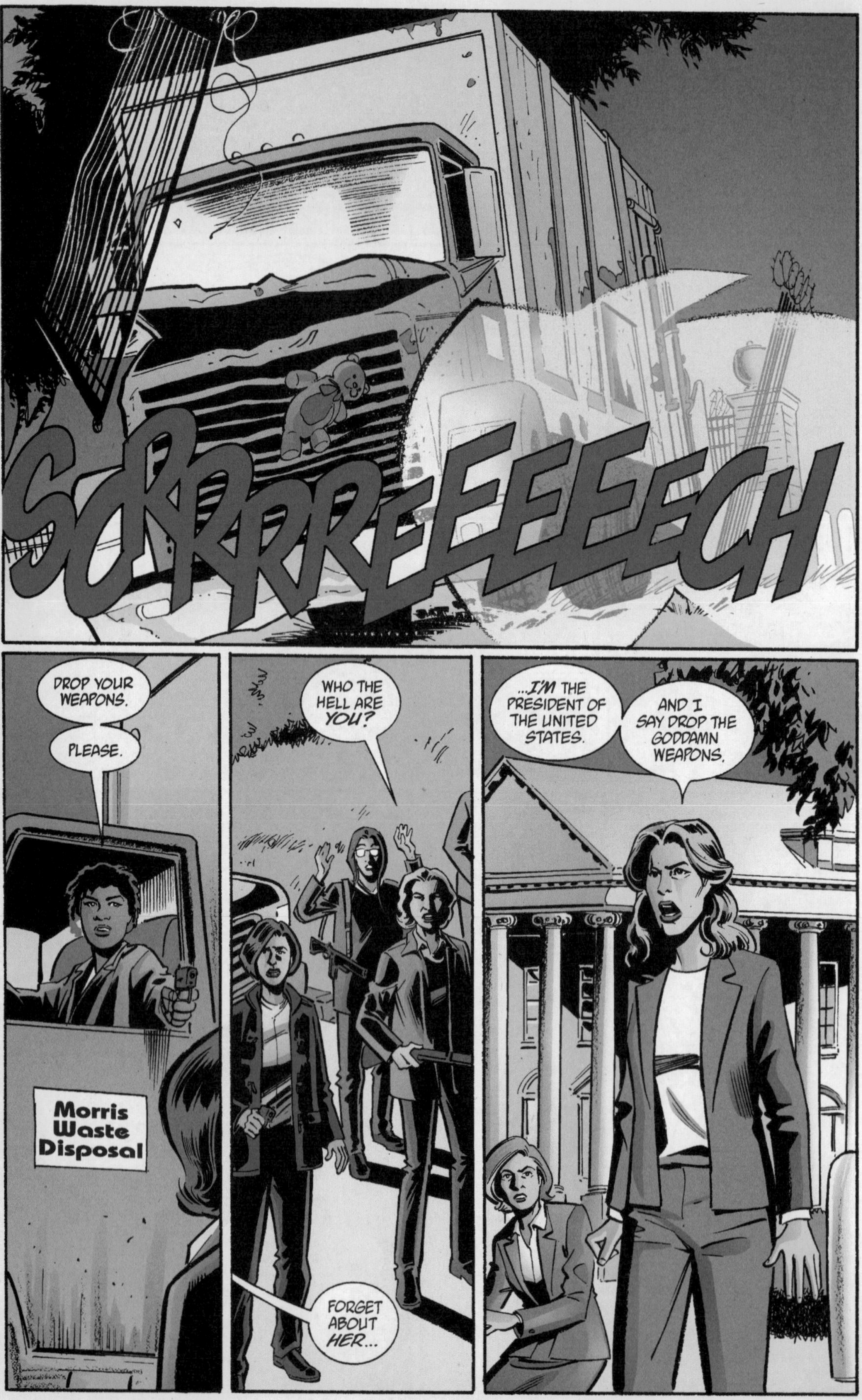
SCRRREEEEECH
DROP YOUR WEAPONS.
PLEASE.
Morris Waste Disposal
WHO THE HELL ARE YOU?
FORGET ABOUT HER...
...I'M THE PRESIDENT OF THE UNITED STATES.
AND I SAY DROP THE GODDAMN WEAPONS.

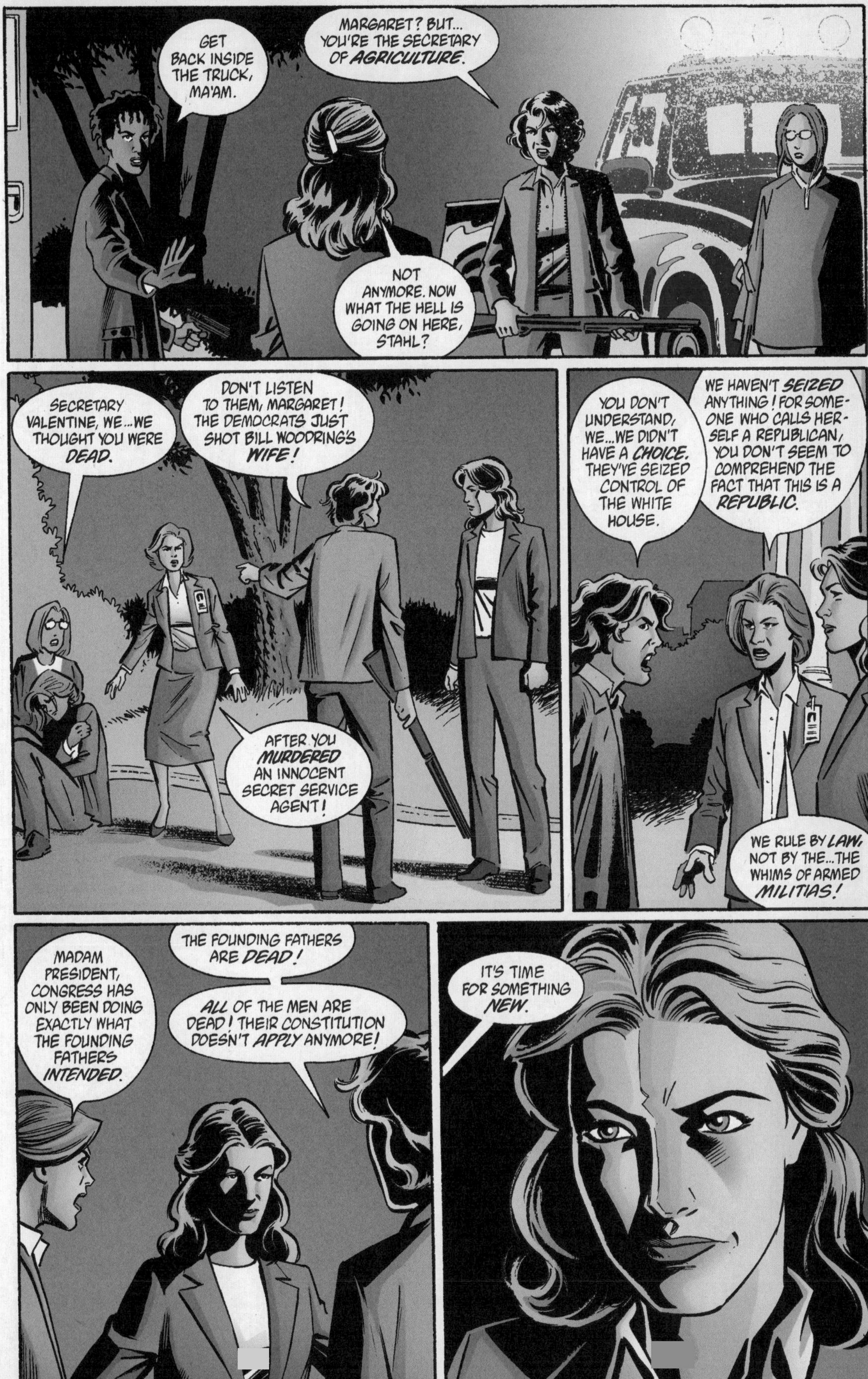
GET BACK INSIDE THE TRUCK, MA'AM.
MARGARET? BUT... YOU'RE THE SECRETARY OF AGRICULTURE.
NOT ANYMORE. NOW WHAT THE HELL IS GOING ON HERE, STAHL?
SECRETARY VALENTINE, WE...WE THOUGHT YOU WERE DEAD.
DON'T LISTEN TO THEM, MARGARET! THE DEMOCRATS JUST SHOT BILL WOODRING'S WIFE!
AFTER YOU MURDERED AN INNOCENT SECRET SERVICE AGENT!
YOU DON'T UNDERSTAND, WE...WE DIDN'T HAVE A CHOICE. THEY'VE SEIZED CONTROL OF THE WHITE HOUSE.
WE HAVEN'T SEIZED ANYTHING! FOR SOME-ONE WHO CALLS HER-SELF A REPUBLICAN, YOU DON'T SEEM TO COMPREHEND THE FACT THAT THIS IS A REPUBLIC.
WE RULE BY LAW, NOT BY THE...THE WHIMS OF ARMED MILITIAS!
MADAM PRESIDENT, CONGRESS HAS ONLY BEEN DOING EXACTLY WHAT THE FOUNDING FATHERS INTENDED.
THE FOUNDING FATHERS ARE DEAD!
ALL OF THE MEN ARE DEAD! THEIR CONSTITUTION DOESN'T APPLY ANYMORE!
IT'S TIME FOR SOMETHING NEW.

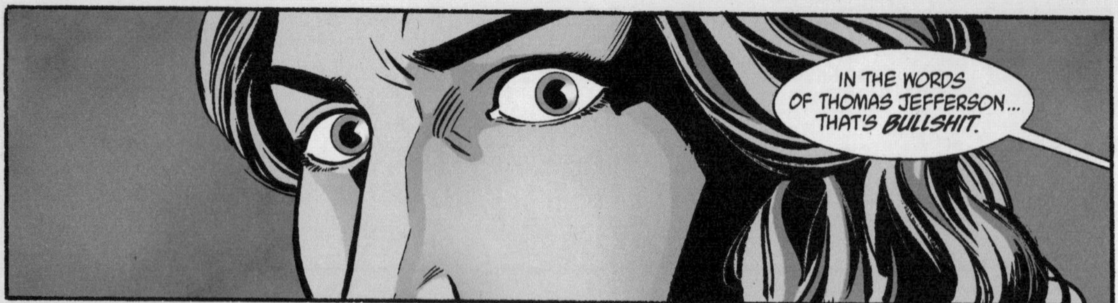
IN THE WORDS OF THOMAS JEFFERSON... THAT'S *BULLSHIT.*

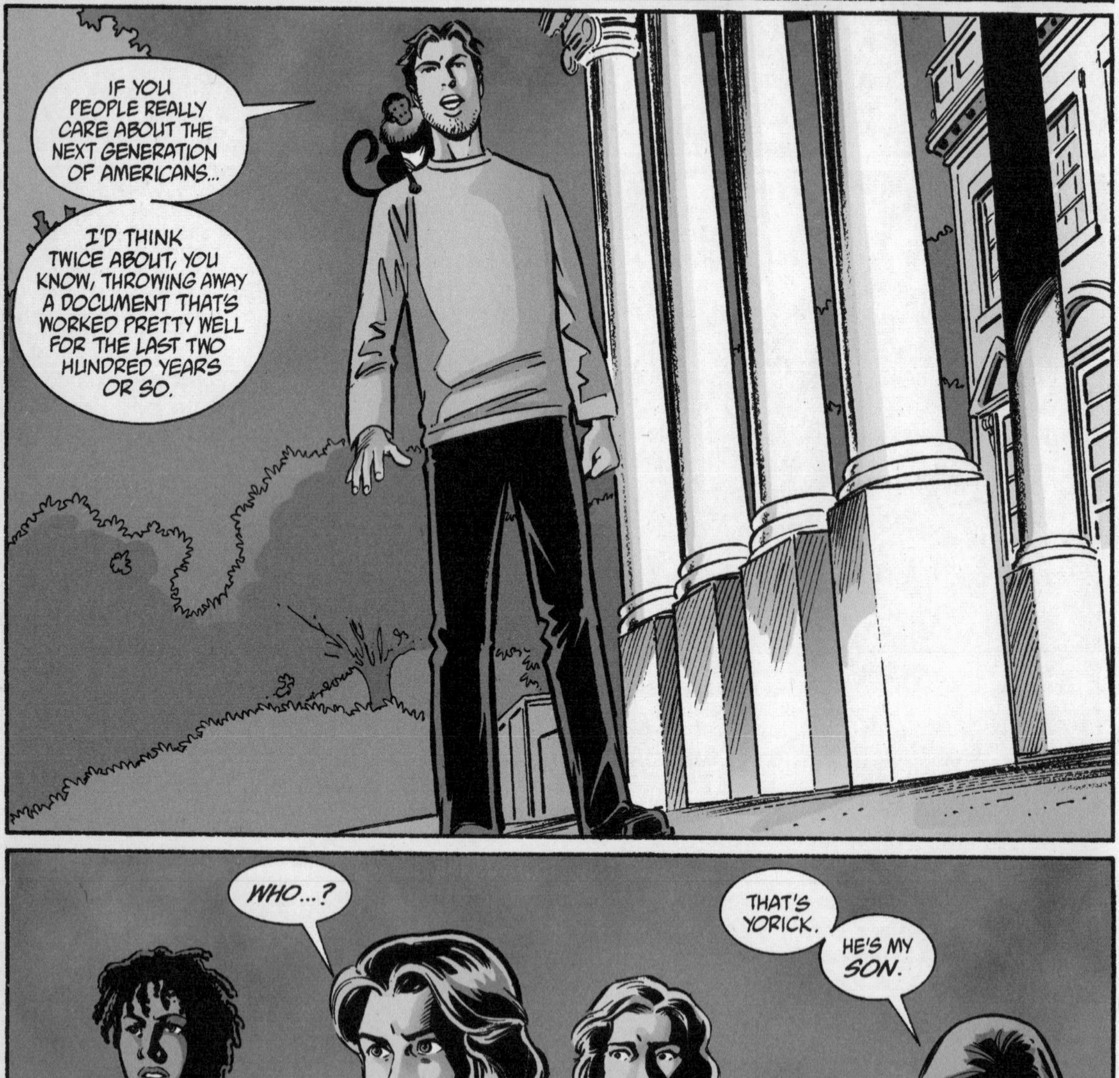
IF YOU PEOPLE REALLY CARE ABOUT THE NEXT GENERATION OF AMERICANS...
I'D THINK TWICE ABOUT, YOU KNOW, THROWING AWAY A DOCUMENT THAT'S WORKED PRETTY WELL FOR THE LAST TWO HUNDRED YEARS OR SO.

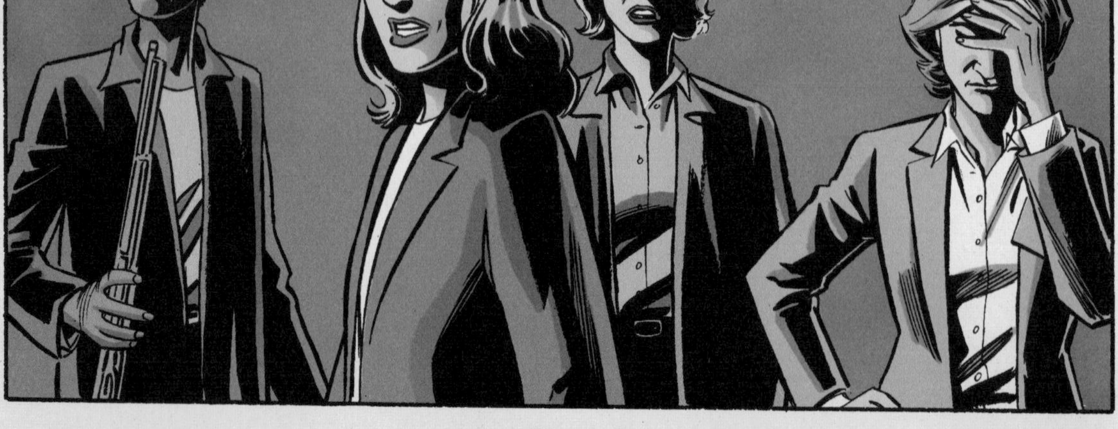
WHO...?
THAT'S YORICK.
HE'S MY *SON.*

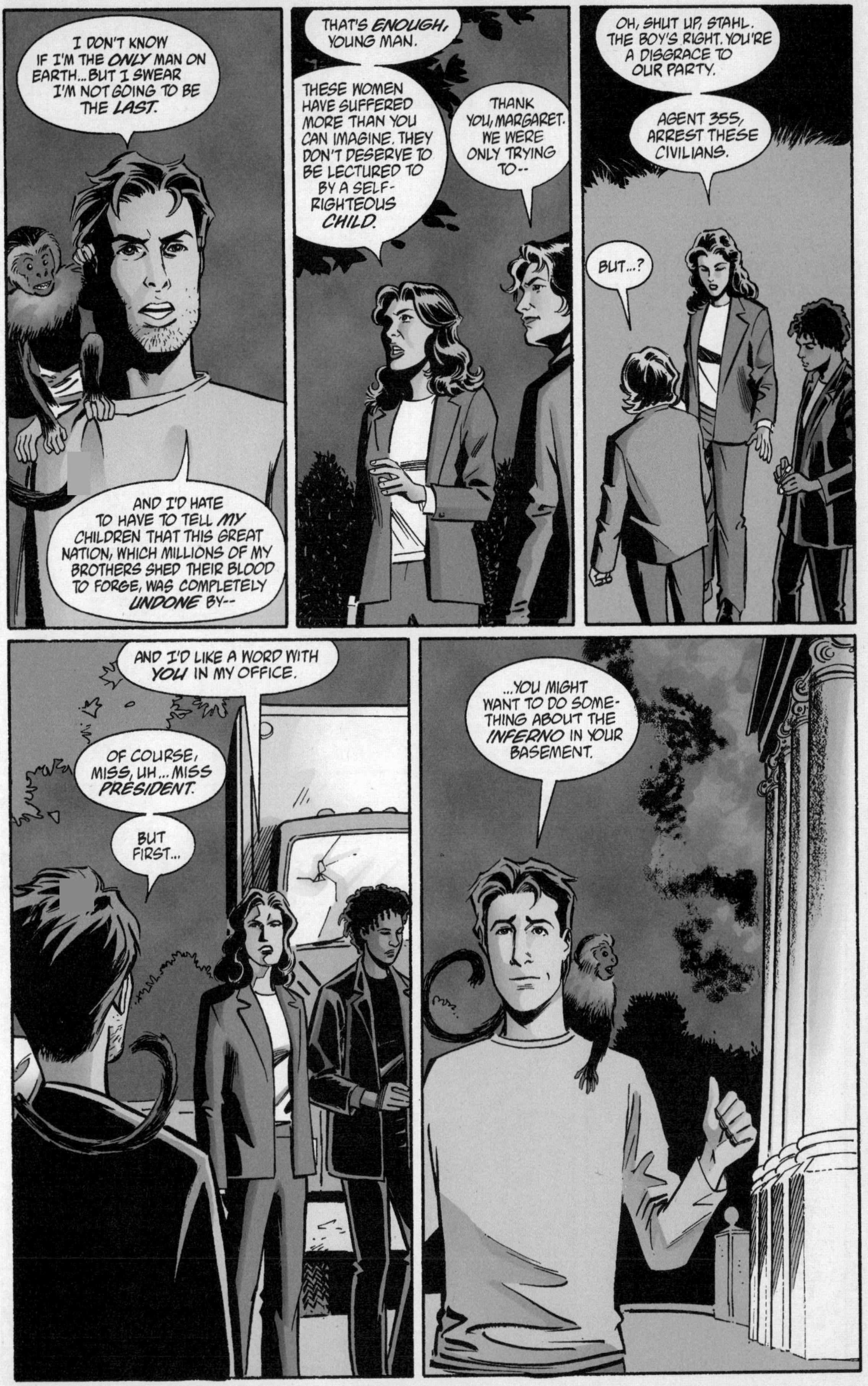
I DON'T KNOW IF I'M THE ONLY MAN ON EARTH... BUT I SWEAR I'M NOT GOING TO BE THE LAST.
AND I'D HATE TO HAVE TO TELL MY CHILDREN THAT THIS GREAT NATION, WHICH MILLIONS OF MY BROTHERS SHED THEIR BLOOD TO FORGE, WAS COMPLETELY UNDONE BY--
THAT'S ENOUGH, YOUNG MAN.
THESE WOMEN HAVE SUFFERED MORE THAN YOU CAN IMAGINE. THEY DON'T DESERVE TO BE LECTURED TO BY A SELF-RIGHTEOUS CHILD.
THANK YOU, MARGARET. WE WERE ONLY TRYING TO--
OH, SHUT UP, STAHL. THE BOY'S RIGHT. YOU'RE A DISGRACE TO OUR PARTY.
AGENT 355, ARREST THESE CIVILIANS.
BUT...?
AND I'D LIKE A WORD WITH YOU IN MY OFFICE.
OF COURSE, MISS, UH... MISS PRESIDENT.
BUT FIRST...
...YOU MIGHT WANT TO DO SOMETHING ABOUT THE INFERNO IN YOUR BASEMENT.

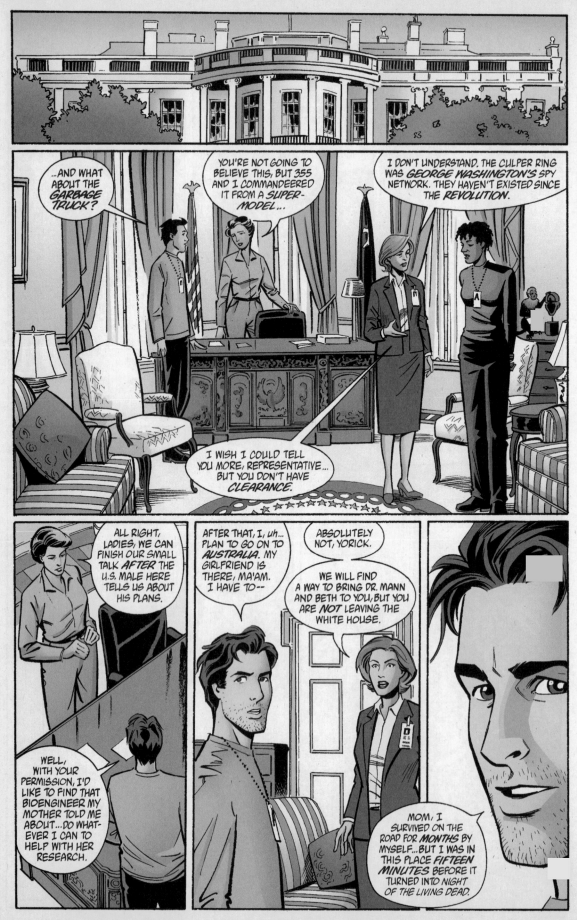

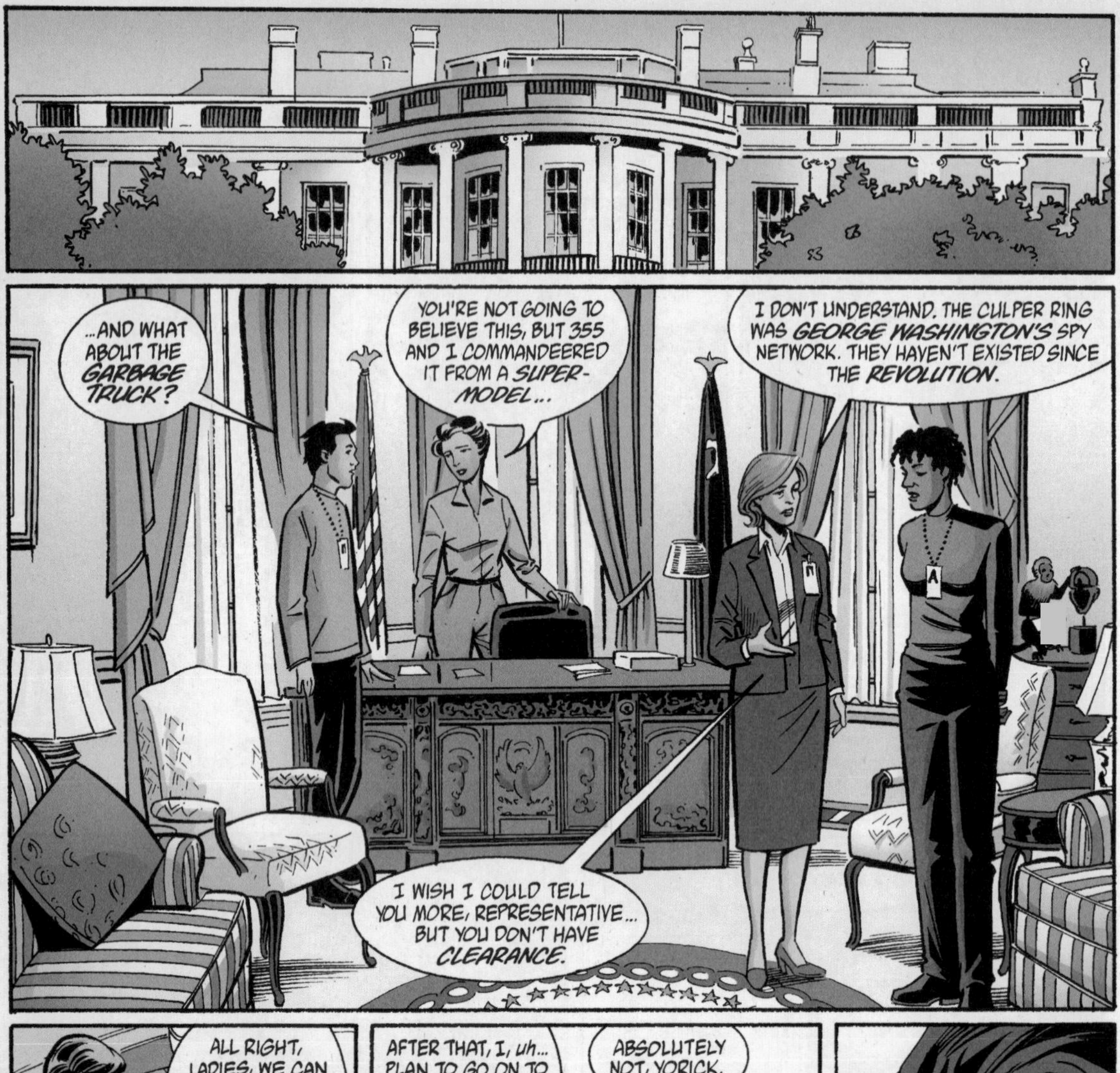
...AND WHAT ABOUT THE GARBAGE TRUCK?
YOU'RE NOT GOING TO BELIEVE THIS, BUT 355 AND I COMMANDEERED IT FROM A SUPER-MODEL...
I DON'T UNDERSTAND. THE CULPER RING WAS GEORGE WASHINGTON'S SPY NETWORK. THEY HAVEN'T EXISTED SINCE THE REVOLUTION.
I WISH I COULD TELL YOU MORE, REPRESENTATIVE... BUT YOU DON'T HAVE CLEARANCE.
ALL RIGHT, LADIES, WE CAN FINISH OUR SMALL TALK AFTER THE U.S. MALE HERE TELLS US ABOUT HIS PLANS.
WELL, WITH YOUR PERMISSION, I'D LIKE TO FIND THAT BIOENGINEER MY MOTHER TOLD ME ABOUT...DO WHAT-EVER I CAN TO HELP WITH HER RESEARCH.
AFTER THAT, I, uh... PLAN TO GO ON TO AUSTRALIA. MY GIRLFRIEND IS THERE, MA'AM. I HAVE TO--
ABSOLUTELY NOT, YORICK.
WE WILL FIND A WAY TO BRING DR. MANN AND BETH TO YOU, BUT YOU ARE NOT LEAVING THE WHITE HOUSE.
MOM, I SURVIVED ON THE ROAD FOR MONTHS BY MYSELF...BUT I WAS IN THIS PLACE FIFTEEN MINUTES BEFORE IT TURNED INTO NIGHT OF THE LIVING DEAD.

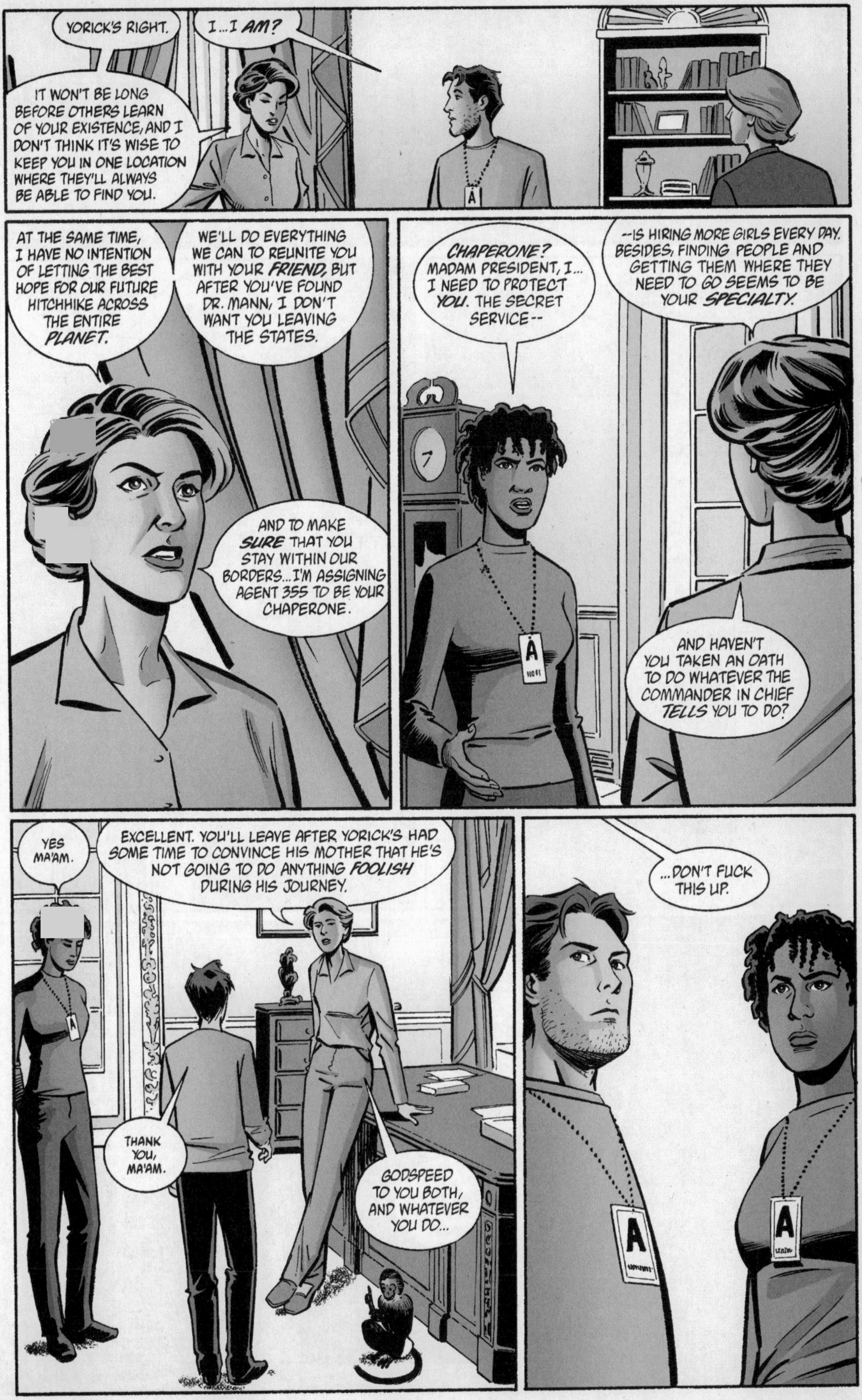
YORICK'S RIGHT.
I...I AM?
IT WON'T BE LONG BEFORE OTHERS LEARN OF YOUR EXISTENCE, AND I DON'T THINK IT'S WISE TO KEEP YOU IN ONE LOCATION WHERE THEY'LL ALWAYS BE ABLE TO FIND YOU.
AT THE SAME TIME, I HAVE NO INTENTION OF LETTING THE BEST HOPE FOR OUR FUTURE HITCHHIKE ACROSS THE ENTIRE PLANET.
WE'LL DO EVERYTHING WE CAN TO REUNITE YOU WITH YOUR FRIEND, BUT AFTER YOU'VE FOUND DR. MANN, I DON'T WANT YOU LEAVING THE STATES.
AND TO MAKE SURE THAT YOU STAY WITHIN OUR BORDERS...I'M ASSIGNING AGENT 355 TO BE YOUR CHAPERONE.
CHAPERONE? MADAM PRESIDENT, I... I NEED TO PROTECT YOU. THE SECRET SERVICE--
--IS HIRING MORE GIRLS EVERY DAY. BESIDES, FINDING PEOPLE AND GETTING THEM WHERE THEY NEED TO GO SEEMS TO BE YOUR SPECIALTY.
AND HAVEN'T YOU TAKEN AN OATH TO DO WHATEVER THE COMMANDER IN CHIEF TELLS YOU TO DO?
YES MA'AM.
EXCELLENT. YOU'LL LEAVE AFTER YORICK'S HAD SOME TIME TO CONVINCE HIS MOTHER THAT HE'S NOT GOING TO DO ANYTHING FOOLISH DURING HIS JOURNEY.
THANK YOU, MA'AM.
GODSPEED TO YOU BOTH, AND WHATEVER YOU DO...
...DON'T FUCK THIS UP.

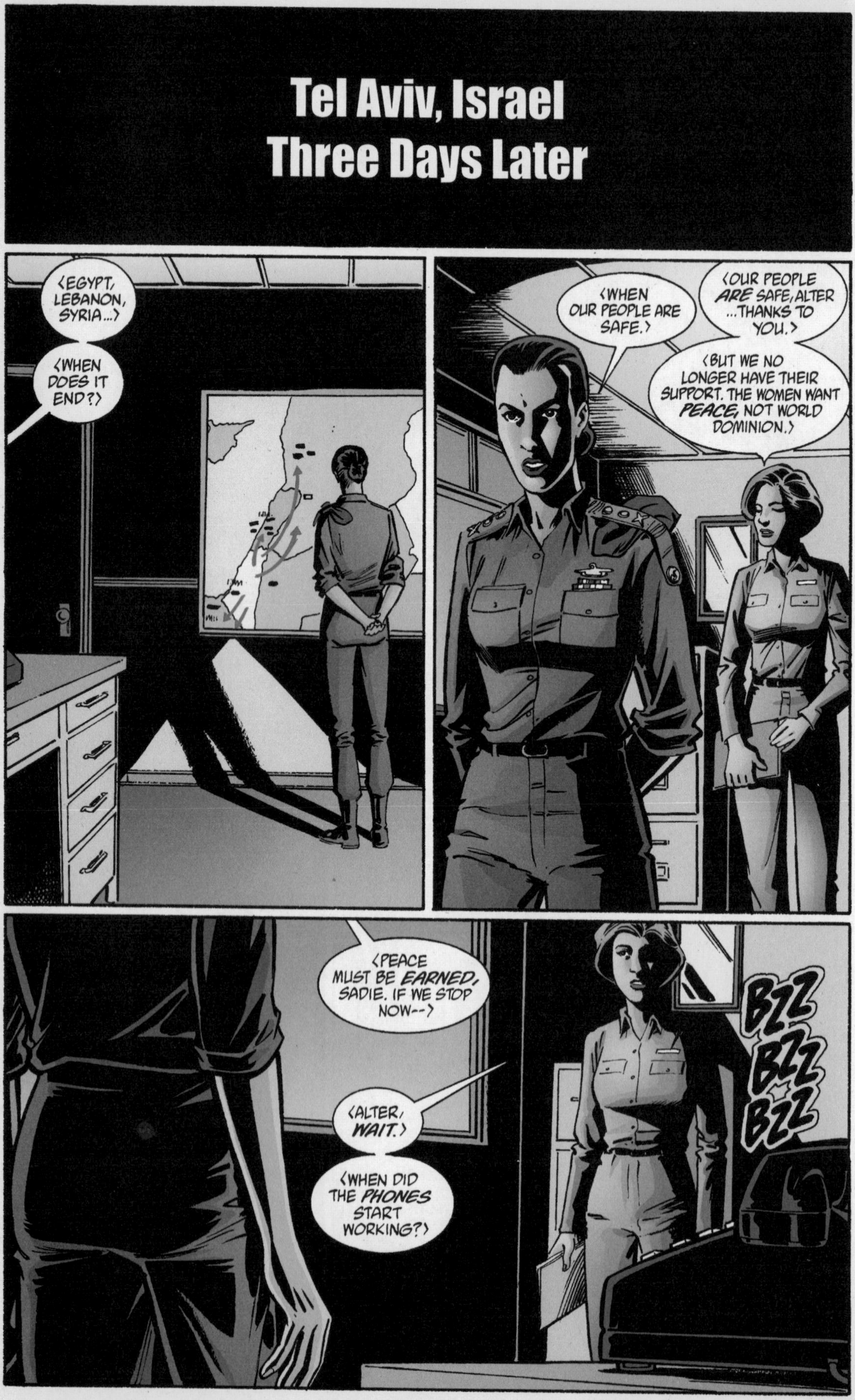
Tel Aviv, Israel
Three Days Later
‹EGYPT, LEBANON, SYRIA...›
‹WHEN DOES IT END?›
‹WHEN OUR PEOPLE ARE SAFE.›
‹OUR PEOPLE ARE SAFE, ALTER ...THANKS TO YOU.›
‹BUT WE NO LONGER HAVE THEIR SUPPORT. THE WOMEN WANT PEACE, NOT WORLD DOMINION.›
‹PEACE MUST BE EARNED, SADIE. IF WE STOP NOW--›
‹ALTER, WAIT.›
‹WHEN DID THE PHONES START WORKING?›
BZZ BZZ BZZ

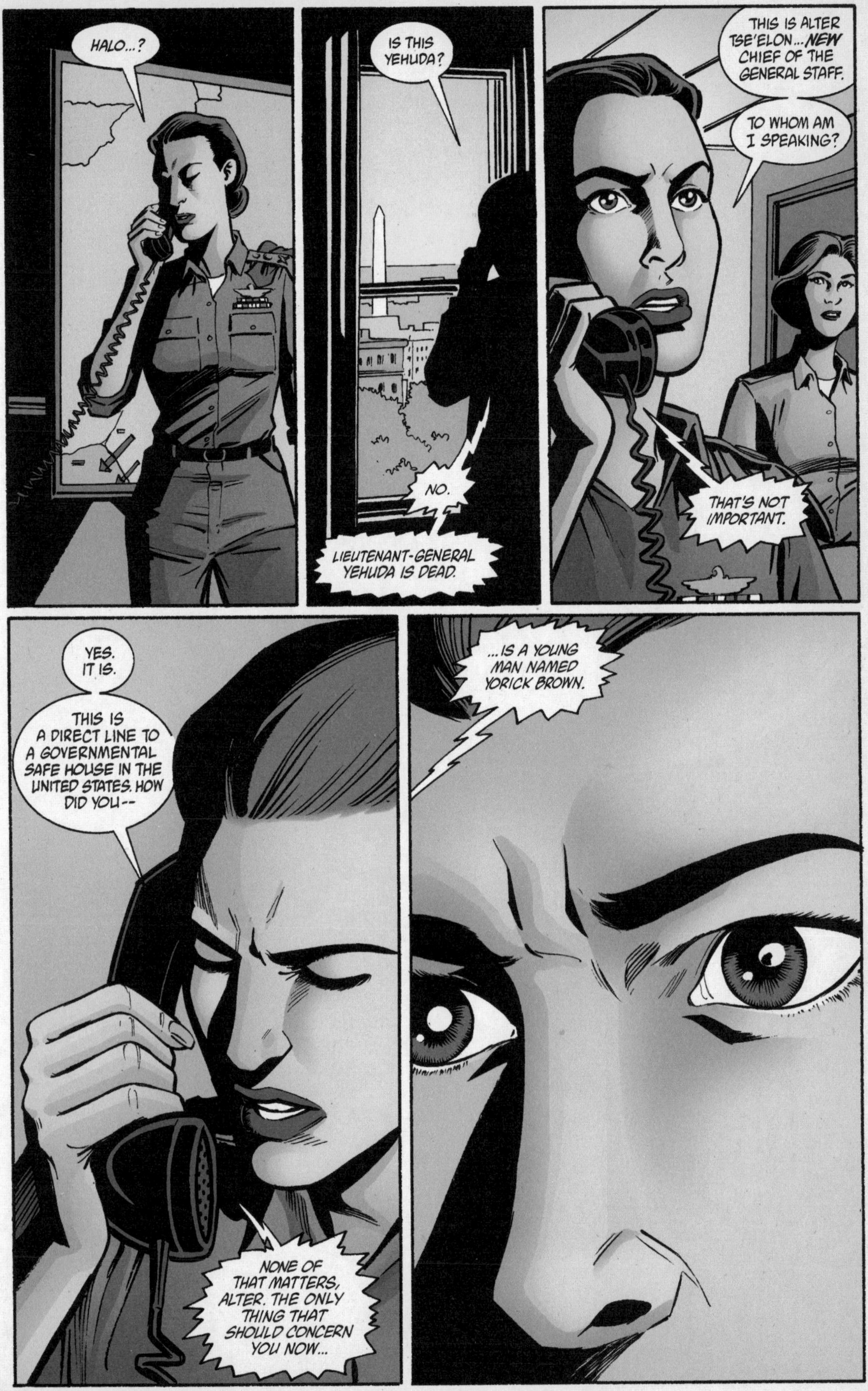
HALO...?
IS THIS YEHUDA?
NO.
LIEUTENANT-GENERAL YEHUDA IS DEAD.
THIS IS ALTER TSE'ELON... NEW CHIEF OF THE GENERAL STAFF.
TO WHOM AM I SPEAKING?
THAT'S NOT IMPORTANT.
YES. IT IS.
THIS IS A DIRECT LINE TO A GOVERNMENTAL SAFE HOUSE IN THE UNITED STATES. HOW DID YOU--
NONE OF THAT MATTERS, ALTER. THE ONLY THING THAT SHOULD CONCERN YOU NOW...
...IS A YOUNG MAN NAMED YORICK BROWN.

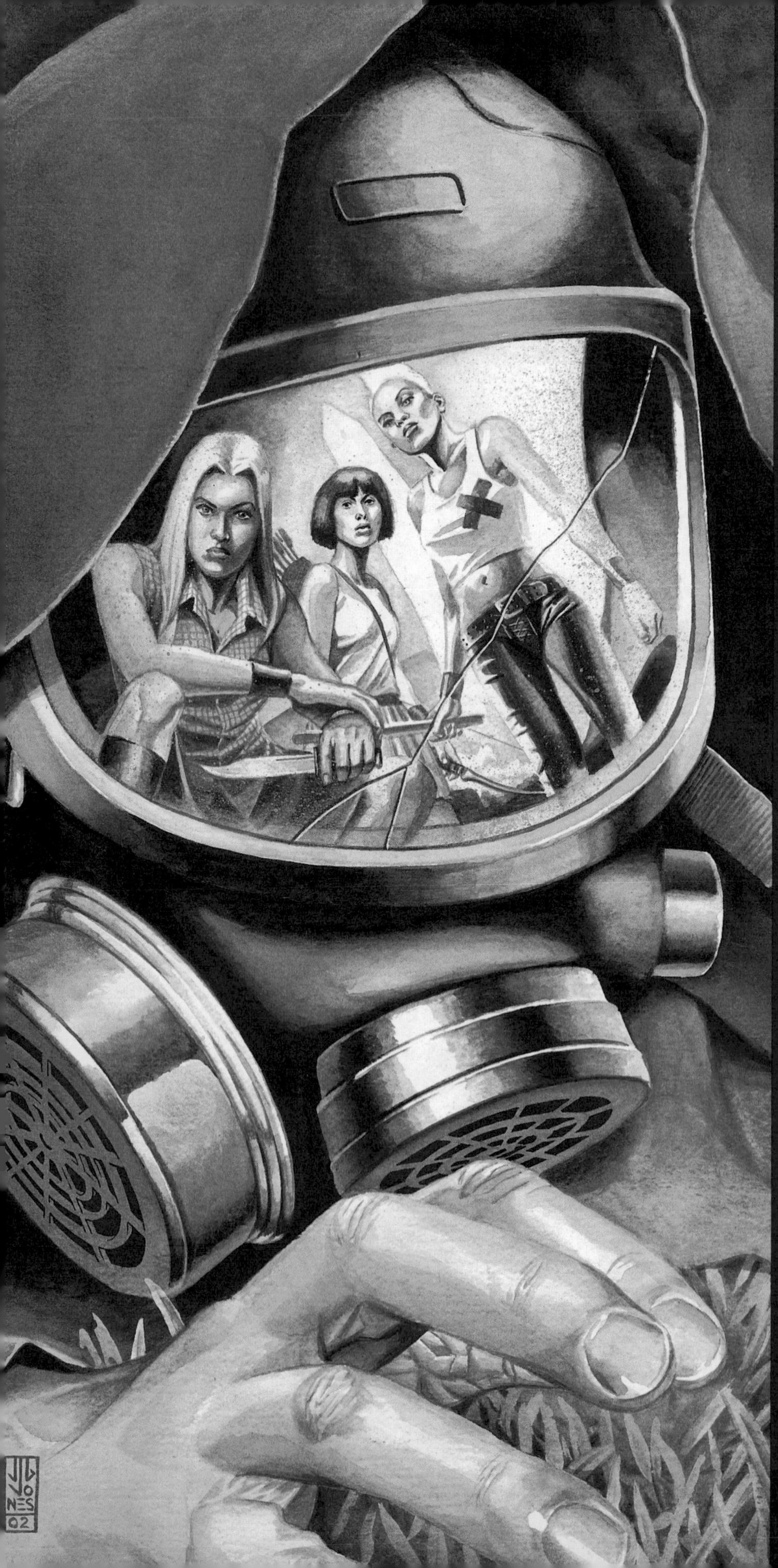
JG JONES 02

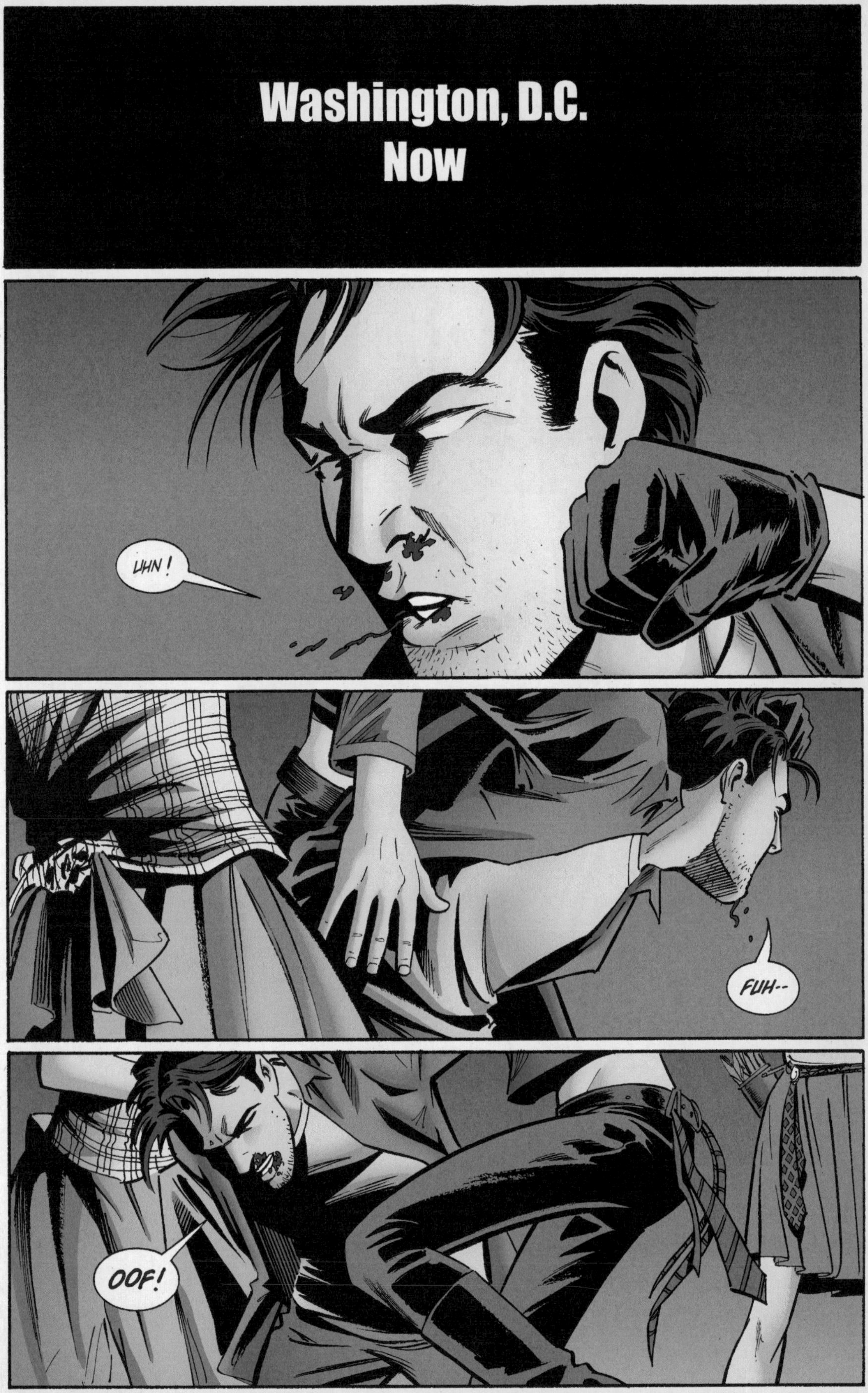
Washington, D.C.
Now
UHN!
FUH--
OOF!

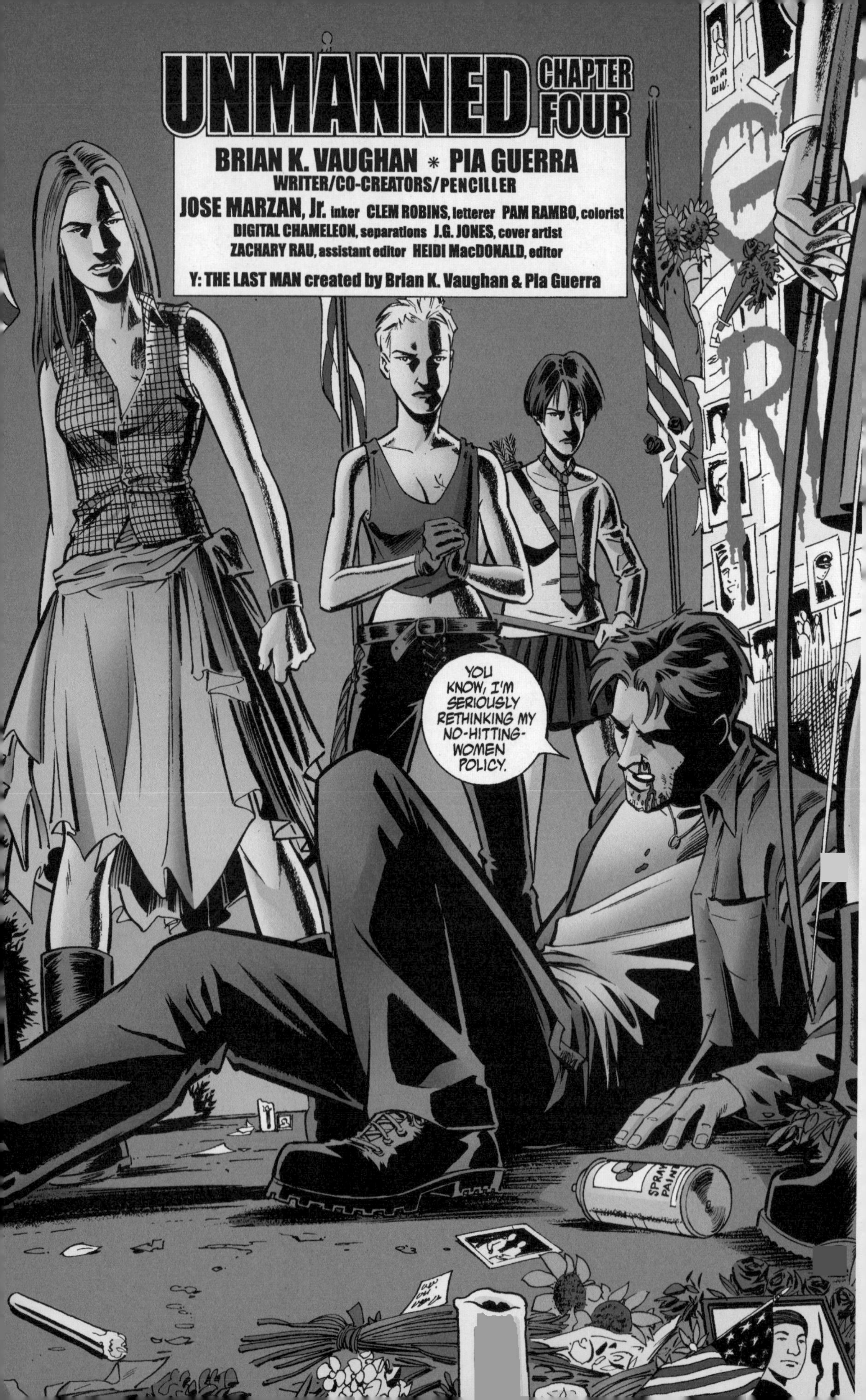
UNMANNED CHAPTER FOUR
BRIAN K. VAUGHAN * PIA GUERRA
WRITER/CO-CREATORS/PENCILLER
JOSE MARZAN, Jr. inker CLEM ROBINS, letterer PAM RAMBO, colorist
DIGITAL CHAMELEON, separations J.G. JONES, cover artist
ZACHARY RAU, assistant editor HEIDI MacDONALD, editor
Y: THE LAST MAN created by Brian K. Vaughan & Pia Guerra
YOU KNOW, I'M SERIOUSLY RETHINKING MY NO-HITTING-WOMEN POLICY.
SPRAY PAINT

Washington, D.C.
One Hour Ago

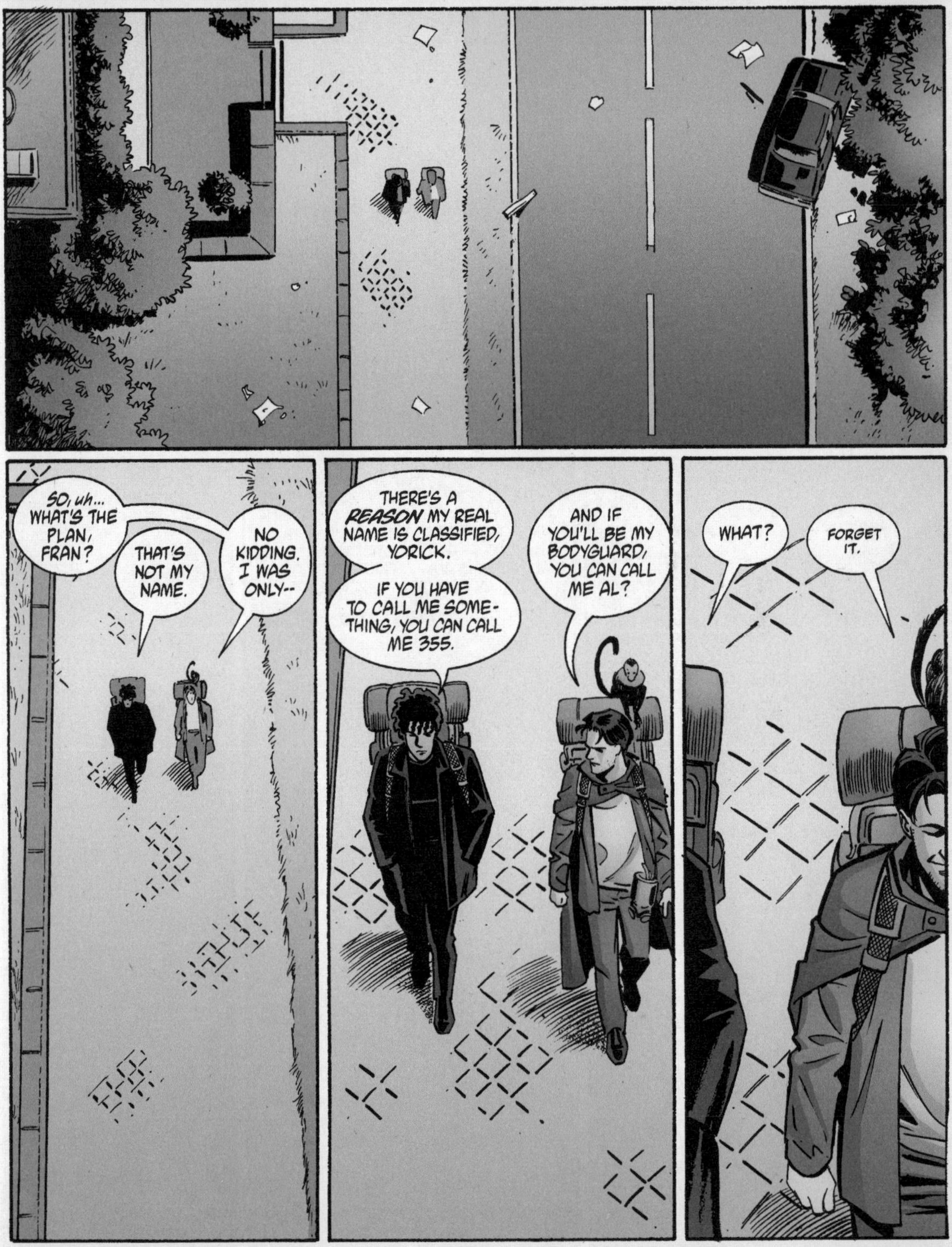

SO, uh... WHAT'S THE PLAN, FRAN?
THAT'S NOT MY NAME.
NO KIDDING. I WAS ONLY--
THERE'S A REASON MY REAL NAME IS CLASSIFIED, YORICK.
IF YOU HAVE TO CALL ME SOMETHING, YOU CAN CALL ME 355.
AND IF YOU'LL BE MY BODYGUARD, YOU CAN CALL ME AL?
WHAT?
FORGET IT.

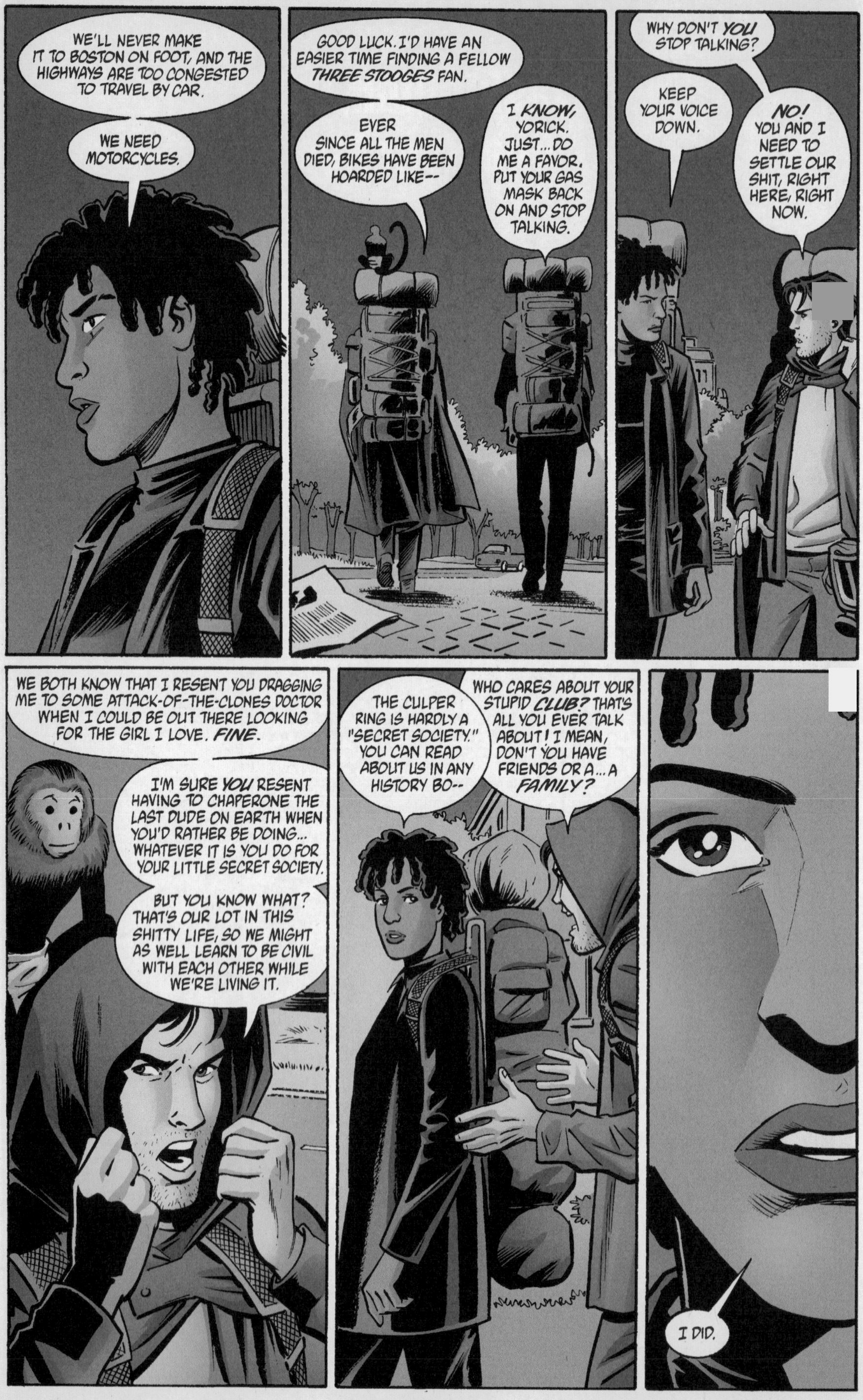

WE'LL NEVER MAKE IT TO BOSTON ON FOOT, AND THE HIGHWAYS ARE TOO CONGESTED TO TRAVEL BY CAR.
WE NEED MOTORCYCLES.
GOOD LUCK. I'D HAVE AN EASIER TIME FINDING A FELLOW THREE STOOGES FAN.
EVER SINCE ALL THE MEN DIED, BIKES HAVE BEEN HOARDED LIKE--
I KNOW, YORICK. JUST... DO ME A FAVOR. PUT YOUR GAS MASK BACK ON AND STOP TALKING.
WHY DON'T YOU STOP TALKING?
KEEP YOUR VOICE DOWN.
NO! YOU AND I NEED TO SETTLE OUR SHIT, RIGHT HERE, RIGHT NOW.
WE BOTH KNOW THAT I RESENT YOU DRAGGING ME TO SOME ATTACK-OF-THE-CLONES DOCTOR WHEN I COULD BE OUT THERE LOOKING FOR THE GIRL I LOVE. FINE.
I'M SURE YOU RESENT HAVING TO CHAPERONE THE LAST DUDE ON EARTH WHEN YOU'D RATHER BE DOING... WHATEVER IT IS YOU DO FOR YOUR LITTLE SECRET SOCIETY.
BUT YOU KNOW WHAT? THAT'S OUR LOT IN THIS SHITTY LIFE, SO WE MIGHT AS WELL LEARN TO BE CIVIL WITH EACH OTHER WHILE WE'RE LIVING IT.
THE CULPER RING IS HARDLY A "SECRET SOCIETY." YOU CAN READ ABOUT US IN ANY HISTORY BO--
WHO CARES ABOUT YOUR STUPID CLUB? THAT'S ALL YOU EVER TALK ABOUT! I MEAN, DON'T YOU HAVE FRIENDS OR A... A FAMILY?
I DID.

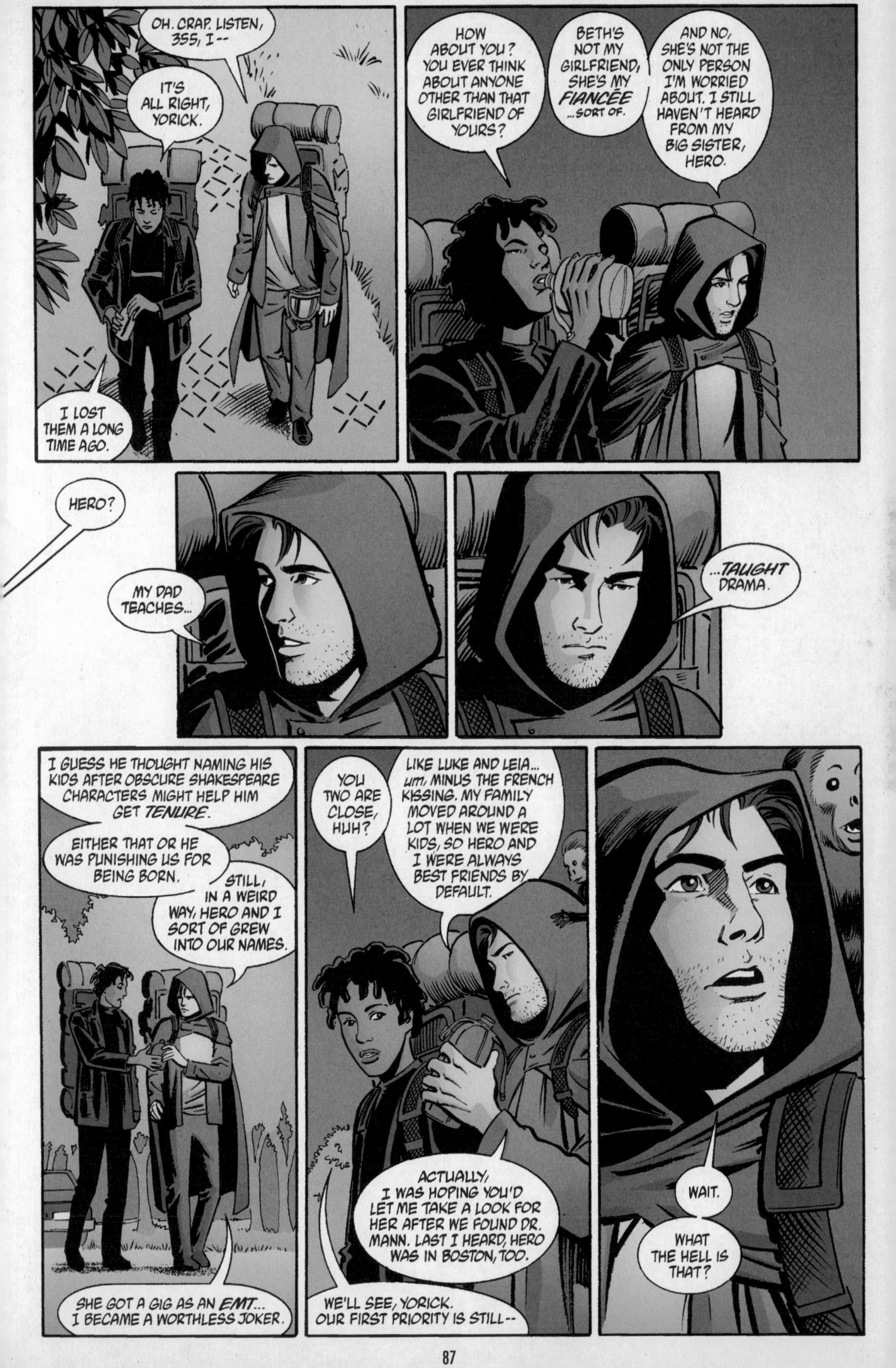
OH. CRAP. LISTEN, 355, I--
IT'S ALL RIGHT, YORICK.
I LOST THEM A LONG TIME AGO.
HOW ABOUT YOU? YOU EVER THINK ABOUT ANYONE OTHER THAN THAT GIRLFRIEND OF YOURS?
BETH'S NOT MY GIRLFRIEND, SHE'S MY FIANCÉE ...SORT OF.
AND NO, SHE'S NOT THE ONLY PERSON I'M WORRIED ABOUT. I STILL HAVEN'T HEARD FROM MY BIG SISTER, HERO.
HERO?
MY DAD TEACHES...
...TAUGHT DRAMA.
I GUESS HE THOUGHT NAMING HIS KIDS AFTER OBSCURE SHAKESPEARE CHARACTERS MIGHT HELP HIM GET TENURE.
EITHER THAT OR HE WAS PUNISHING US FOR BEING BORN.
STILL, IN A WEIRD WAY, HERO AND I SORT OF GREW INTO OUR NAMES.
SHE GOT A GIG AS AN EMT... I BECAME A WORTHLESS JOKER.
YOU TWO ARE CLOSE, HUH?
LIKE LUKE AND LEIA... UM, MINUS THE FRENCH KISSING. MY FAMILY MOVED AROUND A LOT WHEN WE WERE KIDS, SO HERO AND I WERE ALWAYS BEST FRIENDS BY DEFAULT.
ACTUALLY, I WAS HOPING YOU'D LET ME TAKE A LOOK FOR HER AFTER WE FOUND DR. MANN. LAST I HEARD, HERO WAS IN BOSTON, TOO.
WE'LL SEE, YORICK. OUR FIRST PRIORITY IS STILL--
WAIT.
WHAT THE HELL IS THAT?

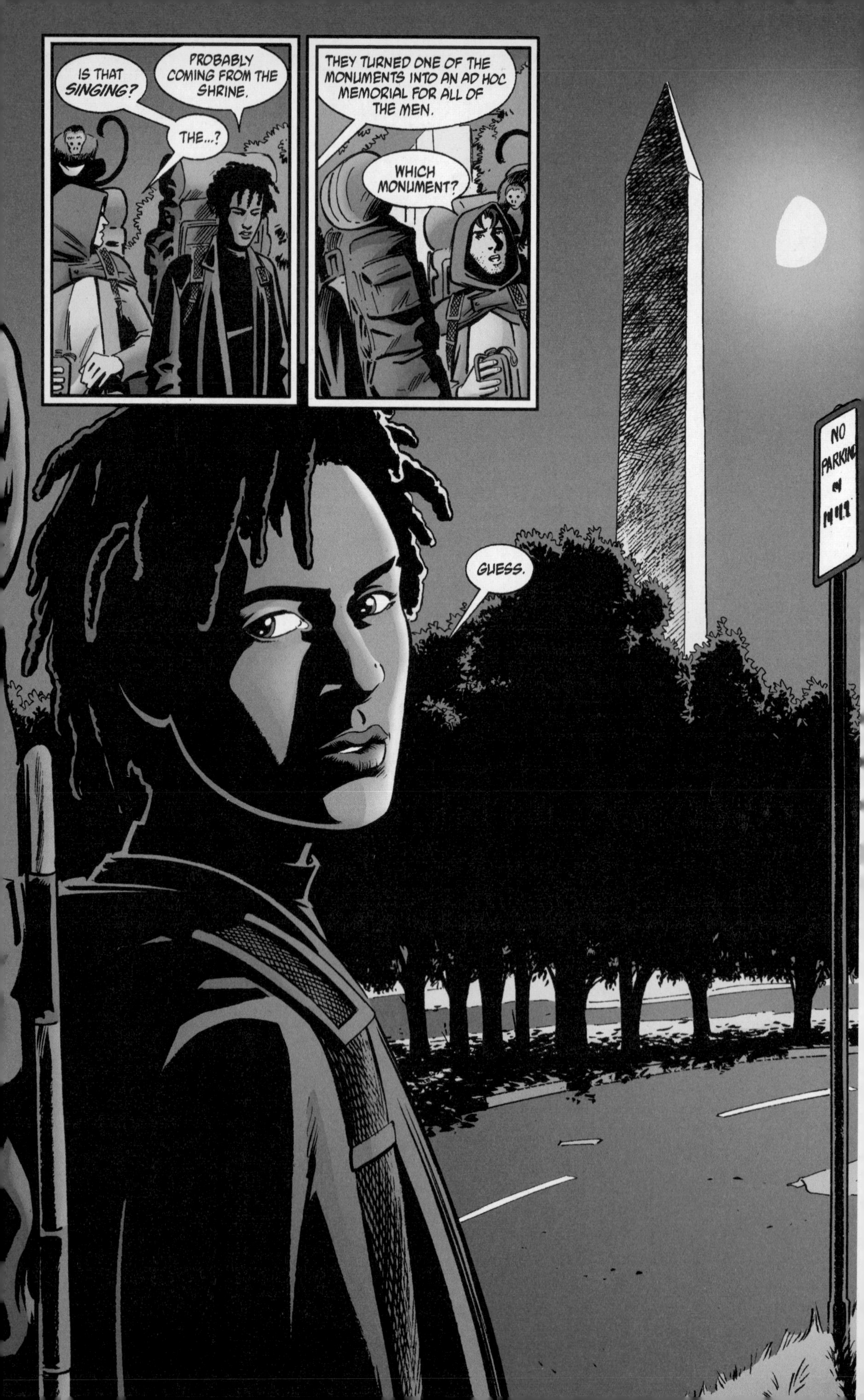
IS THAT SINGING?
PROBABLY COMING FROM THE SHRINE.
THE...?
THEY TURNED ONE OF THE MONUMENTS INTO AN AD HOC MEMORIAL FOR ALL OF THE MEN.
WHICH MONUMENT?
GUESS.
NO PARKING

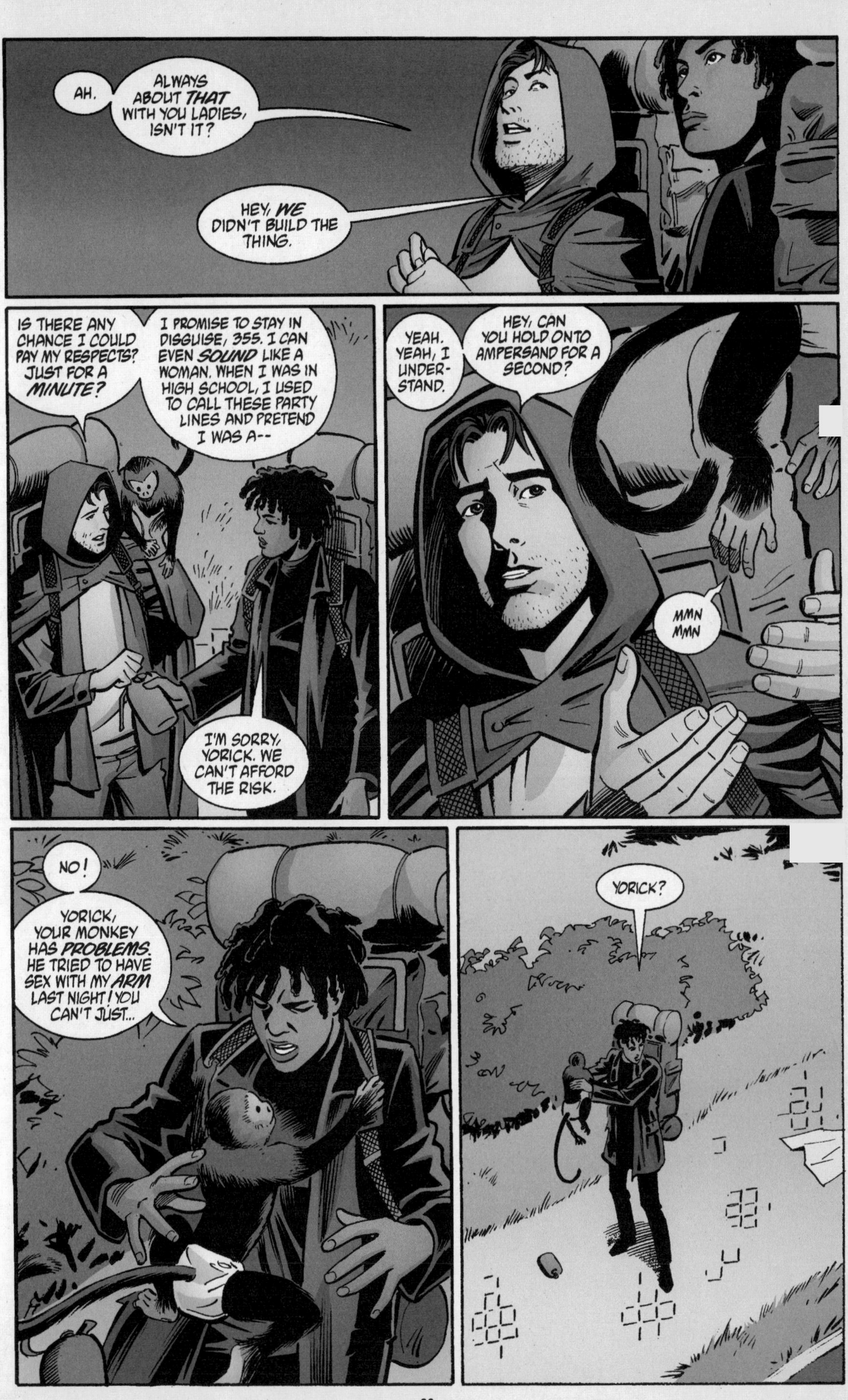
AH.
ALWAYS ABOUT THAT WITH YOU LADIES, ISN'T IT?
HEY, WE DIDN'T BUILD THE THING.
IS THERE ANY CHANCE I COULD PAY MY RESPECTS? JUST FOR A MINUTE?
I PROMISE TO STAY IN DISGUISE, 355. I CAN EVEN SOUND LIKE A WOMAN. WHEN I WAS IN HIGH SCHOOL, I USED TO CALL THESE PARTY LINES AND PRETEND I WAS A--
I'M SORRY, YORICK. WE CAN'T AFFORD THE RISK.
YEAH. YEAH, I UNDER-STAND.
HEY, CAN YOU HOLD ONTO AMPERSAND FOR A SECOND?
MMN MMN
NO!
YORICK, YOUR MONKEY HAS PROBLEMS. HE TRIED TO HAVE SEX WITH MY ARM LAST NIGHT! YOU CAN'T JUST...
YORICK?

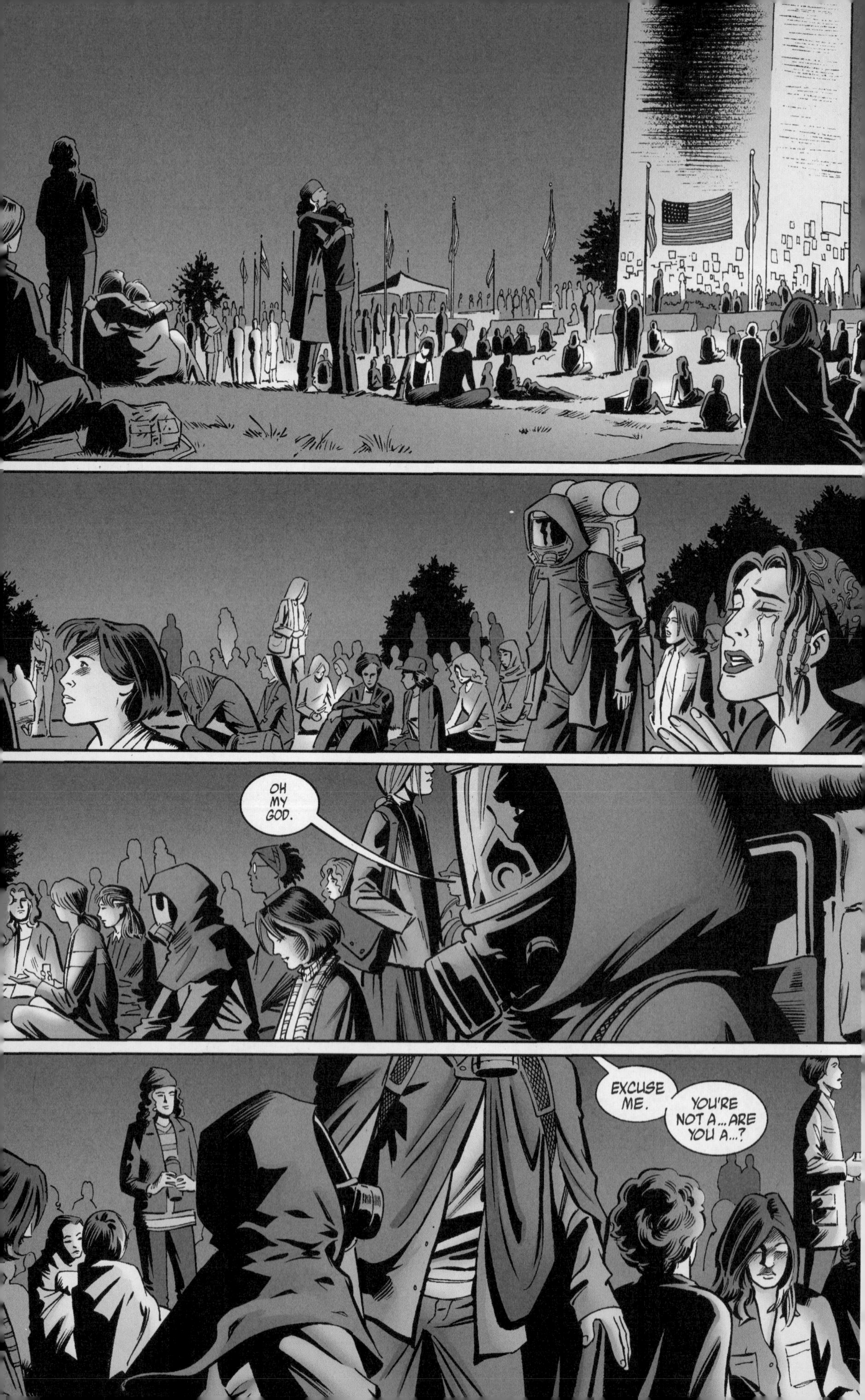
OH MY GOD.
EXCUSE ME.
YOU'RE NOT A...ARE YOU A...?

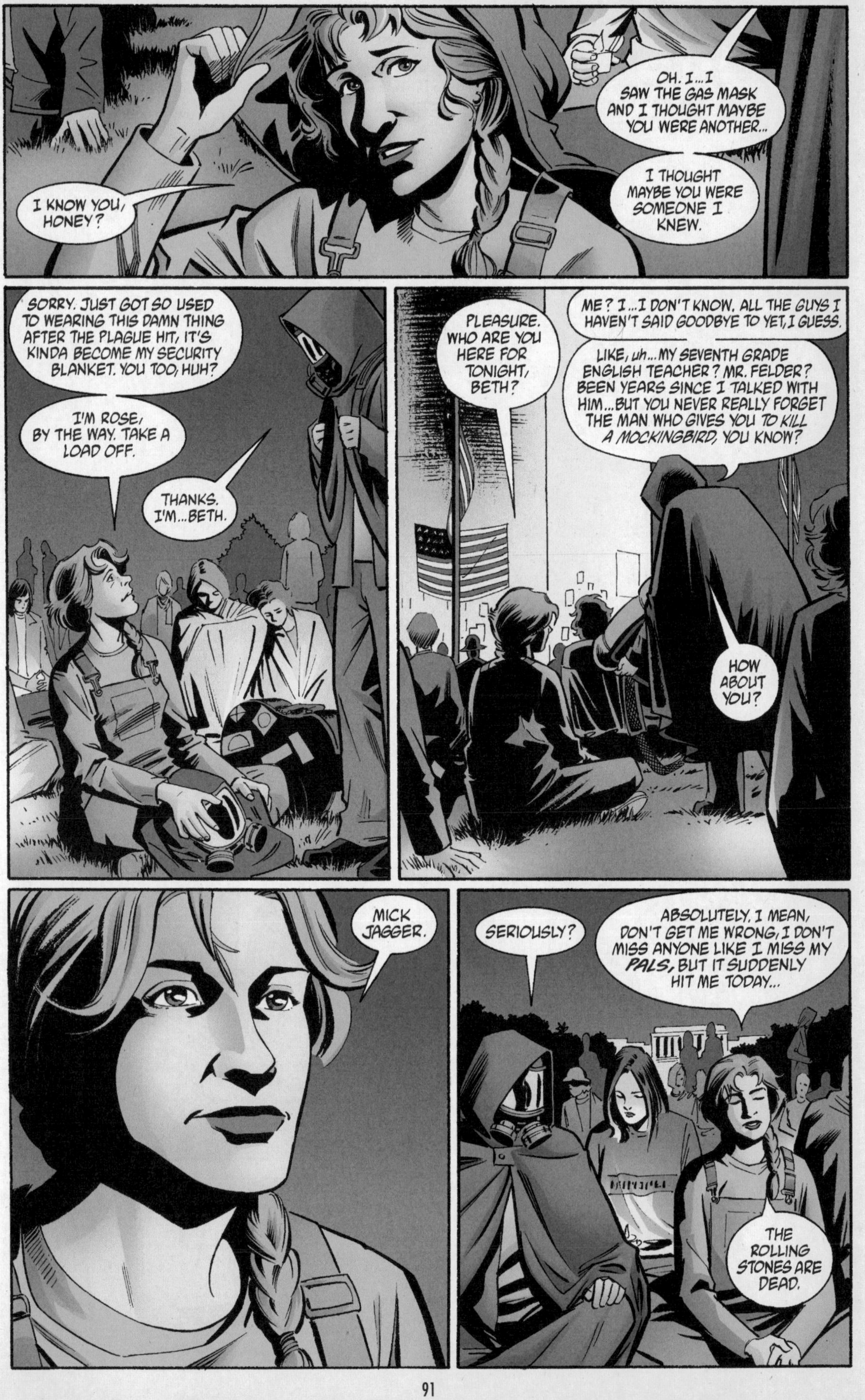
I KNOW YOU, HONEY?
OH. I...I SAW THE GAS MASK AND I THOUGHT MAYBE YOU WERE ANOTHER...
I THOUGHT MAYBE YOU WERE SOMEONE I KNEW.
SORRY. JUST GOT SO USED TO WEARING THIS DAMN THING AFTER THE PLAGUE HIT, IT'S KINDA BECOME MY SECURITY BLANKET. YOU TOO, HUH?
I'M ROSE, BY THE WAY. TAKE A LOAD OFF.
THANKS. I'M...BETH.
PLEASURE. WHO ARE YOU HERE FOR TONIGHT, BETH?
ME? I...I DON'T KNOW. ALL THE GUYS I HAVEN'T SAID GOODBYE TO YET, I GUESS.
LIKE, uh... MY SEVENTH GRADE ENGLISH TEACHER? MR. FELDER? BEEN YEARS SINCE I TALKED WITH HIM...BUT YOU NEVER REALLY FORGET THE MAN WHO GIVES YOU TO KILL A MOCKINGBIRD, YOU KNOW?
HOW ABOUT YOU?
MICK JAGGER.
SERIOUSLY?
ABSOLUTELY. I MEAN, DON'T GET ME WRONG, I DON'T MISS ANYONE LIKE I MISS MY PALS, BUT IT SUDDENLY HIT ME TODAY...
THE ROLLING STONES ARE DEAD.

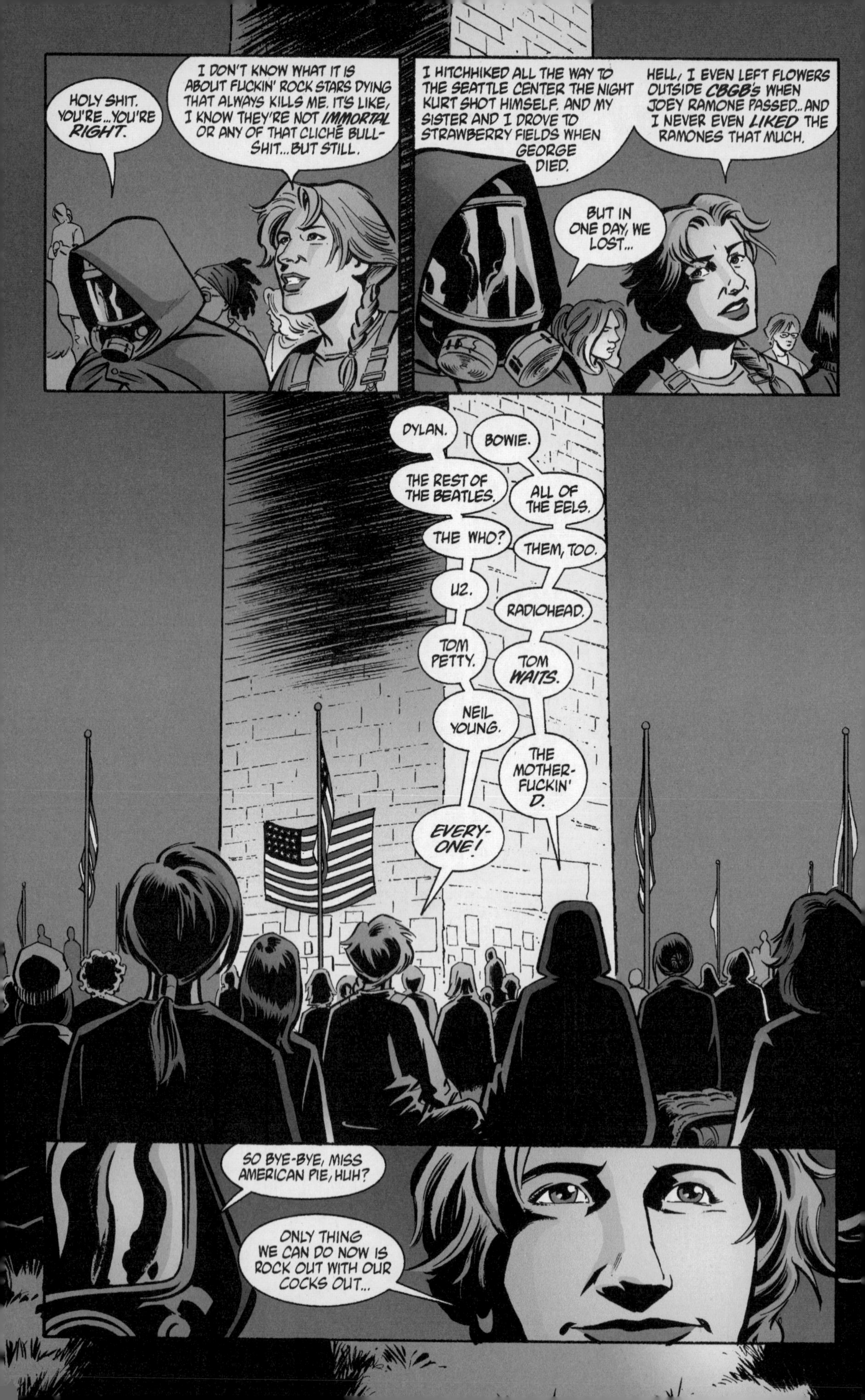
HOLY SHIT. YOU'RE...YOU'RE RIGHT.
I DON'T KNOW WHAT IT IS ABOUT FUCKIN' ROCK STARS DYING THAT ALWAYS KILLS ME. IT'S LIKE, I KNOW THEY'RE NOT IMMORTAL OR ANY OF THAT CLICHÉ BULL-SHIT...BUT STILL.
I HITCHHIKED ALL THE WAY TO THE SEATTLE CENTER THE NIGHT KURT SHOT HIMSELF. AND MY SISTER AND I DROVE TO STRAWBERRY FIELDS WHEN GEORGE DIED.
HELL, I EVEN LEFT FLOWERS OUTSIDE CBGB'S WHEN JOEY RAMONE PASSED...AND I NEVER EVEN LIKED THE RAMONES THAT MUCH.
BUT IN ONE DAY, WE LOST...
DYLAN.
BOWIE.
THE REST OF THE BEATLES.
ALL OF THE EELS.
THE WHO?
THEM, TOO.
U2.
RADIOHEAD.
TOM PETTY.
TOM WAITS.
NEIL YOUNG.
THE MOTHER-FUCKIN' D.
EVERY-ONE!
SO BYE-BYE, MISS AMERICAN PIE, HUH?
ONLY THING WE CAN DO NOW IS ROCK OUT WITH OUR COCKS OUT...

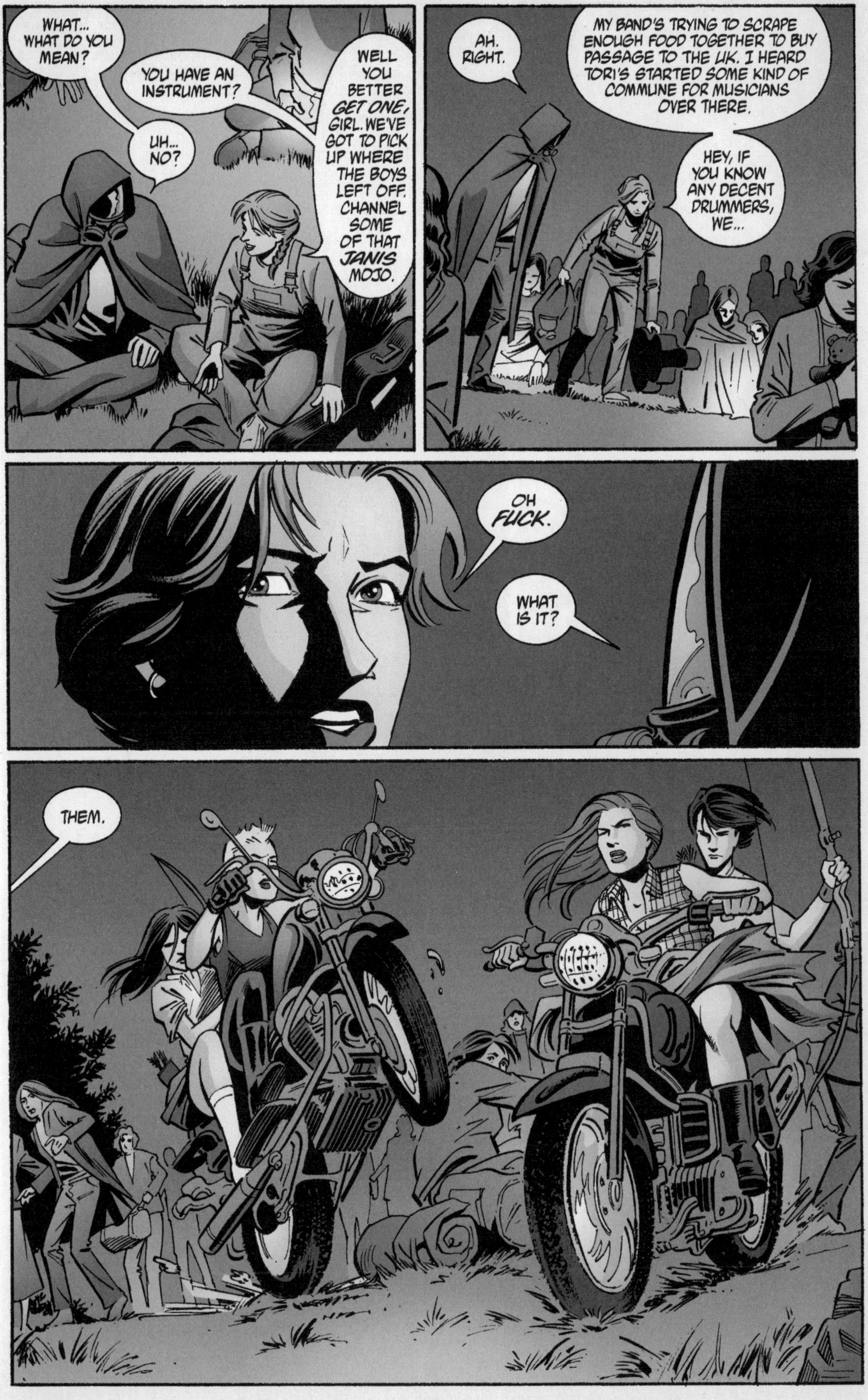
WHAT... WHAT DO YOU MEAN?
YOU HAVE AN INSTRUMENT?
UH... NO?
WELL YOU BETTER GET ONE, GIRL. WE'VE GOT TO PICK UP WHERE THE BOYS LEFT OFF. CHANNEL SOME OF THAT JANIS MOJO.
AH. RIGHT.
MY BAND'S TRYING TO SCRAPE ENOUGH FOOD TOGETHER TO BUY PASSAGE TO THE UK. I HEARD TORI'S STARTED SOME KIND OF COMMUNE FOR MUSICIANS OVER THERE.
HEY, IF YOU KNOW ANY DECENT DRUMMERS, WE...
OH FUCK.
WHAT IS IT?
THEM.

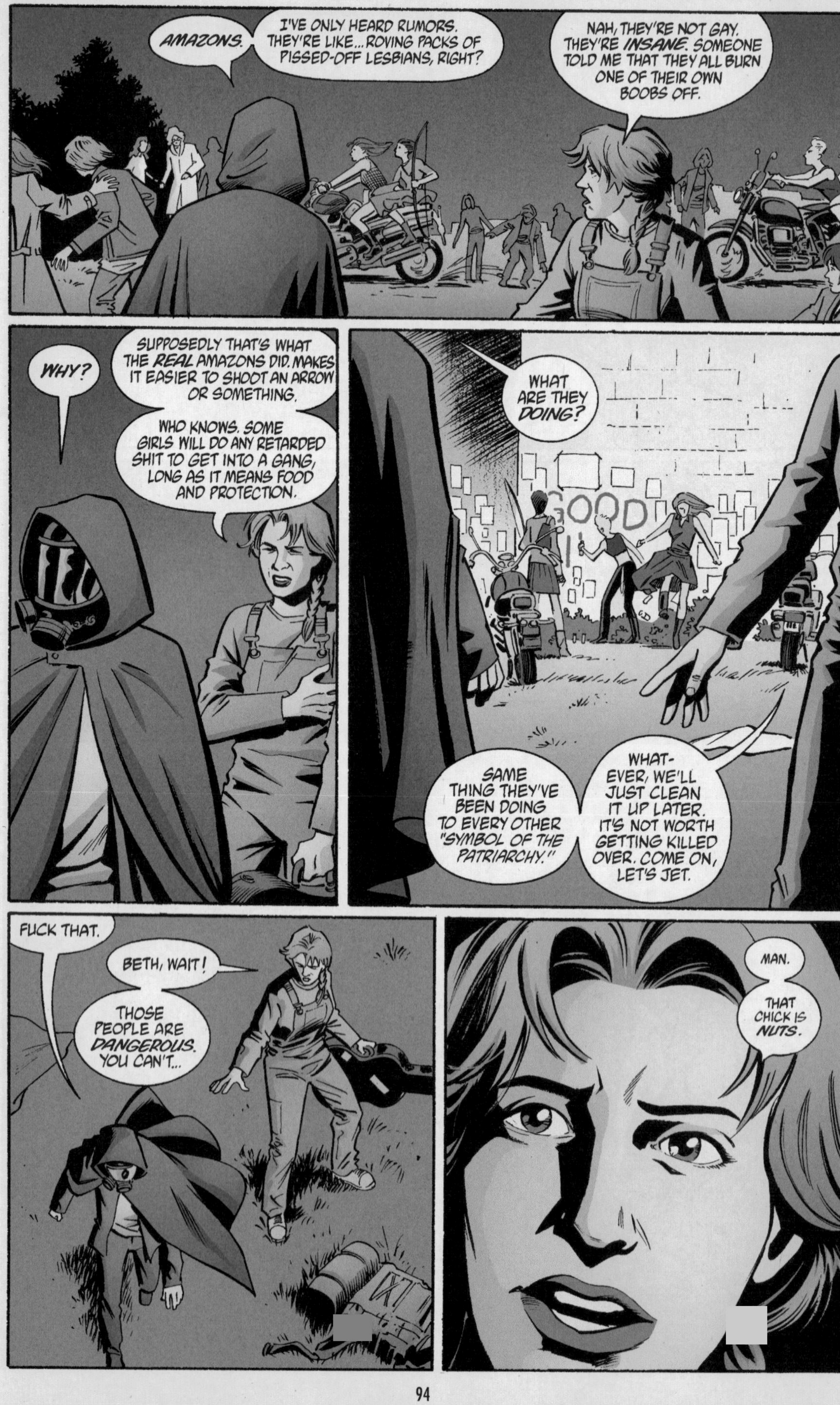
AMAZONS.
I'VE ONLY HEARD RUMORS. THEY'RE LIKE... ROVING PACKS OF PISSED-OFF LESBIANS, RIGHT?
NAH, THEY'RE NOT GAY. THEY'RE INSANE. SOMEONE TOLD ME THAT THEY ALL BURN ONE OF THEIR OWN BOOBS OFF.
WHY?
SUPPOSEDLY THAT'S WHAT THE REAL AMAZONS DID. MAKES IT EASIER TO SHOOT AN ARROW OR SOMETHING.
WHO KNOWS. SOME GIRLS WILL DO ANY RETARDED SHIT TO GET INTO A GANG, LONG AS IT MEANS FOOD AND PROTECTION.
WHAT ARE THEY DOING?
GOOD
SAME THING THEY'VE BEEN DOING TO EVERY OTHER "SYMBOL OF THE PATRIARCHY."
WHAT-EVER, WE'LL JUST CLEAN IT UP LATER. IT'S NOT WORTH GETTING KILLED OVER. COME ON, LET'S JET.
FUCK THAT.
BETH, WAIT!
THOSE PEOPLE ARE DANGEROUS. YOU CAN'T...
MAN.
THAT CHICK IS NUTS.

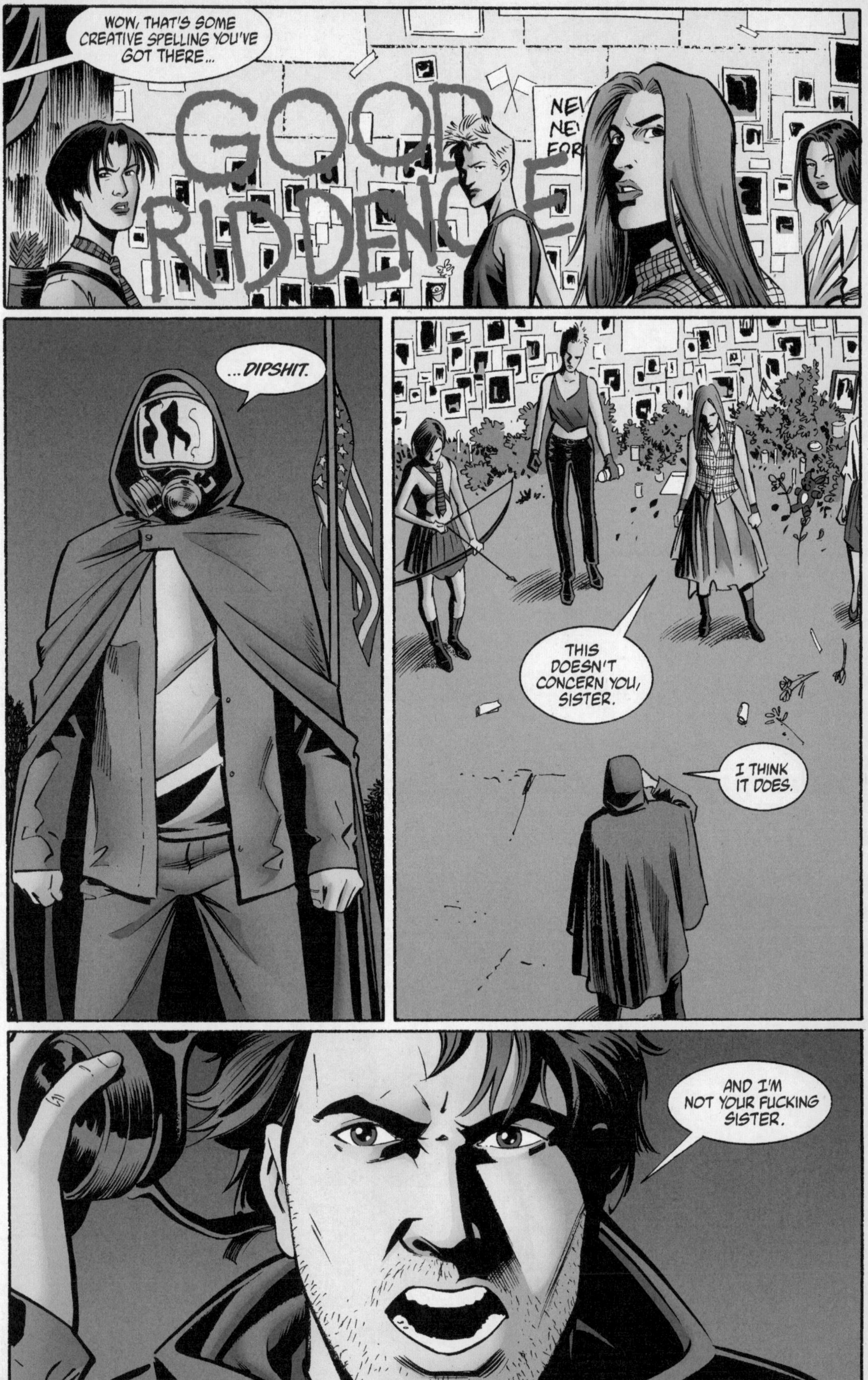
WOW, THAT'S SOME CREATIVE SPELLING YOU'VE GOT THERE...
GOOD RIDDENCE
...DIPSHIT.
THIS DOESN'T CONCERN YOU, SISTER.
I THINK IT DOES.
AND I'M NOT YOUR FUCKING SISTER.

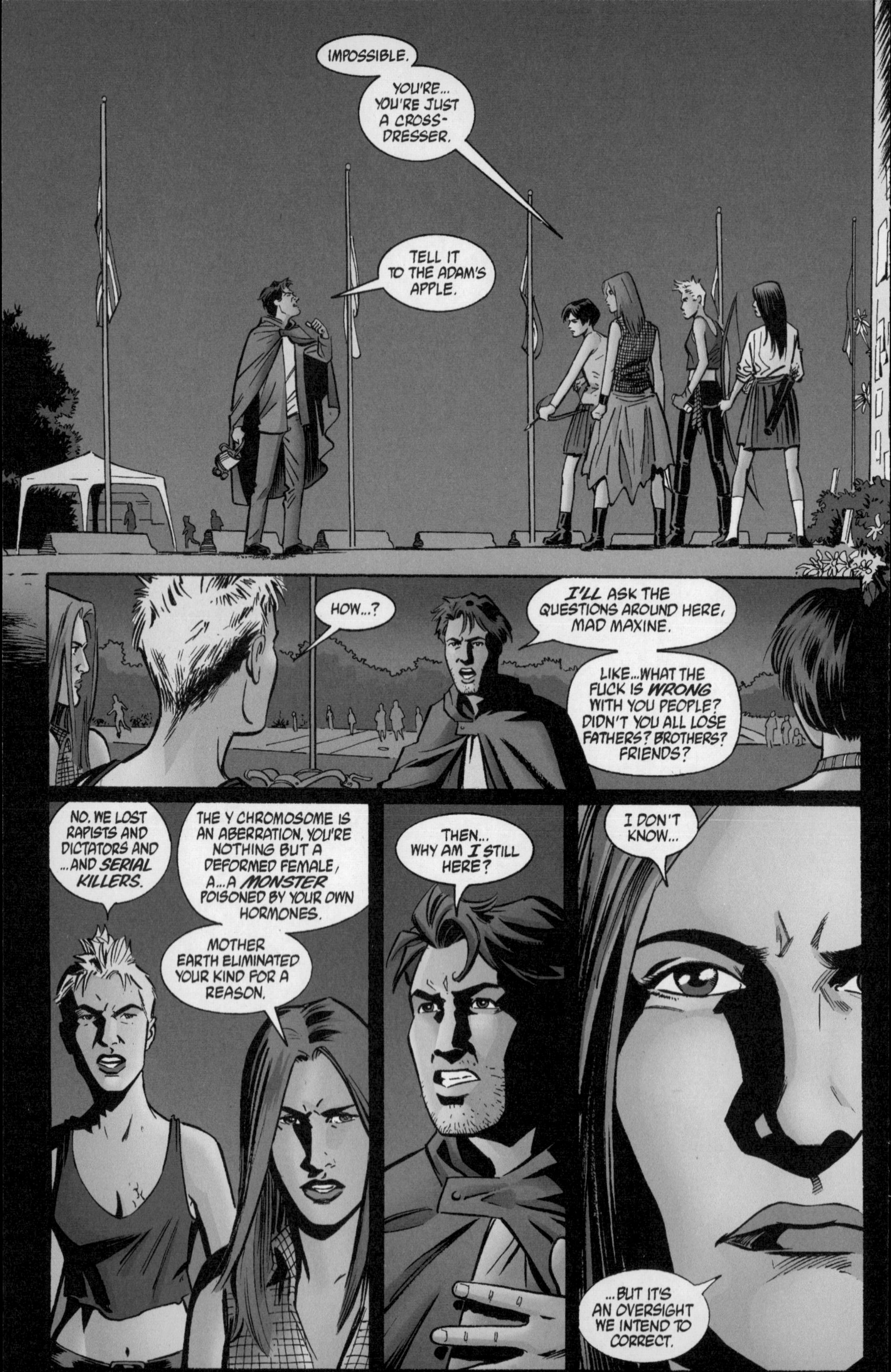
IMPOSSIBLE.
YOU'RE... YOU'RE JUST A CROSS-DRESSER.
TELL IT TO THE ADAM'S APPLE.
HOW...?
I'LL ASK THE QUESTIONS AROUND HERE, MAD MAXINE.
LIKE...WHAT THE FUCK IS WRONG WITH YOU PEOPLE? DIDN'T YOU ALL LOSE FATHERS? BROTHERS? FRIENDS?
NO. WE LOST RAPISTS AND DICTATORS AND ...AND SERIAL KILLERS.
THE Y CHROMOSOME IS AN ABERRATION. YOU'RE NOTHING BUT A DEFORMED FEMALE, A...A MONSTER POISONED BY YOUR OWN HORMONES.
MOTHER EARTH ELIMINATED YOUR KIND FOR A REASON.
THEN... WHY AM I STILL HERE?
I DON'T KNOW...
...BUT IT'S AN OVERSIGHT WE INTEND TO CORRECT.

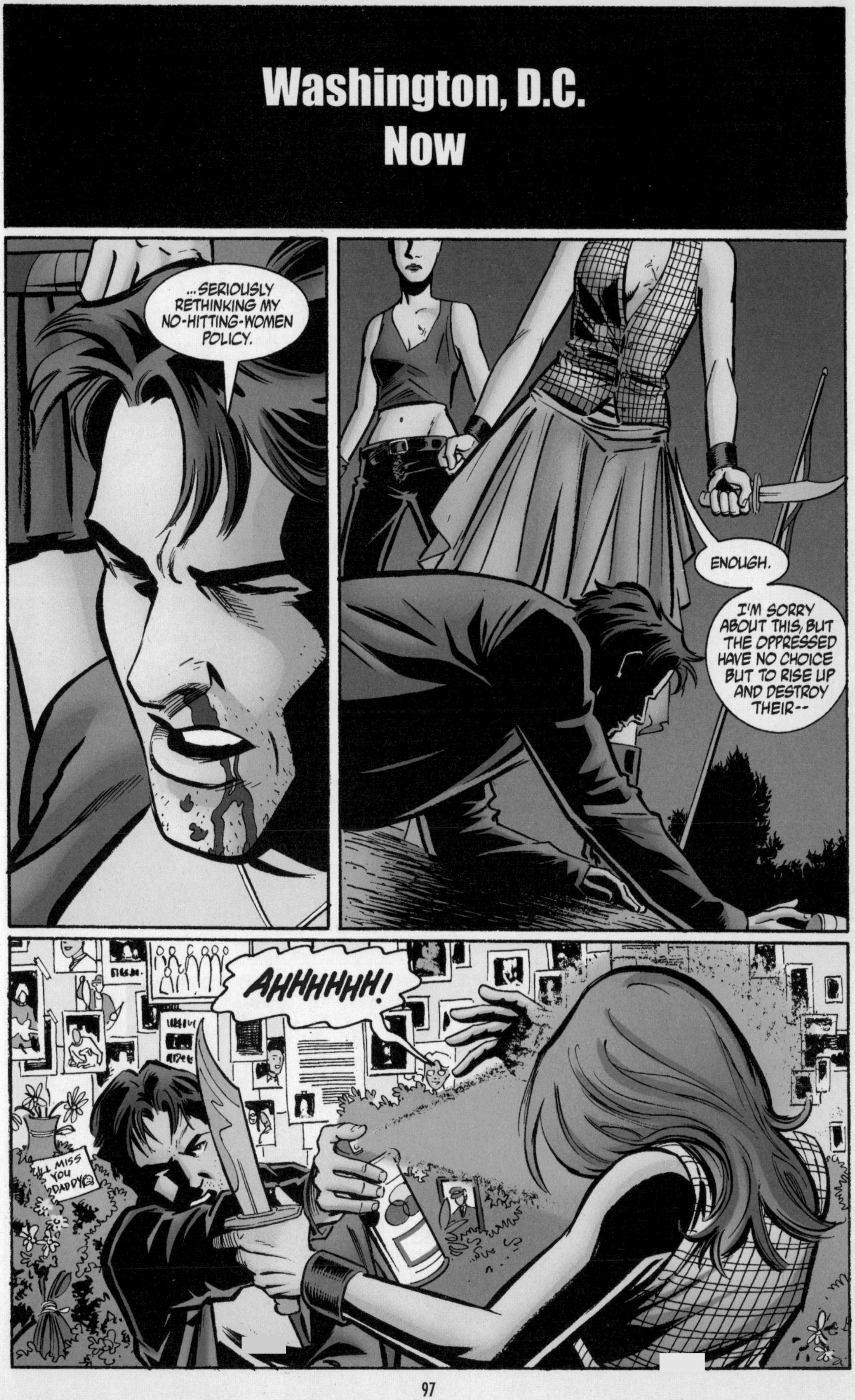
Washington, D.C.
Now
...SERIOUSLY RETHINKING MY NO-HITTING-WOMEN POLICY.
ENOUGH.
I'M SORRY ABOUT THIS, BUT THE OPPRESSED HAVE NO CHOICE BUT TO RISE UP AND DESTROY THEIR--
AHHHHHH!
LL MISS YOU DADDY

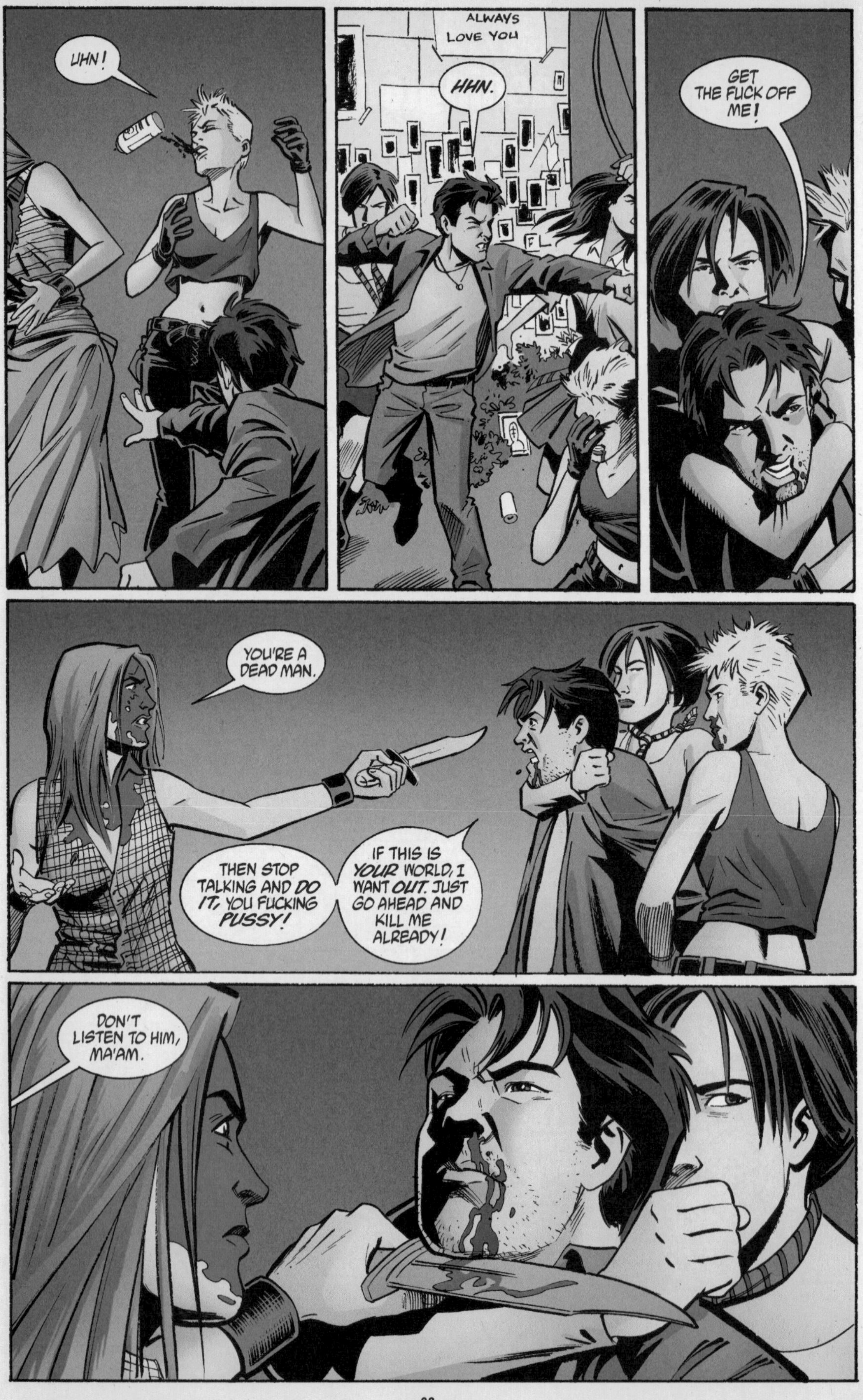
UHN!
ALWAYS LOVE YOU
HHN.
GET THE FUCK OFF ME!
YOU'RE A DEAD MAN.
THEN STOP TALKING AND DO IT, YOU FUCKING PUSSY!
IF THIS IS YOUR WORLD, I WANT OUT. JUST GO AHEAD AND KILL ME ALREADY!
DON'T LISTEN TO HIM, MA'AM.

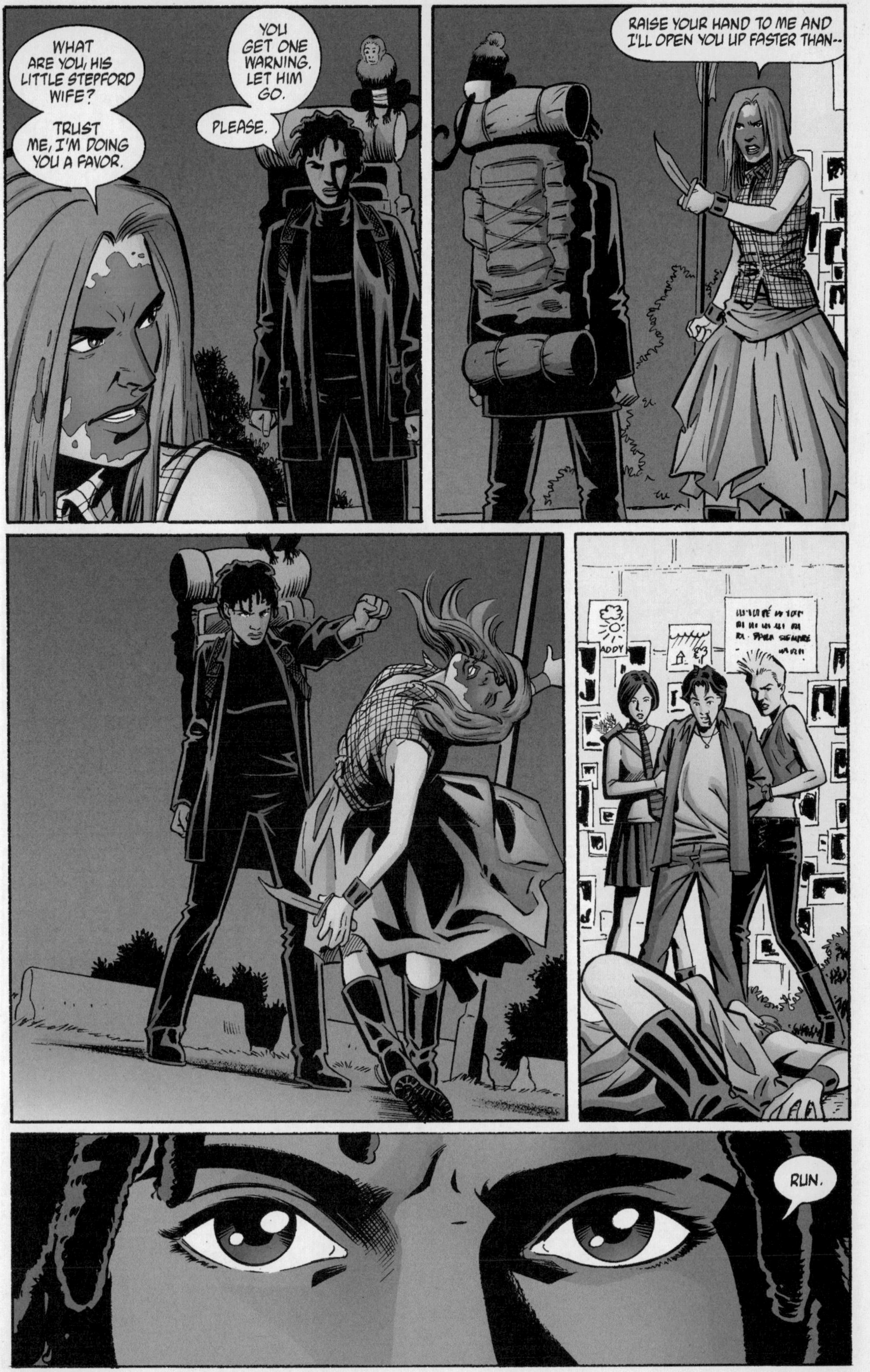
WHAT ARE YOU, HIS LITTLE STEPFORD WIFE?
TRUST ME, I'M DOING YOU A FAVOR.
YOU GET ONE WARNING. LET HIM GO.
PLEASE.
RAISE YOUR HAND TO ME AND I'LL OPEN YOU UP FASTER THAN--
RUN.

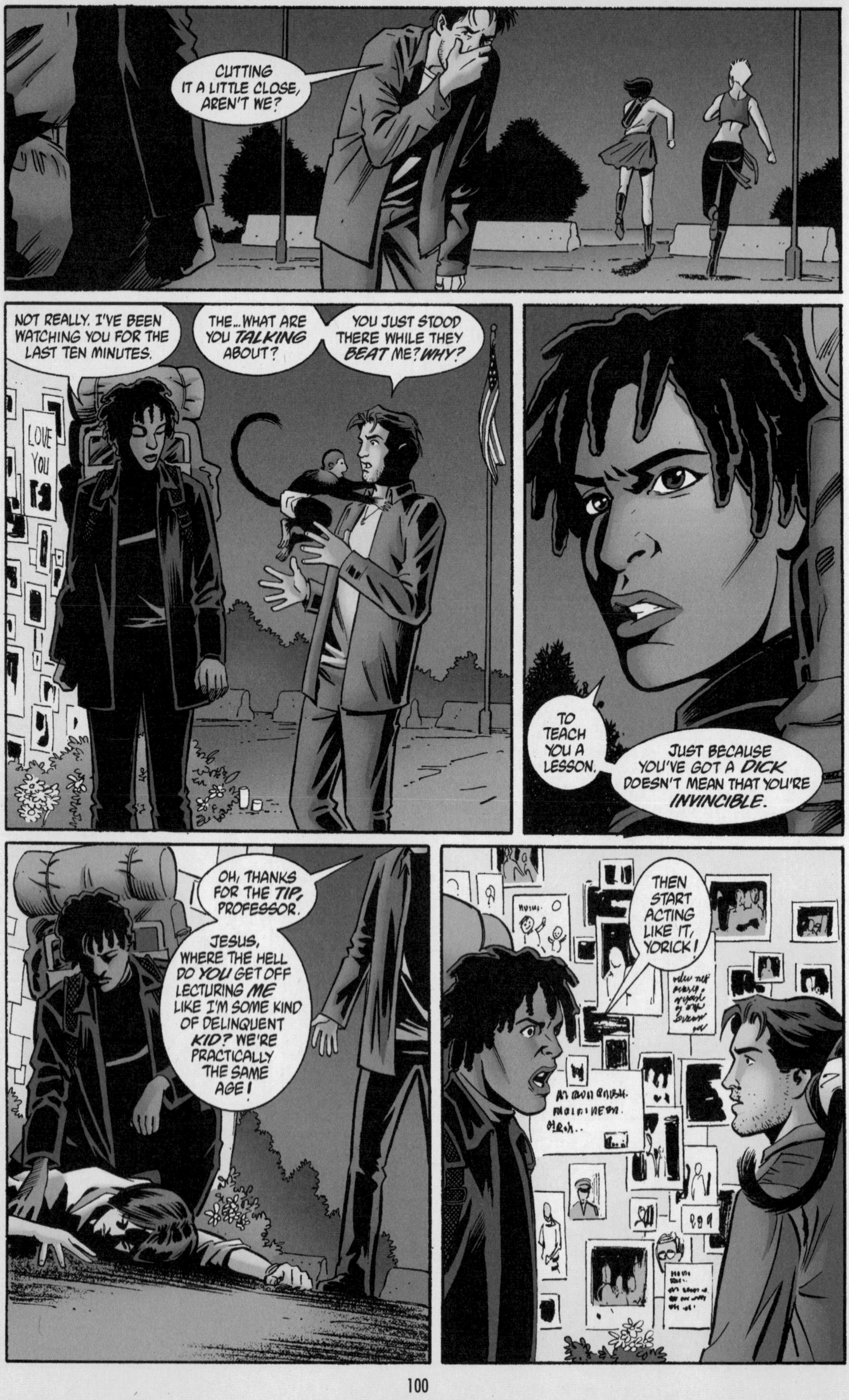
CUTTING IT A LITTLE CLOSE, AREN'T WE?
NOT REALLY. I'VE BEEN WATCHING YOU FOR THE LAST TEN MINUTES.
THE...WHAT ARE YOU TALKING ABOUT?
YOU JUST STOOD THERE WHILE THEY BEAT ME? WHY?
LOVE YOU
TO TEACH YOU A LESSON.
JUST BECAUSE YOU'VE GOT A DICK DOESN'T MEAN THAT YOU'RE INVINCIBLE.
OH, THANKS FOR THE TIP, PROFESSOR.
JESUS, WHERE THE HELL DO YOU GET OFF LECTURING ME LIKE I'M SOME KIND OF DELINQUENT KID? WE'RE PRACTICALLY THE SAME AGE!
THEN START ACTING LIKE IT, YORICK!

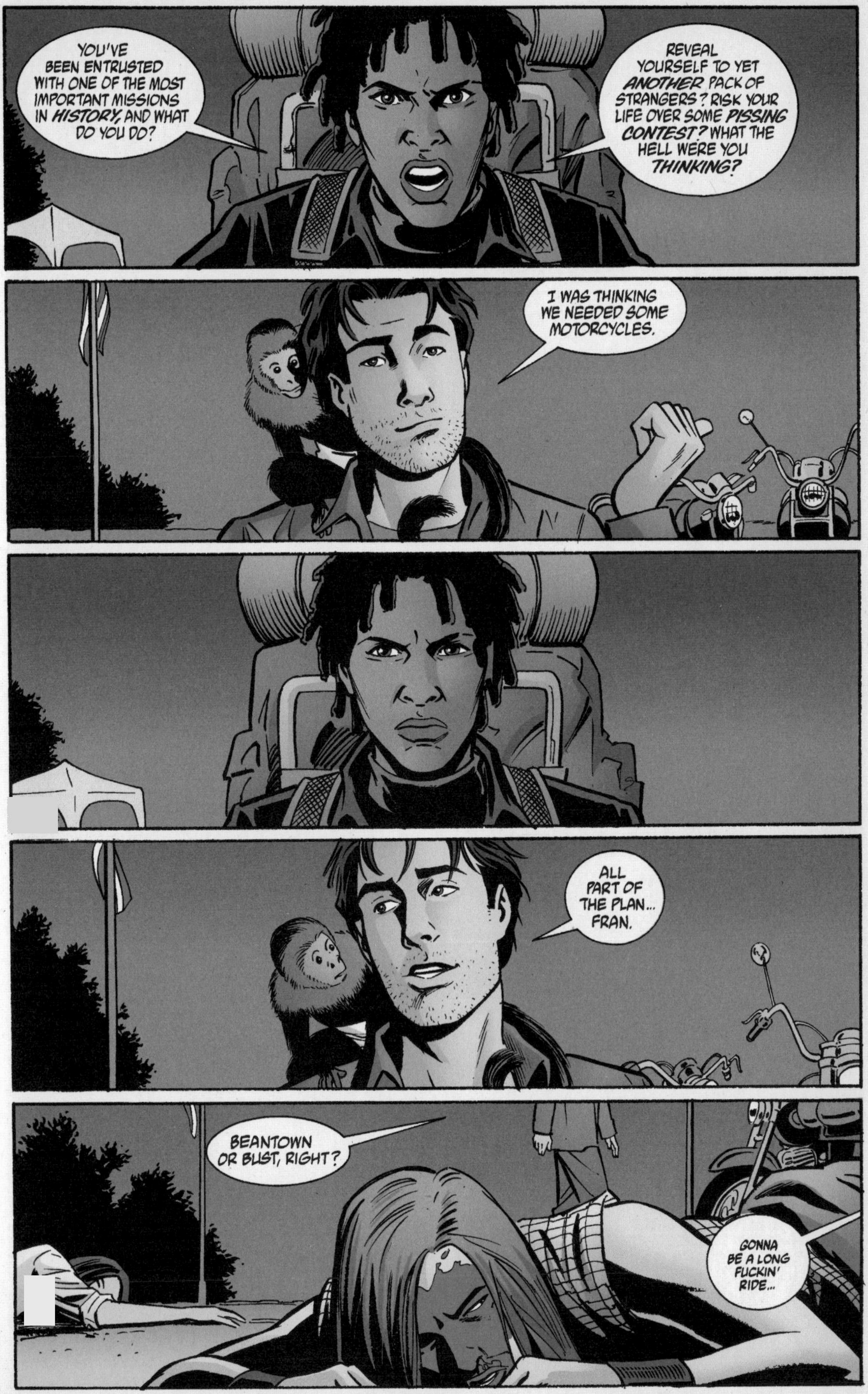
YOU'VE BEEN ENTRUSTED WITH ONE OF THE MOST IMPORTANT MISSIONS IN HISTORY, AND WHAT DO YOU DO?
REVEAL YOURSELF TO YET ANOTHER PACK OF STRANGERS? RISK YOUR LIFE OVER SOME PISSING CONTEST? WHAT THE HELL WERE YOU THINKING?
I WAS THINKING WE NEEDED SOME MOTORCYCLES.
ALL PART OF THE PLAN... FRAN.
BEANTOWN OR BUST, RIGHT?
GONNA BE A LONG FUCKIN' RIDE...

Baltimore Convention Center
Six Hours Later

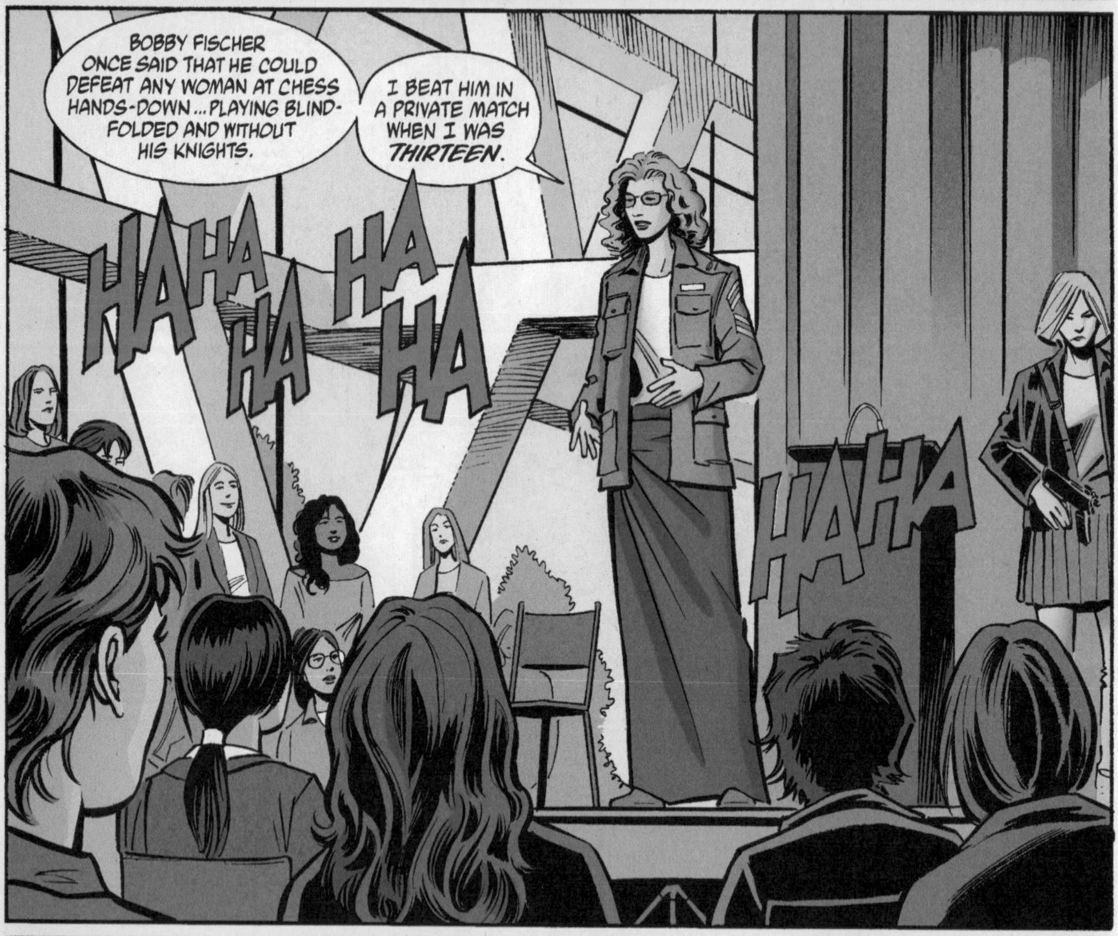
BOBBY FISCHER ONCE SAID THAT HE COULD DEFEAT ANY WOMAN AT CHESS HANDS-DOWN...PLAYING BLIND-FOLDED AND WITHOUT HIS KNIGHTS.
I BEAT HIM IN A PRIVATE MATCH WHEN I WAS THIRTEEN.
HAHA HA HA HA
HAHA

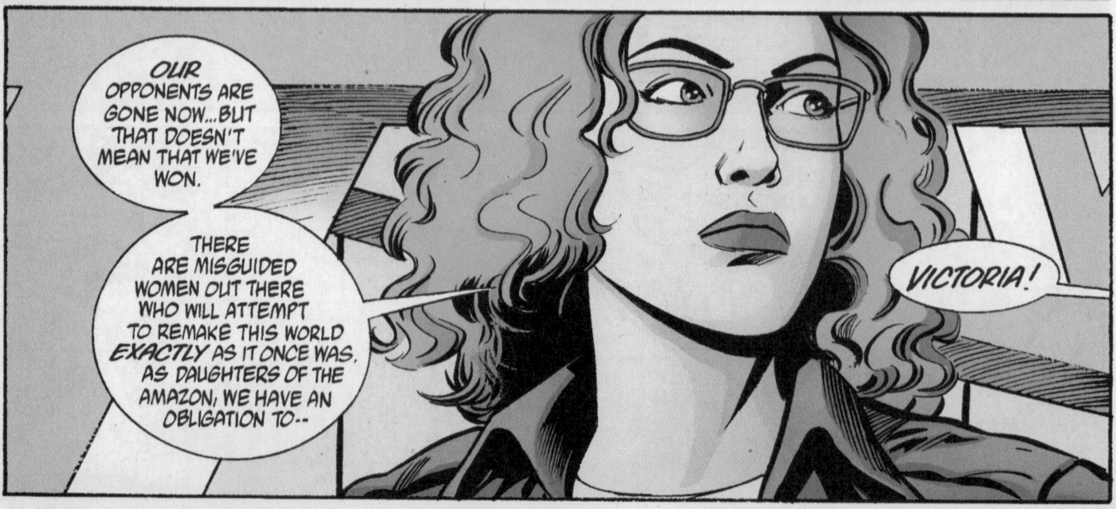
OUR OPPONENTS ARE GONE NOW...BUT THAT DOESN'T MEAN THAT WE'VE WON.
THERE ARE MISGUIDED WOMEN OUT THERE WHO WILL ATTEMPT TO REMAKE THIS WORLD EXACTLY AS IT ONCE WAS. AS DAUGHTERS OF THE AMAZON, WE HAVE AN OBLIGATION TO--
VICTORIA!

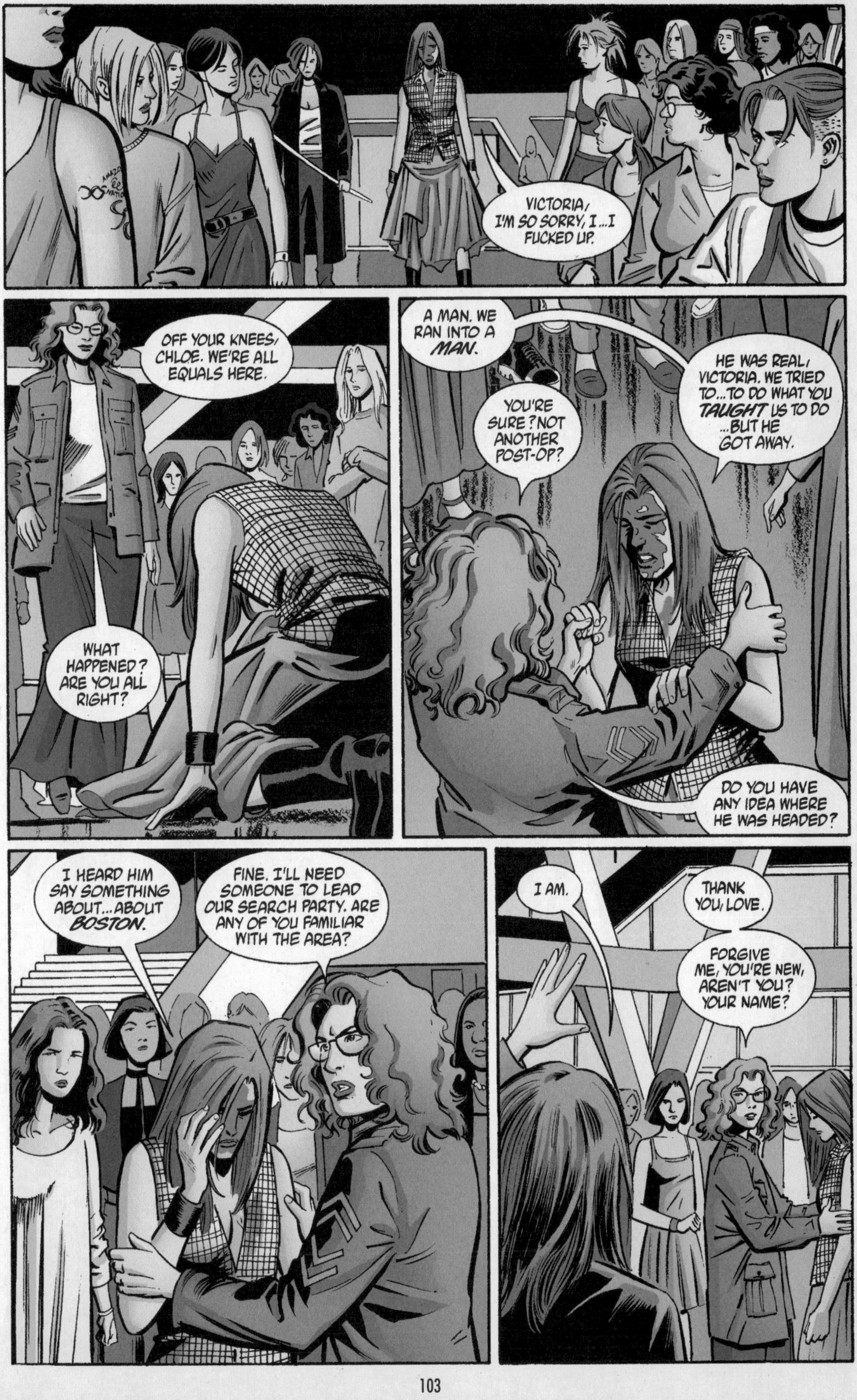
VICTORIA, I'M SO SORRY, I...I FUCKED UP.
OFF YOUR KNEES, CHLOE. WE'RE ALL EQUALS HERE.
WHAT HAPPENED? ARE YOU ALL RIGHT?
A MAN. WE RAN INTO A *MAN*.
YOU'RE SURE? NOT ANOTHER POST-OP?
HE WAS REAL, VICTORIA. WE TRIED TO...TO DO WHAT YOU *TAUGHT* US TO DO ...BUT HE GOT AWAY.
DO YOU HAVE ANY IDEA WHERE HE WAS HEADED?
I HEARD HIM SAY SOMETHING ABOUT...ABOUT *BOSTON*.
FINE. I'LL NEED SOMEONE TO LEAD OUR SEARCH PARTY. ARE ANY OF YOU FAMILIAR WITH THE AREA?
I AM.
THANK YOU, LOVE.
FORGIVE ME, YOU'RE NEW, AREN'T YOU? YOUR NAME?

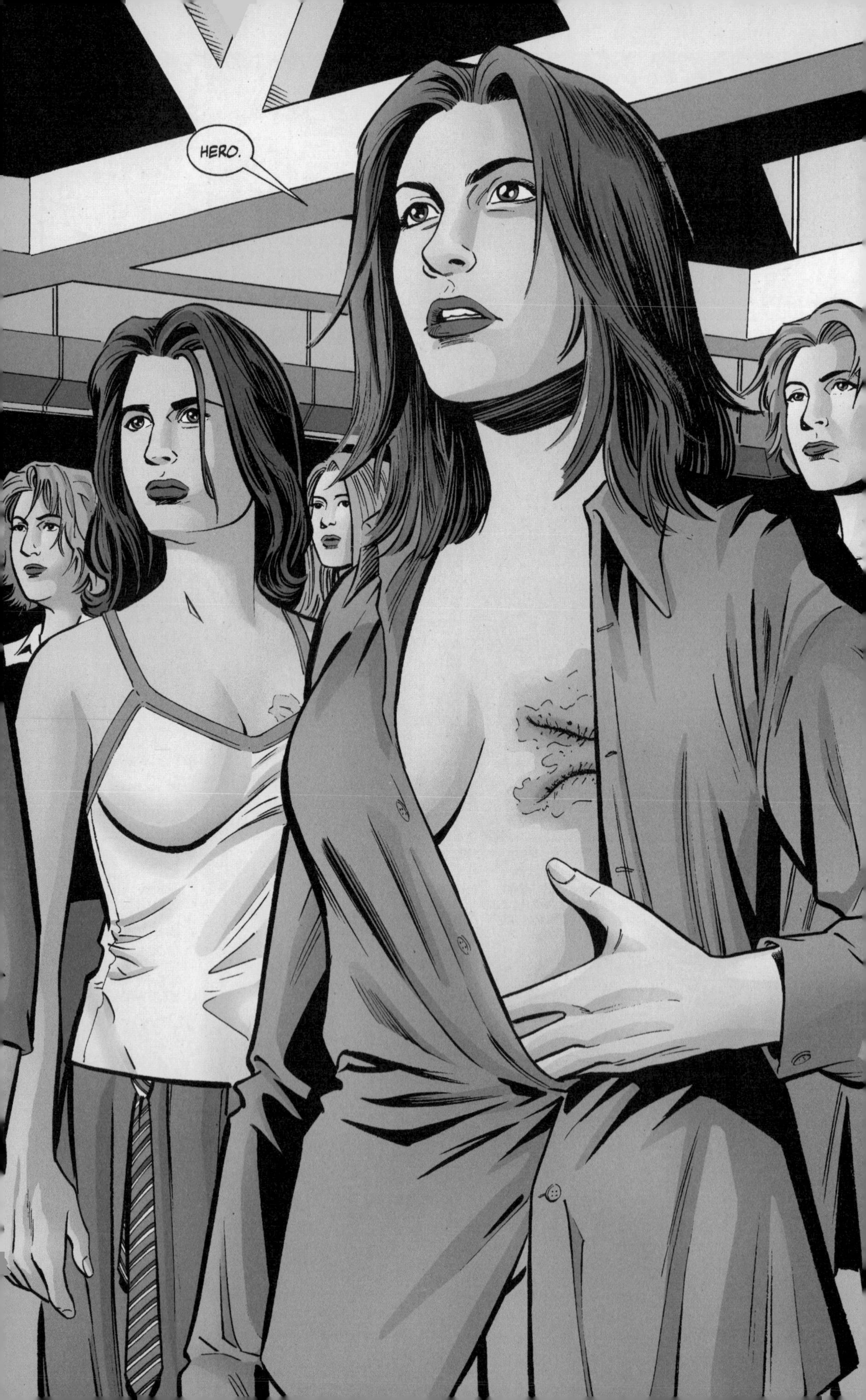
HERO.

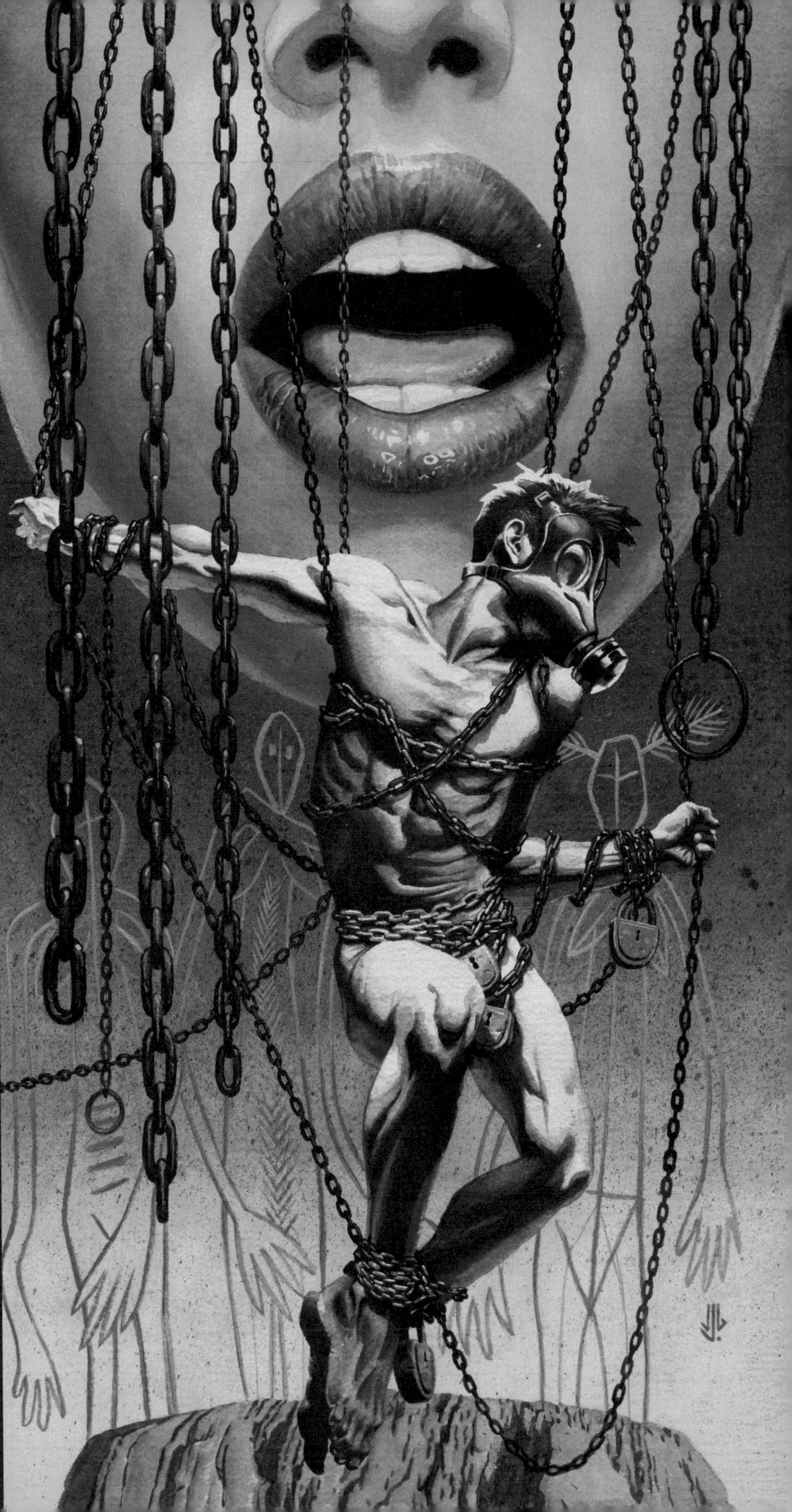

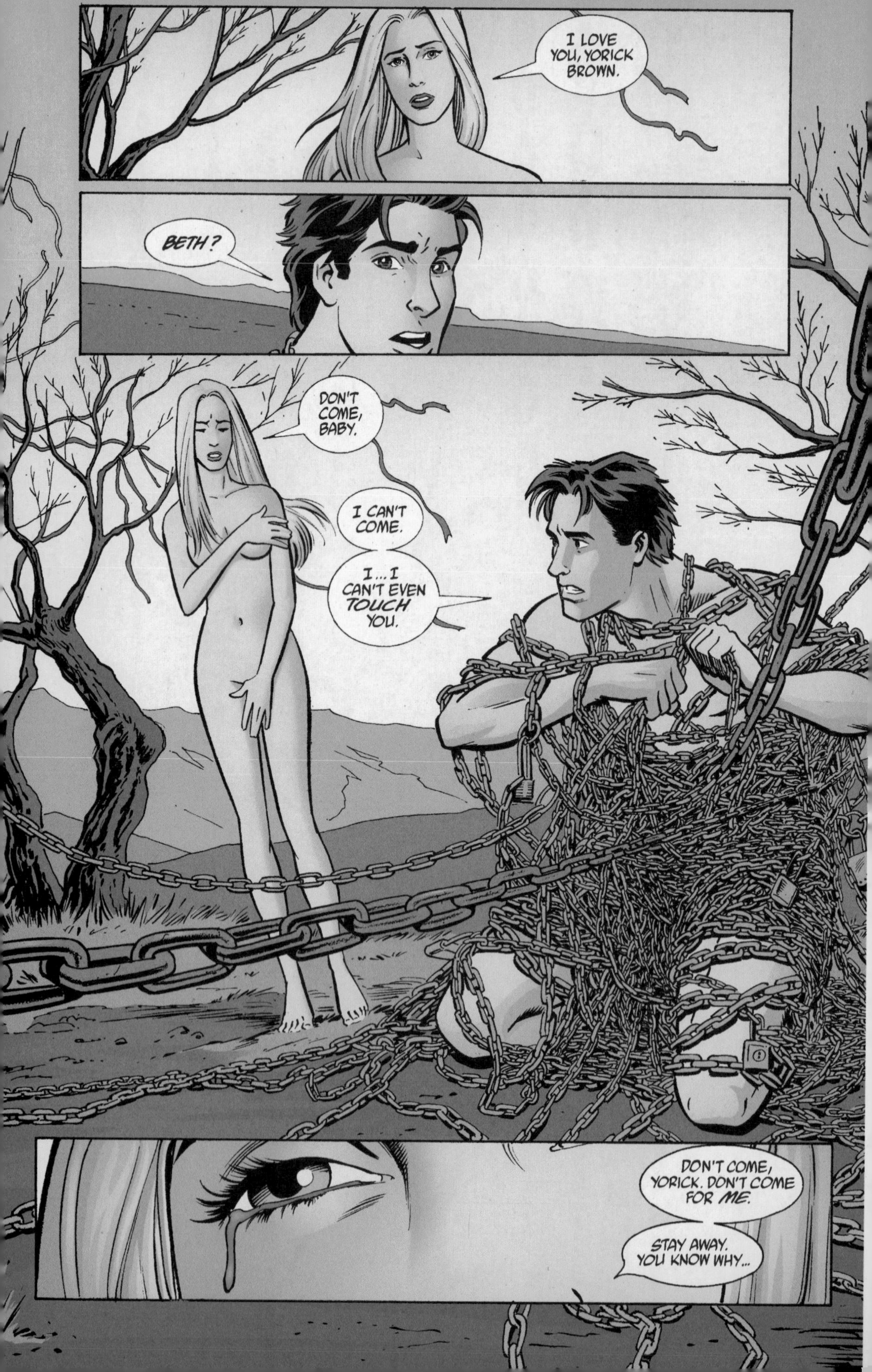
I LOVE YOU, YORICK BROWN.
BETH?
DON'T COME, BABY.
I CAN'T COME.
I... I CAN'T EVEN TOUCH YOU.
DON'T COME, YORICK. DON'T COME FOR ME.
STAY AWAY. YOU KNOW WHY...

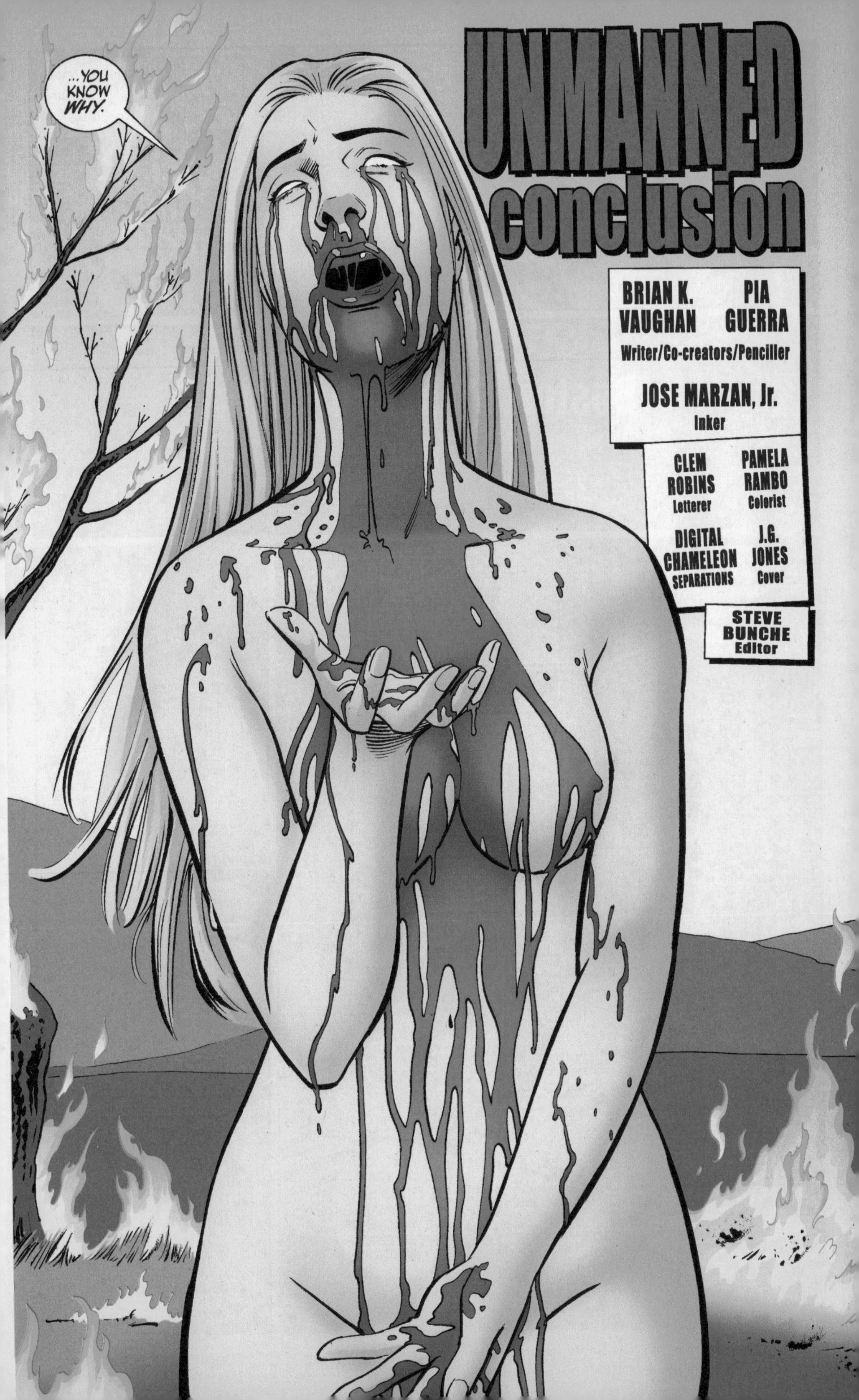
...YOU KNOW WHY.
UNMANNED
conclusion
BRIAN K. VAUGHAN PIA GUERRA
Writer/Co-creators/Penciller
JOSE MARZAN, Jr.
Inker
CLEM ROBINS
Letterer
PAMELA RAMBO
Colorist
DIGITAL CHAMELEON
SEPARATIONS
J.G. JONES
Cover
STEVE BUNCHE
Editor

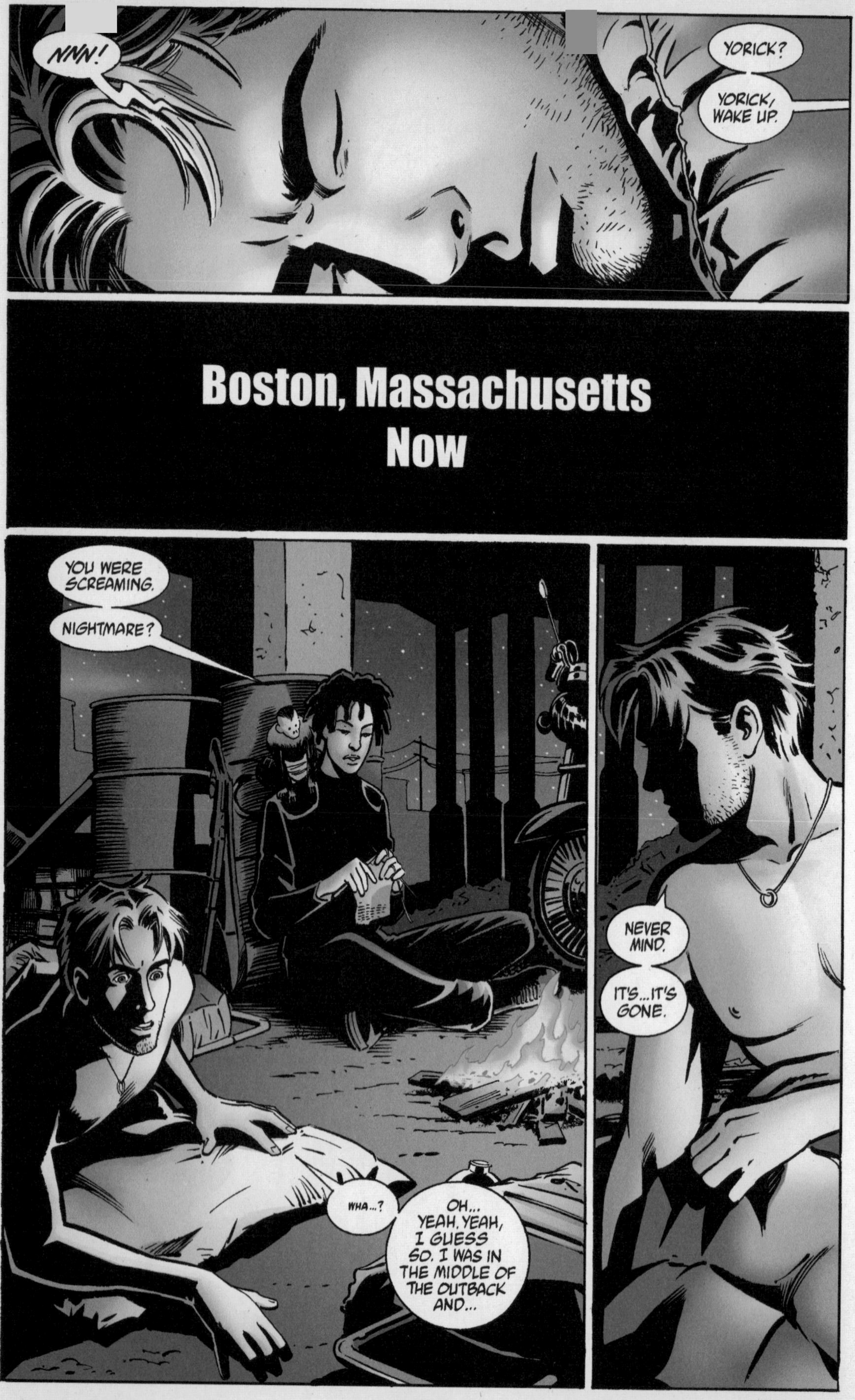
NNN!
YORICK?
YORICK, WAKE UP.
Boston, Massachusetts
Now
YOU WERE SCREAMING.
NIGHTMARE?
WHA...?
OH... YEAH. YEAH, I GUESS SO. I WAS IN THE MIDDLE OF THE OUTBACK AND...
NEVER MIND.
IT'S...IT'S GONE.

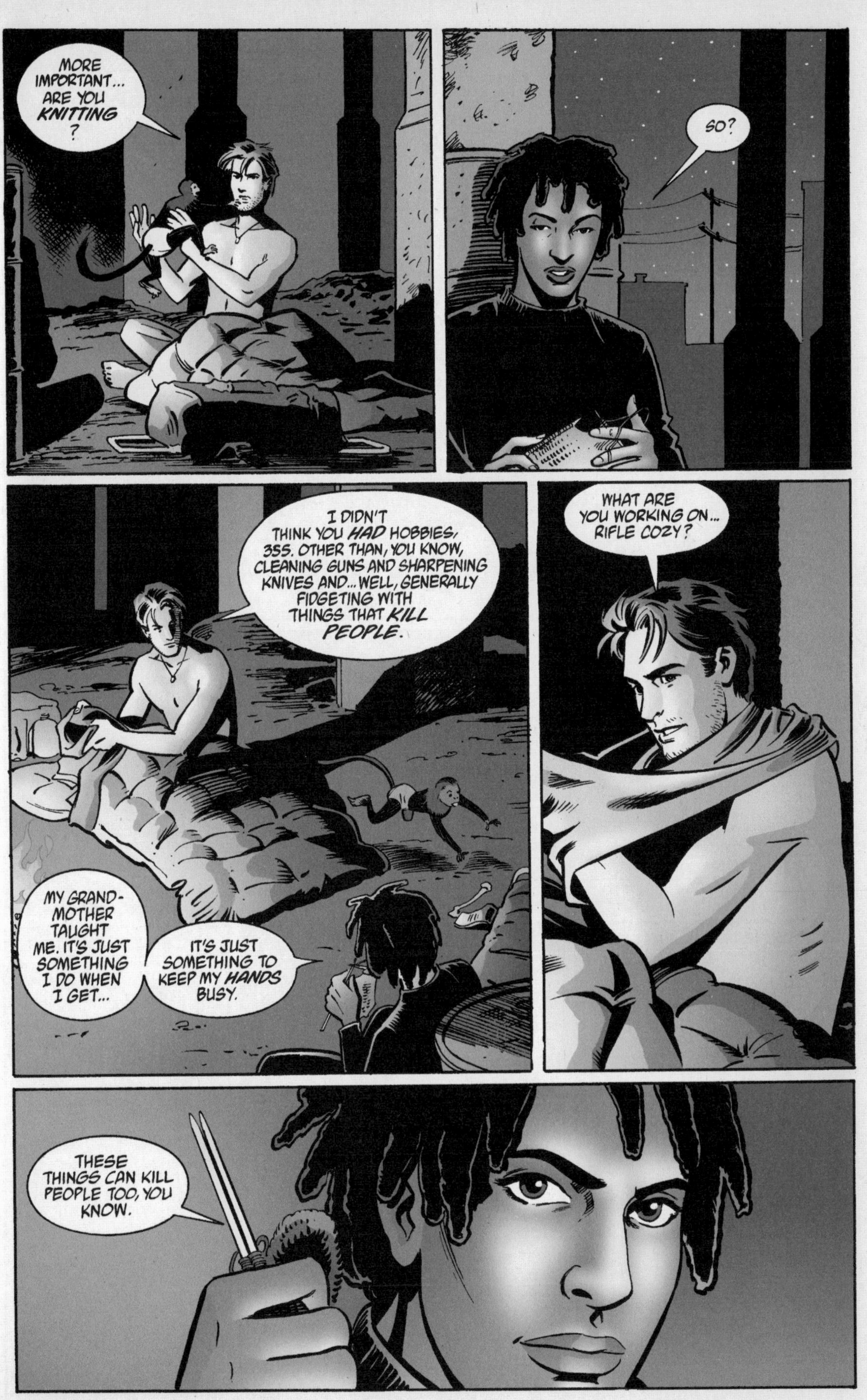
MORE IMPORTANT... ARE YOU KNITTING ?
SO?
I DIDN'T THINK YOU HAD HOBBIES, 355. OTHER THAN, YOU KNOW, CLEANING GUNS AND SHARPENING KNIVES AND... WELL, GENERALLY FIDGETING WITH THINGS THAT KILL PEOPLE.
MY GRANDMOTHER TAUGHT ME. IT'S JUST SOMETHING I DO WHEN I GET...
IT'S JUST SOMETHING TO KEEP MY HANDS BUSY.
WHAT ARE YOU WORKING ON... RIFLE COZY?
THESE THINGS CAN KILL PEOPLE TOO, YOU KNOW.

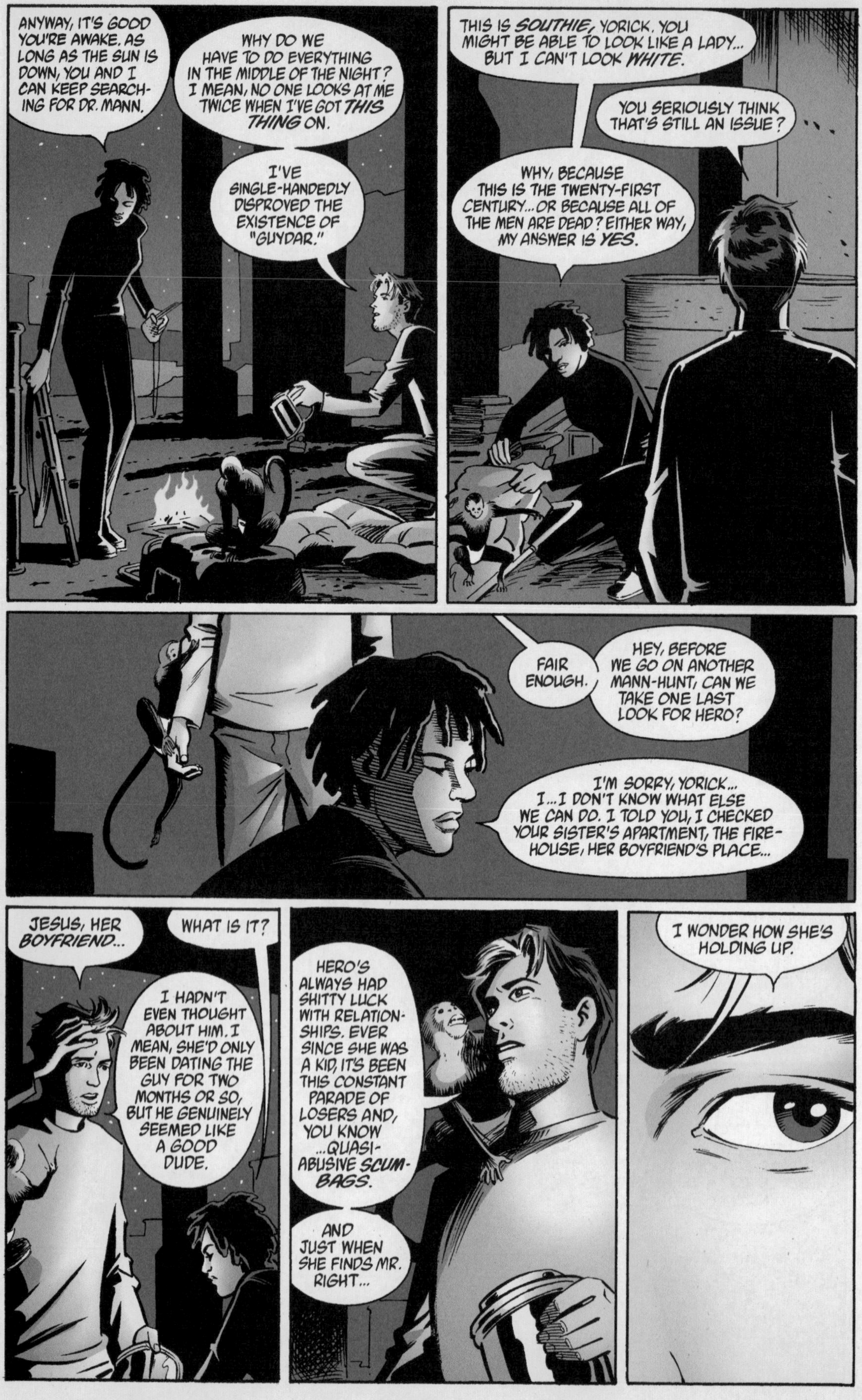
ANYWAY, IT'S GOOD YOU'RE AWAKE. AS LONG AS THE SUN IS DOWN, YOU AND I CAN KEEP SEARCHING FOR DR. MANN.
WHY DO WE HAVE TO DO EVERYTHING IN THE MIDDLE OF THE NIGHT? I MEAN, NO ONE LOOKS AT ME TWICE WHEN I'VE GOT THIS THING ON.
I'VE SINGLE-HANDEDLY DISPROVED THE EXISTENCE OF "GUYDAR."
THIS IS SOUTHIE, YORICK. YOU MIGHT BE ABLE TO LOOK LIKE A LADY... BUT I CAN'T LOOK WHITE.
YOU SERIOUSLY THINK THAT'S STILL AN ISSUE?
WHY, BECAUSE THIS IS THE TWENTY-FIRST CENTURY... OR BECAUSE ALL OF THE MEN ARE DEAD? EITHER WAY, MY ANSWER IS YES.
FAIR ENOUGH.
HEY, BEFORE WE GO ON ANOTHER MANN-HUNT, CAN WE TAKE ONE LAST LOOK FOR HERO?
I'M SORRY, YORICK... I... I DON'T KNOW WHAT ELSE WE CAN DO. I TOLD YOU, I CHECKED YOUR SISTER'S APARTMENT, THE FIRE-HOUSE, HER BOYFRIEND'S PLACE...
JESUS, HER BOYFRIEND...
WHAT IS IT?
I HADN'T EVEN THOUGHT ABOUT HIM. I MEAN, SHE'D ONLY BEEN DATING THE GUY FOR TWO MONTHS OR SO, BUT HE GENUINELY SEEMED LIKE A GOOD DUDE.
HERO'S ALWAYS HAD SHITTY LUCK WITH RELATION-SHIPS. EVER SINCE SHE WAS A KID, IT'S BEEN THIS CONSTANT PARADE OF LOSERS AND, YOU KNOW ...QUASI-ABUSIVE SCUM-BAGS.
AND JUST WHEN SHE FINDS MR. RIGHT...
I WONDER HOW SHE'S HOLDING UP.

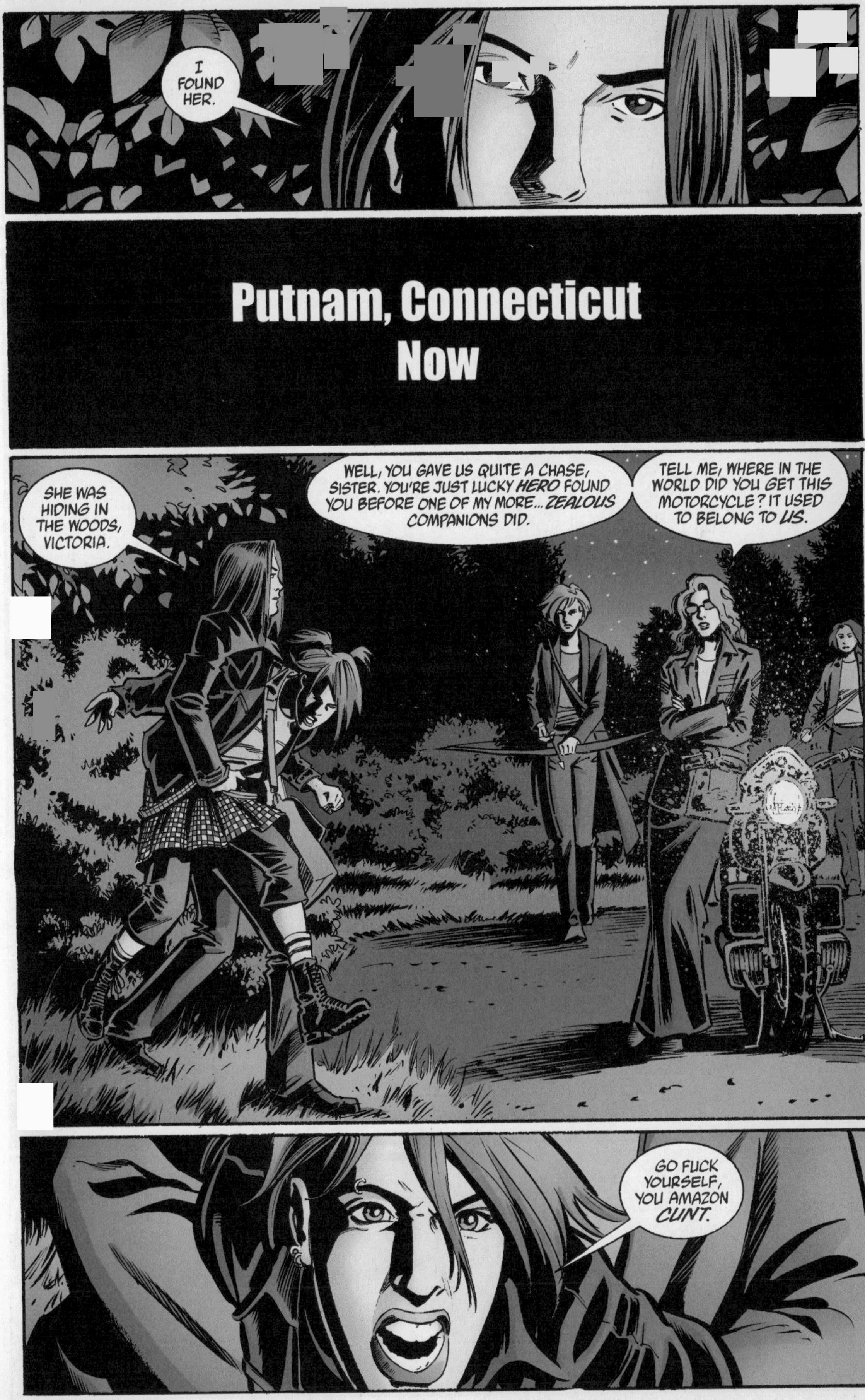
I FOUND HER.
Putnam, Connecticut
Now
SHE WAS HIDING IN THE WOODS, VICTORIA.
WELL, YOU GAVE US QUITE A CHASE, SISTER. YOU'RE JUST LUCKY HERO FOUND YOU BEFORE ONE OF MY MORE... ZEALOUS COMPANIONS DID.
TELL ME, WHERE IN THE WORLD DID YOU GET THIS MOTORCYCLE? IT USED TO BELONG TO US.
GO FUCK YOURSELF, YOU AMAZON CUNT.

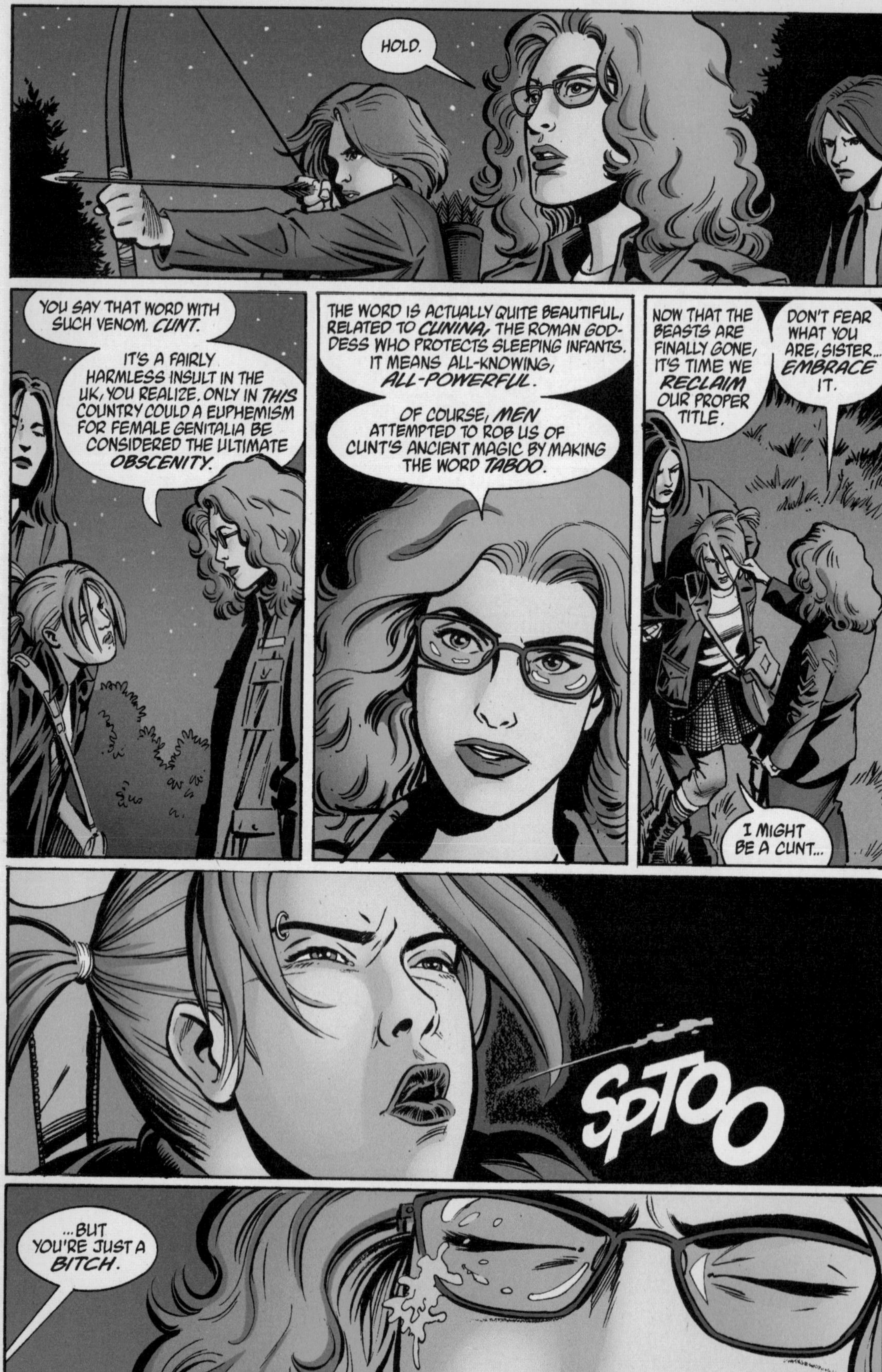
HOLD.
YOU SAY THAT WORD WITH SUCH VENOM. CUNT.
IT'S A FAIRLY HARMLESS INSULT IN THE UK, YOU REALIZE. ONLY IN THIS COUNTRY COULD A EUPHEMISM FOR FEMALE GENITALIA BE CONSIDERED THE ULTIMATE OBSCENITY.
THE WORD IS ACTUALLY QUITE BEAUTIFUL, RELATED TO CUNINA, THE ROMAN GOD-DESS WHO PROTECTS SLEEPING INFANTS. IT MEANS ALL-KNOWING, ALL-POWERFUL.
OF COURSE, MEN ATTEMPTED TO ROB US OF CUNT'S ANCIENT MAGIC BY MAKING THE WORD TABOO.
NOW THAT THE BEASTS ARE FINALLY GONE, IT'S TIME WE RECLAIM OUR PROPER TITLE.
DON'T FEAR WHAT YOU ARE, SISTER... EMBRACE IT.
I MIGHT BE A CUNT...
SPTOO
...BUT YOU'RE JUST A BITCH.

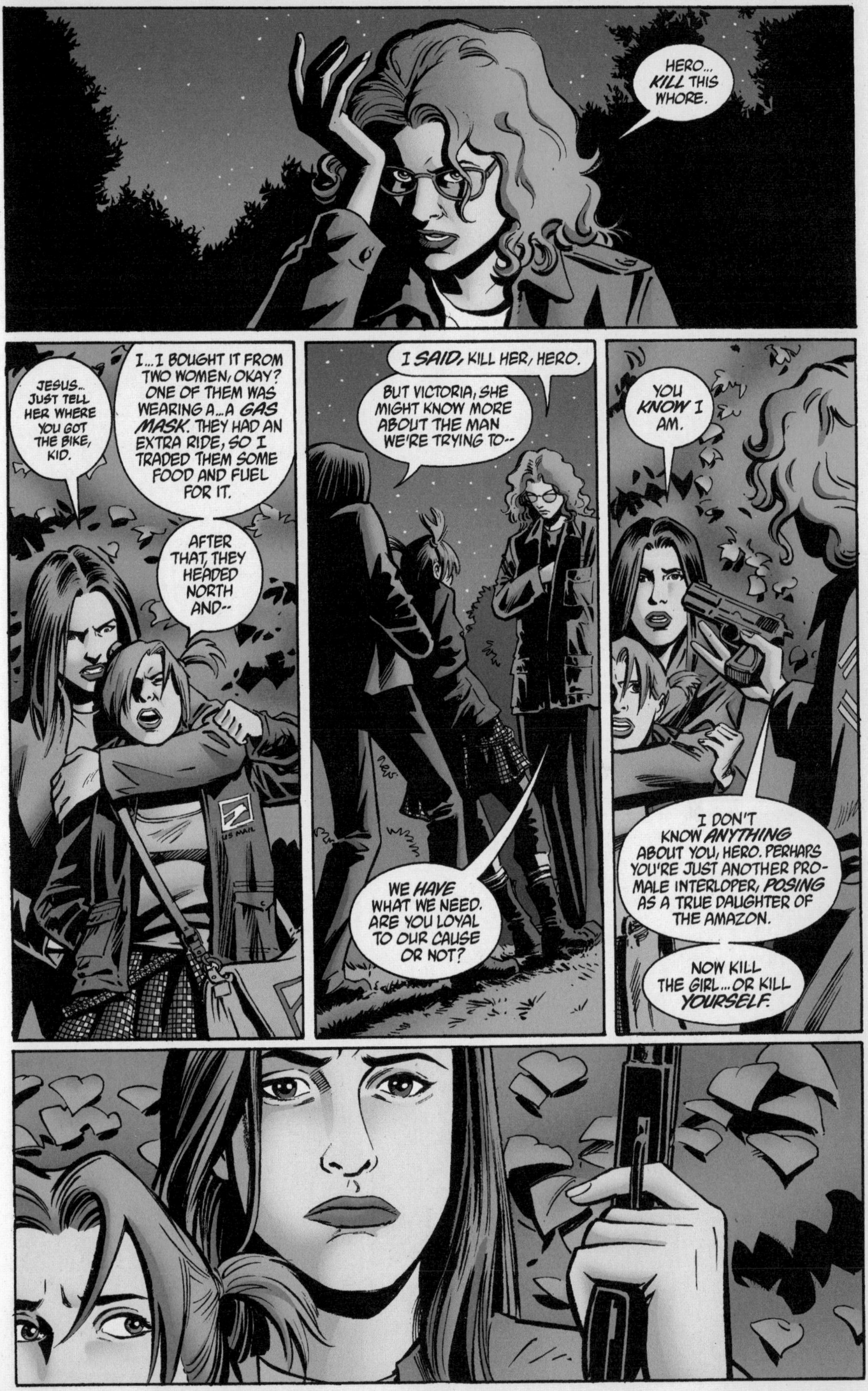
HERO... KILL THIS WHORE.
JESUS.. JUST TELL HER WHERE YOU GOT THE BIKE, KID.
I...I BOUGHT IT FROM TWO WOMEN, OKAY? ONE OF THEM WAS WEARING A...A GAS MASK. THEY HAD AN EXTRA RIDE, SO I TRADED THEM SOME FOOD AND FUEL FOR IT.
AFTER THAT, THEY HEADED NORTH AND--
US MAIL
I SAID, KILL HER, HERO.
BUT VICTORIA, SHE MIGHT KNOW MORE ABOUT THE MAN WE'RE TRYING TO--
WE HAVE WHAT WE NEED. ARE YOU LOYAL TO OUR CAUSE OR NOT?
YOU KNOW I AM.
I DON'T KNOW ANYTHING ABOUT YOU, HERO. PERHAPS YOU'RE JUST ANOTHER PRO-MALE INTERLOPER, POSING AS A TRUE DAUGHTER OF THE AMAZON.
NOW KILL THE GIRL...OR KILL YOURSELF.

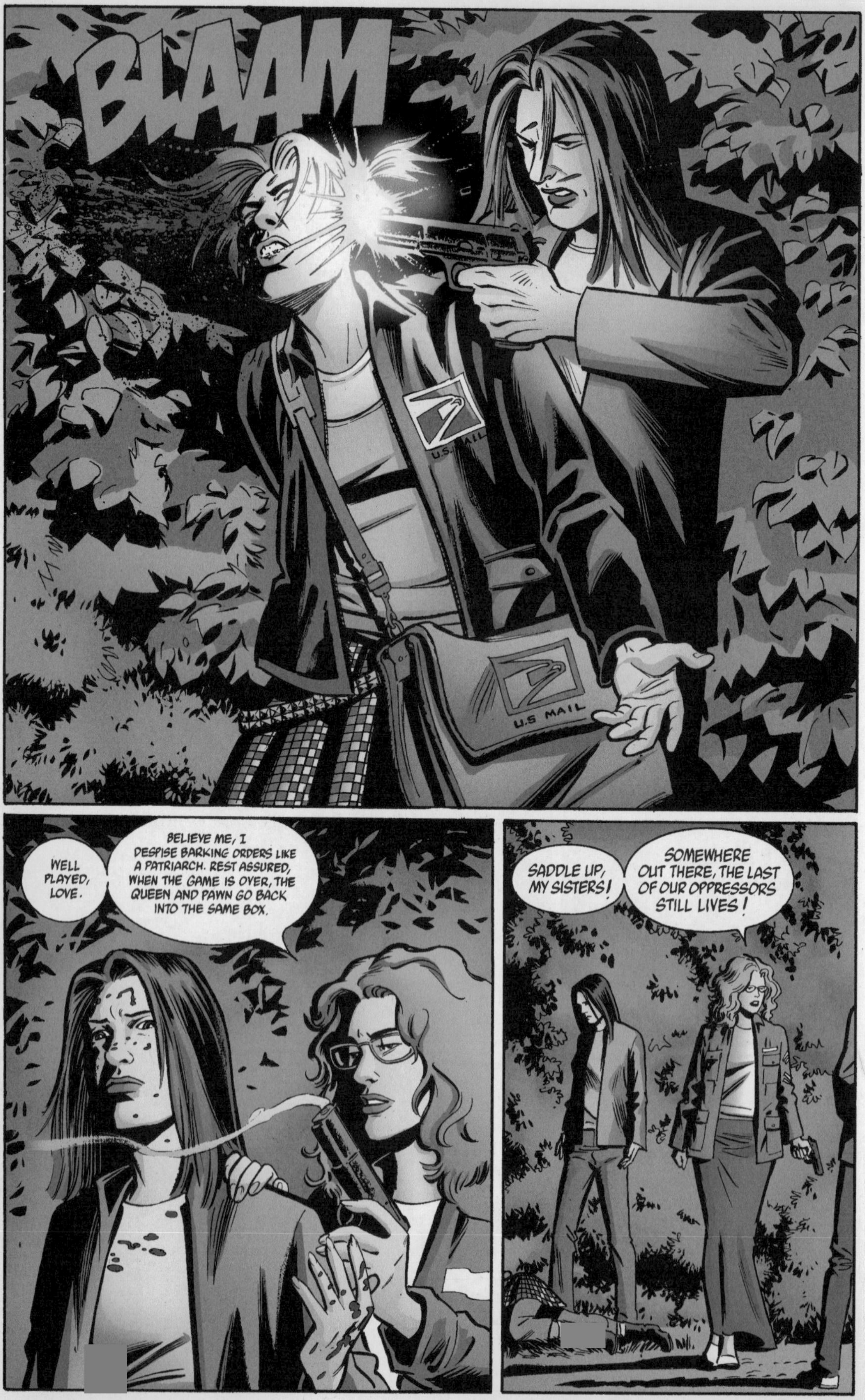
BLAAM
U.S. MAIL
U.S MAIL
WELL PLAYED, LOVE.
BELIEVE ME, I DESPISE BARKING ORDERS LIKE A PATRIARCH. REST ASSURED, WHEN THE GAME IS OVER, THE QUEEN AND PAWN GO BACK INTO THE SAME BOX.
SADDLE UP, MY SISTERS!
SOMEWHERE OUT THERE, THE LAST OF OUR OPPRESSORS STILL LIVES!

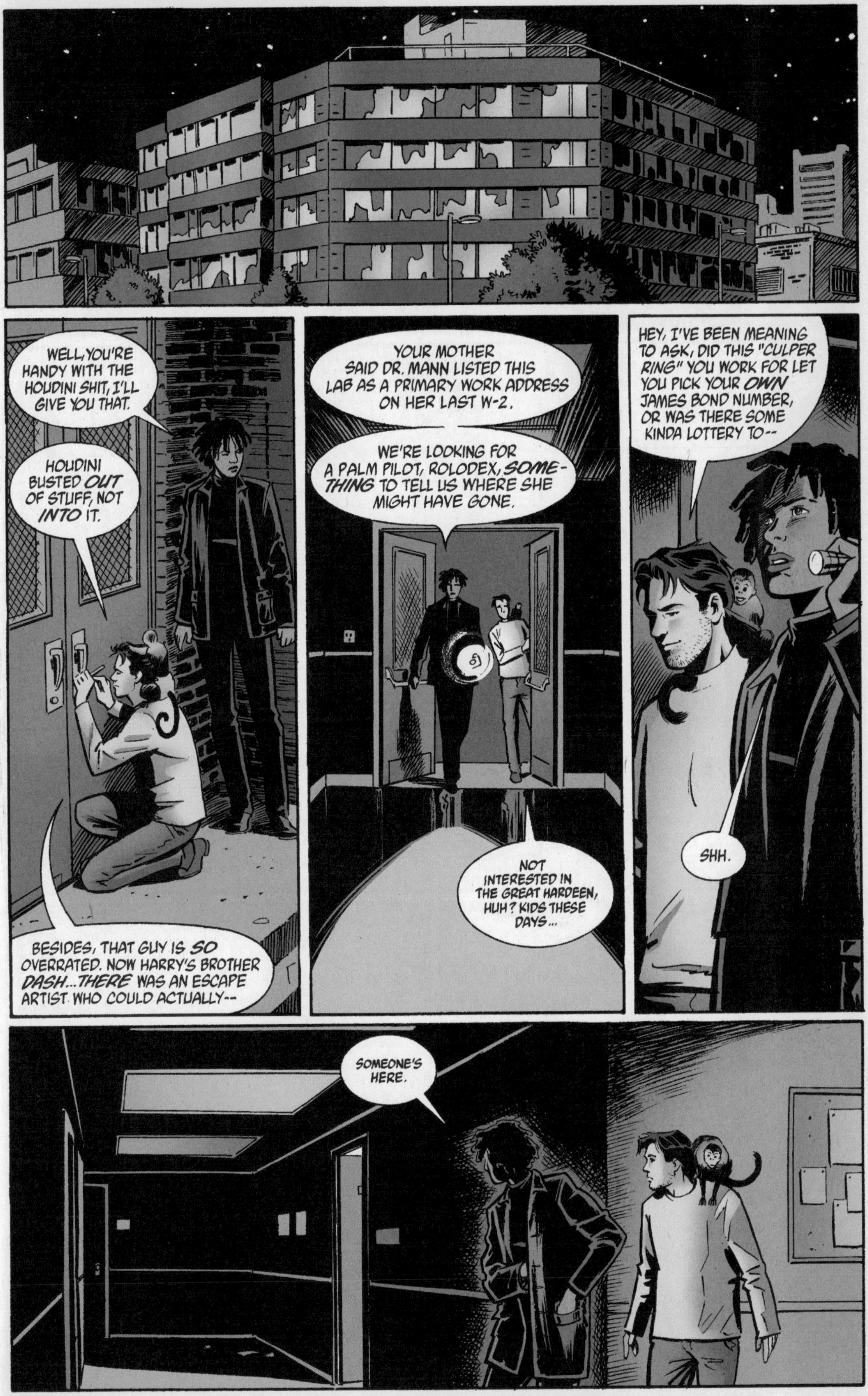
WELL, YOU'RE HANDY WITH THE HOUDINI SHIT, I'LL GIVE YOU THAT.
HOUDINI BUSTED OUT OF STUFF, NOT INTO IT.
BESIDES, THAT GUY IS SO OVERRATED. NOW HARRY'S BROTHER DASH...THERE WAS AN ESCAPE ARTIST WHO COULD ACTUALLY--
YOUR MOTHER SAID DR. MANN LISTED THIS LAB AS A PRIMARY WORK ADDRESS ON HER LAST W-2.
WE'RE LOOKING FOR A PALM PILOT, ROLODEX, SOMETHING TO TELL US WHERE SHE MIGHT HAVE GONE.
NOT INTERESTED IN THE GREAT HARDEEN, HUH? KIDS THESE DAYS...
HEY, I'VE BEEN MEANING TO ASK, DID THIS "CULPER RING" YOU WORK FOR LET YOU PICK YOUR OWN JAMES BOND NUMBER, OR WAS THERE SOME KINDA LOTTERY TO--
SHH.
SOMEONE'S HERE.

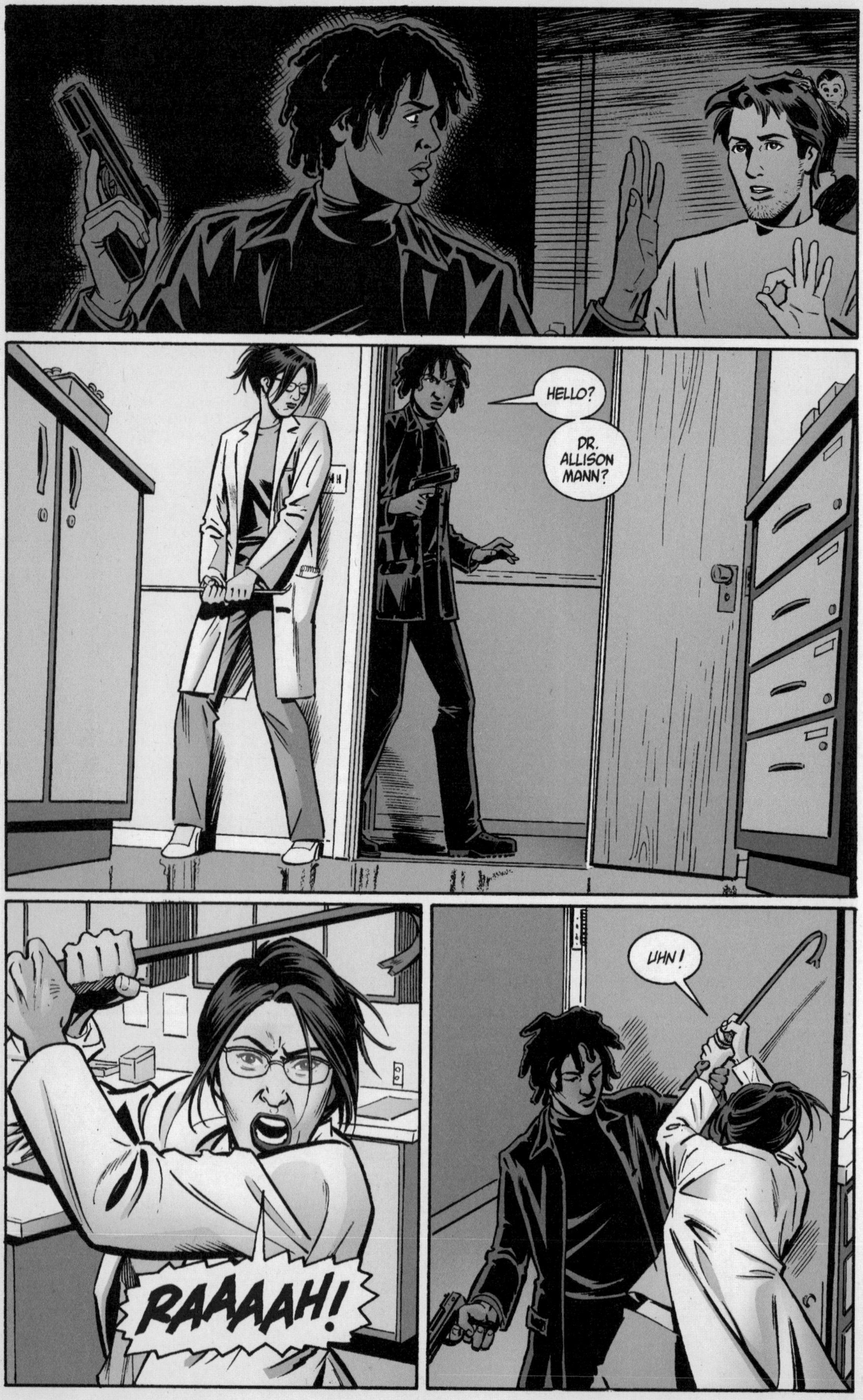
HELLO?
DR. ALLISON MANN?
RAAAAH!
UHN!

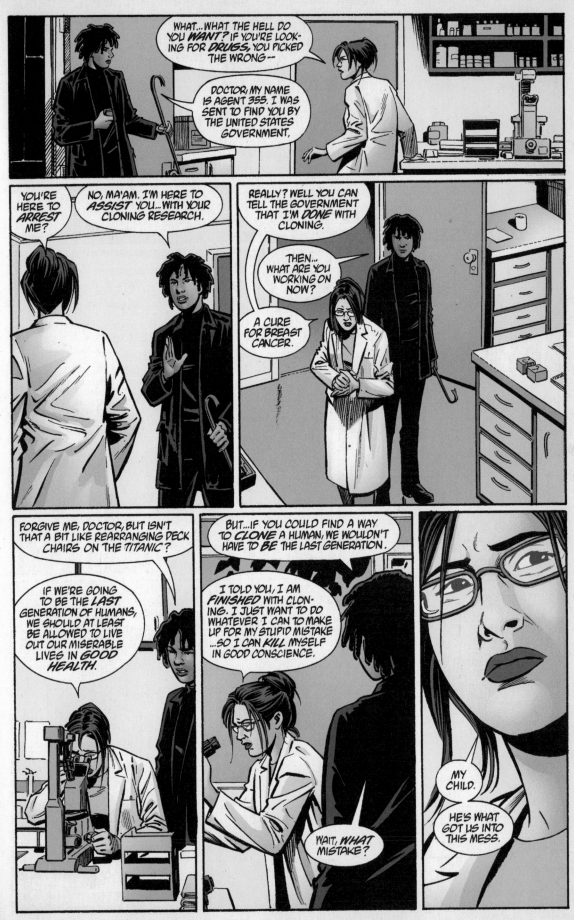

WHAT...WHAT THE HELL DO YOU *WANT*? IF YOU'RE LOOKING FOR *DRUGS*, YOU PICKED THE WRONG--

DOCTOR, MY NAME IS AGENT 355. I WAS SENT TO FIND YOU BY THE UNITED STATES GOVERNMENT.

YOU'RE HERE TO *ARREST* ME?

NO, MA'AM. I'M HERE TO *ASSIST* YOU...WITH YOUR CLONING RESEARCH.

REALLY? WELL YOU CAN TELL THE GOVERNMENT THAT I'M *DONE* WITH CLONING.

THEN... WHAT ARE YOU WORKING ON NOW?

A CURE FOR BREAST CANCER.

FORGIVE ME, DOCTOR, BUT ISN'T THAT A BIT LIKE REARRANGING DECK CHAIRS ON THE *TITANIC*?

IF WE'RE GOING TO BE THE *LAST* GENERATION OF HUMANS, WE SHOULD AT LEAST BE ALLOWED TO LIVE OUT OUR MISERABLE LIVES IN *GOOD HEALTH*.

BUT...IF YOU COULD FIND A WAY TO *CLONE* A HUMAN, WE WOULDN'T HAVE TO *BE* THE LAST GENERATION.

I TOLD YOU, I AM *FINISHED* WITH CLONING. I JUST WANT TO DO WHATEVER I CAN TO MAKE UP FOR MY STUPID MISTAKE ...SO I CAN *KILL* MYSELF IN GOOD CONSCIENCE.

WAIT, *WHAT* MISTAKE?

MY CHILD.

HE'S WHAT GOT US INTO THIS MESS.

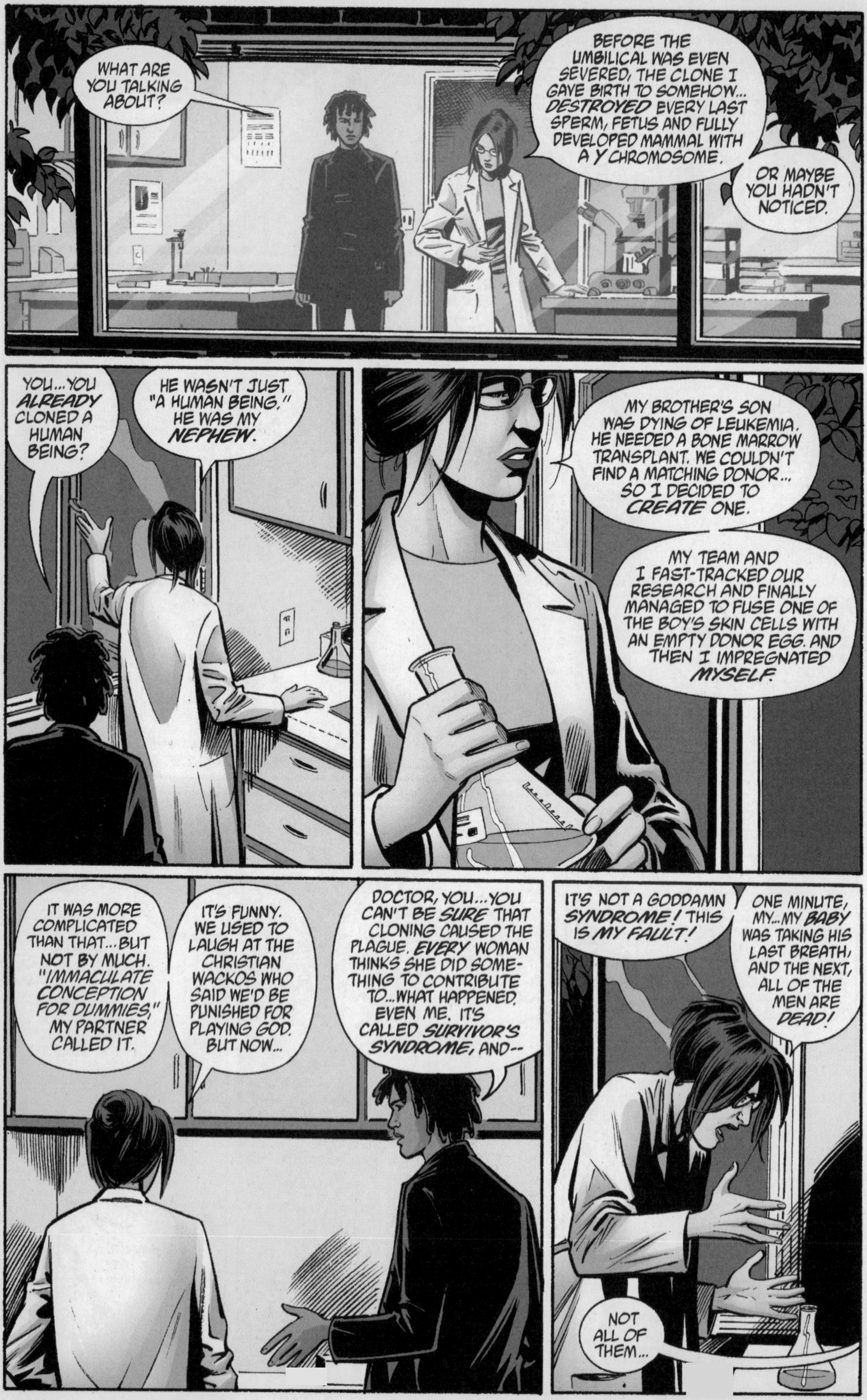
WHAT ARE YOU TALKING ABOUT?
BEFORE THE UMBILICAL WAS EVEN SEVERED, THE CLONE I GAVE BIRTH TO SOMEHOW... DESTROYED EVERY LAST SPERM, FETUS AND FULLY DEVELOPED MAMMAL WITH A Y CHROMOSOME.
OR MAYBE YOU HADN'T NOTICED.
YOU...YOU ALREADY CLONED A HUMAN BEING?
HE WASN'T JUST "A HUMAN BEING." HE WAS MY NEPHEW.
MY BROTHER'S SON WAS DYING OF LEUKEMIA. HE NEEDED A BONE MARROW TRANSPLANT. WE COULDN'T FIND A MATCHING DONOR... SO I DECIDED TO CREATE ONE.
MY TEAM AND I FAST-TRACKED OUR RESEARCH AND FINALLY MANAGED TO FUSE ONE OF THE BOY'S SKIN CELLS WITH AN EMPTY DONOR EGG. AND THEN I IMPREGNATED MYSELF.
IT WAS MORE COMPLICATED THAN THAT...BUT NOT BY MUCH. "IMMACULATE CONCEPTION FOR DUMMIES," MY PARTNER CALLED IT.
IT'S FUNNY. WE USED TO LAUGH AT THE CHRISTIAN WACKOS WHO SAID WE'D BE PUNISHED FOR PLAYING GOD. BUT NOW...
DOCTOR, YOU...YOU CAN'T BE SURE THAT CLONING CAUSED THE PLAGUE. EVERY WOMAN THINKS SHE DID SOMETHING TO CONTRIBUTE TO...WHAT HAPPENED. EVEN ME. IT'S CALLED SURVIVOR'S SYNDROME, AND--
IT'S NOT A GODDAMN SYNDROME! THIS IS MY FAULT!
ONE MINUTE, MY...MY BABY WAS TAKING HIS LAST BREATH, AND THE NEXT, ALL OF THE MEN ARE DEAD!
NOT ALL OF THEM...

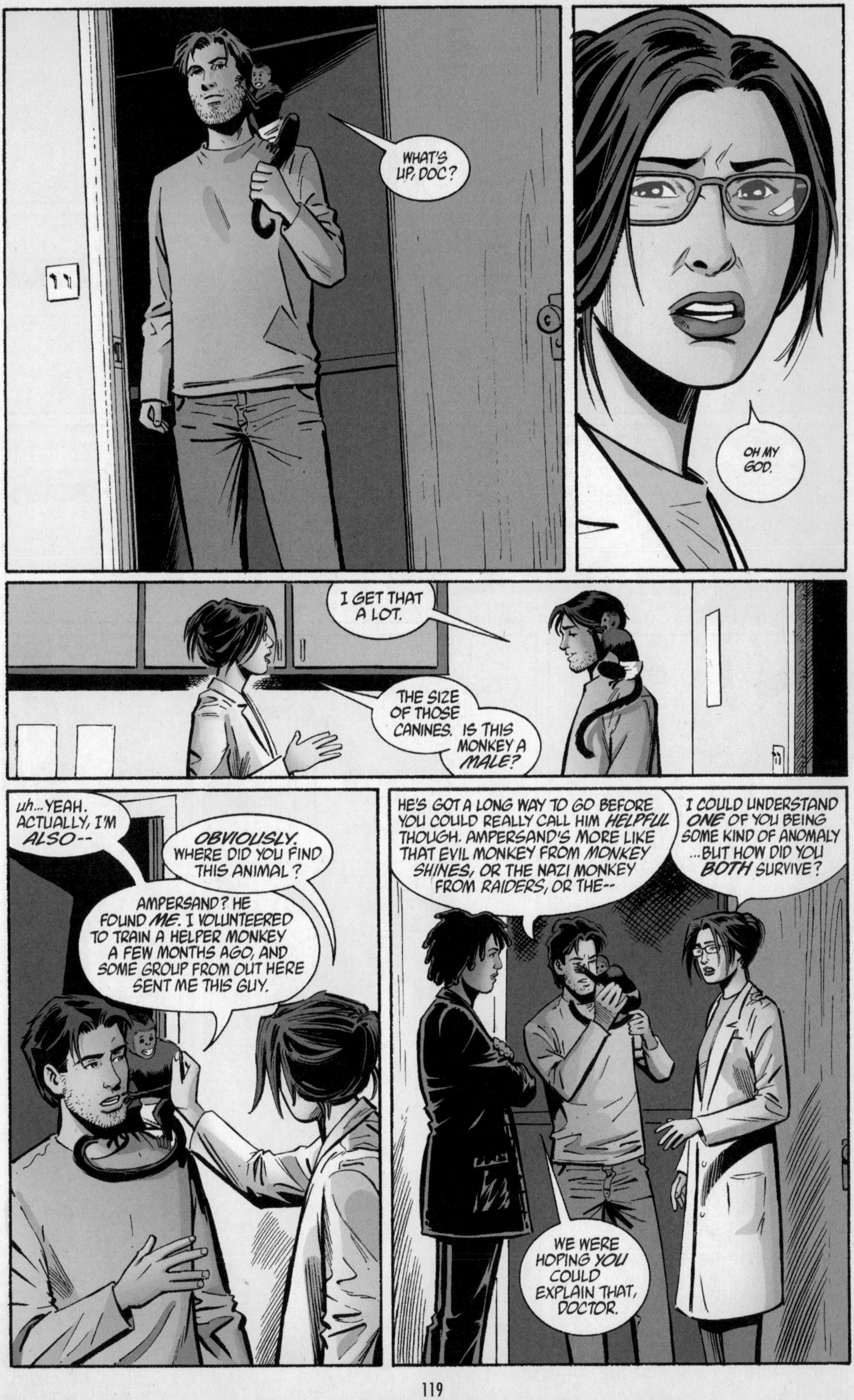
WHAT'S UP, DOC?
OH MY GOD.
I GET THAT A LOT.
THE SIZE OF THOSE CANINES. IS THIS MONKEY A *MALE*?
uh...YEAH. ACTUALLY, I'M *ALSO*--
OBVIOUSLY. WHERE DID YOU FIND THIS ANIMAL?
AMPERSAND? HE FOUND *ME*. I VOLUNTEERED TO TRAIN A HELPER MONKEY A FEW MONTHS AGO, AND SOME GROUP FROM OUT HERE SENT ME THIS GUY.
HE'S GOT A LONG WAY TO GO BEFORE YOU COULD REALLY CALL HIM *HELPFUL* THOUGH. AMPERSAND'S MORE LIKE THAT EVIL MONKEY FROM *MONKEY SHINES*, OR THE NAZI MONKEY FROM *RAIDERS*, OR THE--
I COULD UNDERSTAND *ONE* OF YOU BEING SOME KIND OF ANOMALY ...BUT HOW DID YOU *BOTH* SURVIVE?
WE WERE HOPING *YOU* COULD EXPLAIN THAT, DOCTOR.

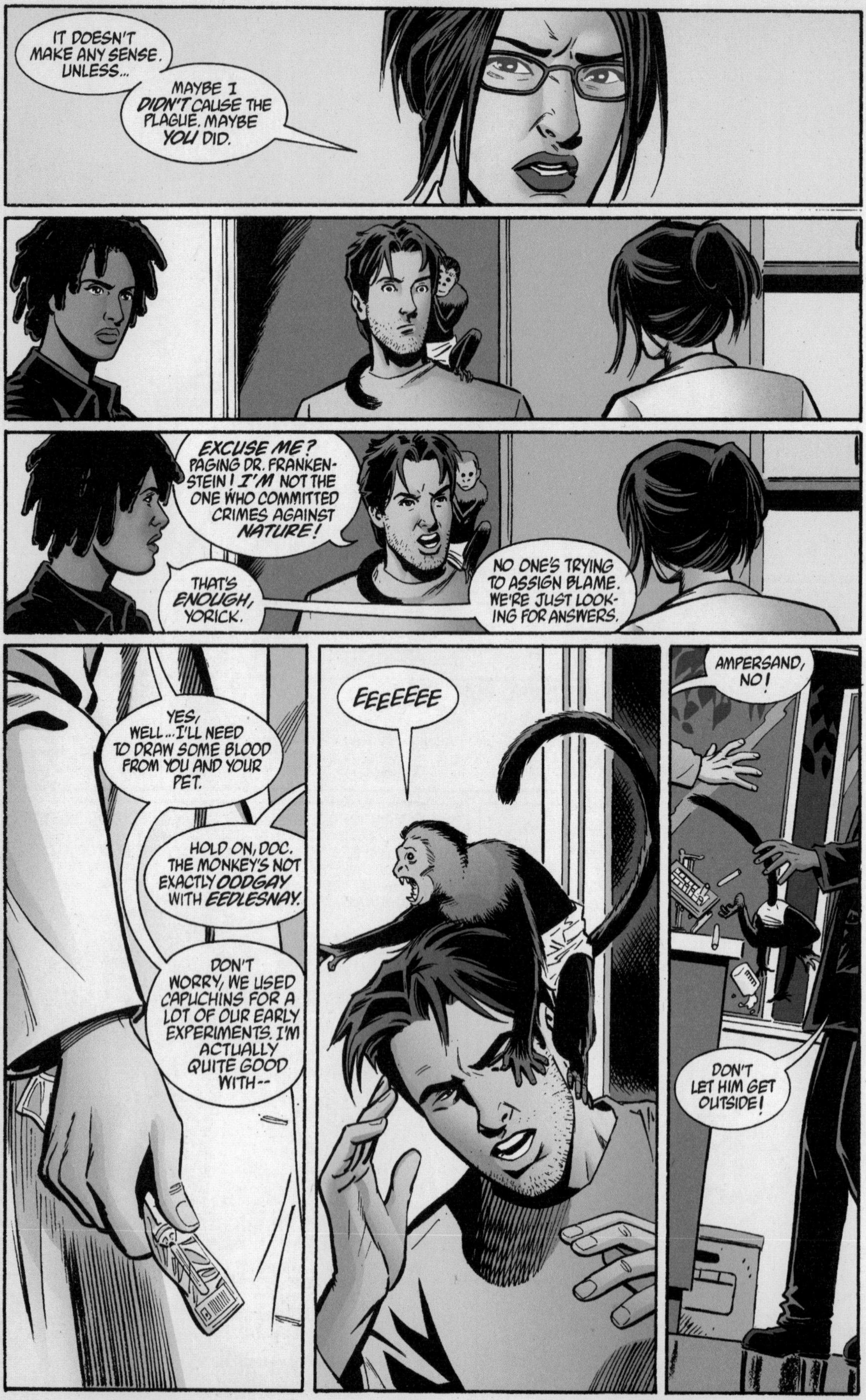
IT DOESN'T MAKE ANY SENSE. UNLESS...
MAYBE I DIDN'T CAUSE THE PLAGUE. MAYBE YOU DID.
EXCUSE ME? PAGING DR. FRANKENSTEIN! I'M NOT THE ONE WHO COMMITTED CRIMES AGAINST NATURE!
THAT'S ENOUGH, YORICK.
NO ONE'S TRYING TO ASSIGN BLAME. WE'RE JUST LOOKING FOR ANSWERS.
YES, WELL...I'LL NEED TO DRAW SOME BLOOD FROM YOU AND YOUR PET.
HOLD ON, DOC. THE MONKEY'S NOT EXACTLY OODGAY WITH EEDLESNAY.
DON'T WORRY, WE USED CAPUCHINS FOR A LOT OF OUR EARLY EXPERIMENTS. I'M ACTUALLY QUITE GOOD WITH--
EEEEEEE
AMPERSAND, NO!
DON'T LET HIM GET OUTSIDE!

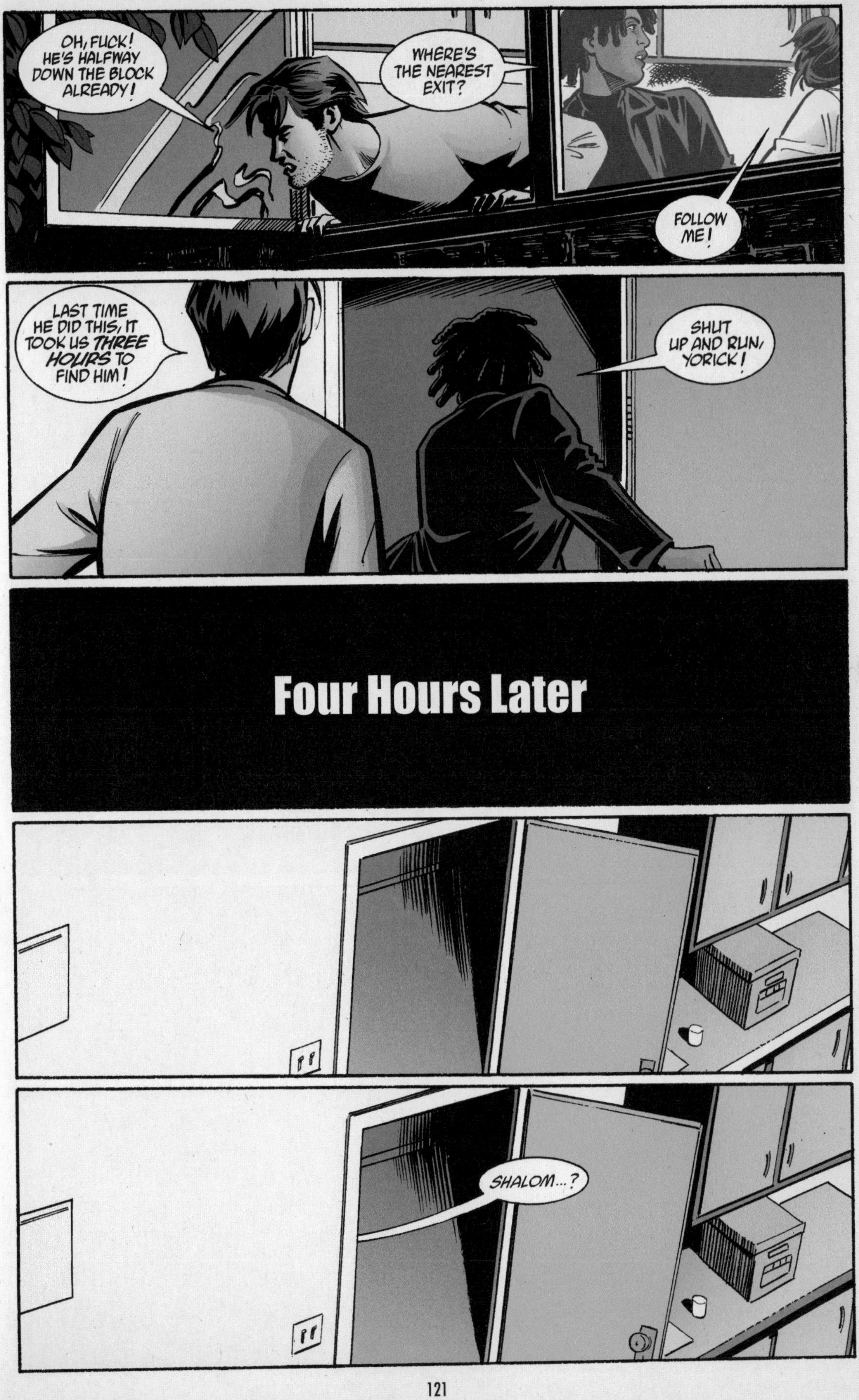
OH, FUCK! HE'S HALFWAY DOWN THE BLOCK ALREADY!
WHERE'S THE NEAREST EXIT?
FOLLOW ME!
LAST TIME HE DID THIS, IT TOOK US THREE HOURS TO FIND HIM!
SHUT UP AND RUN, YORICK!
Four Hours Later
SHALOM...?

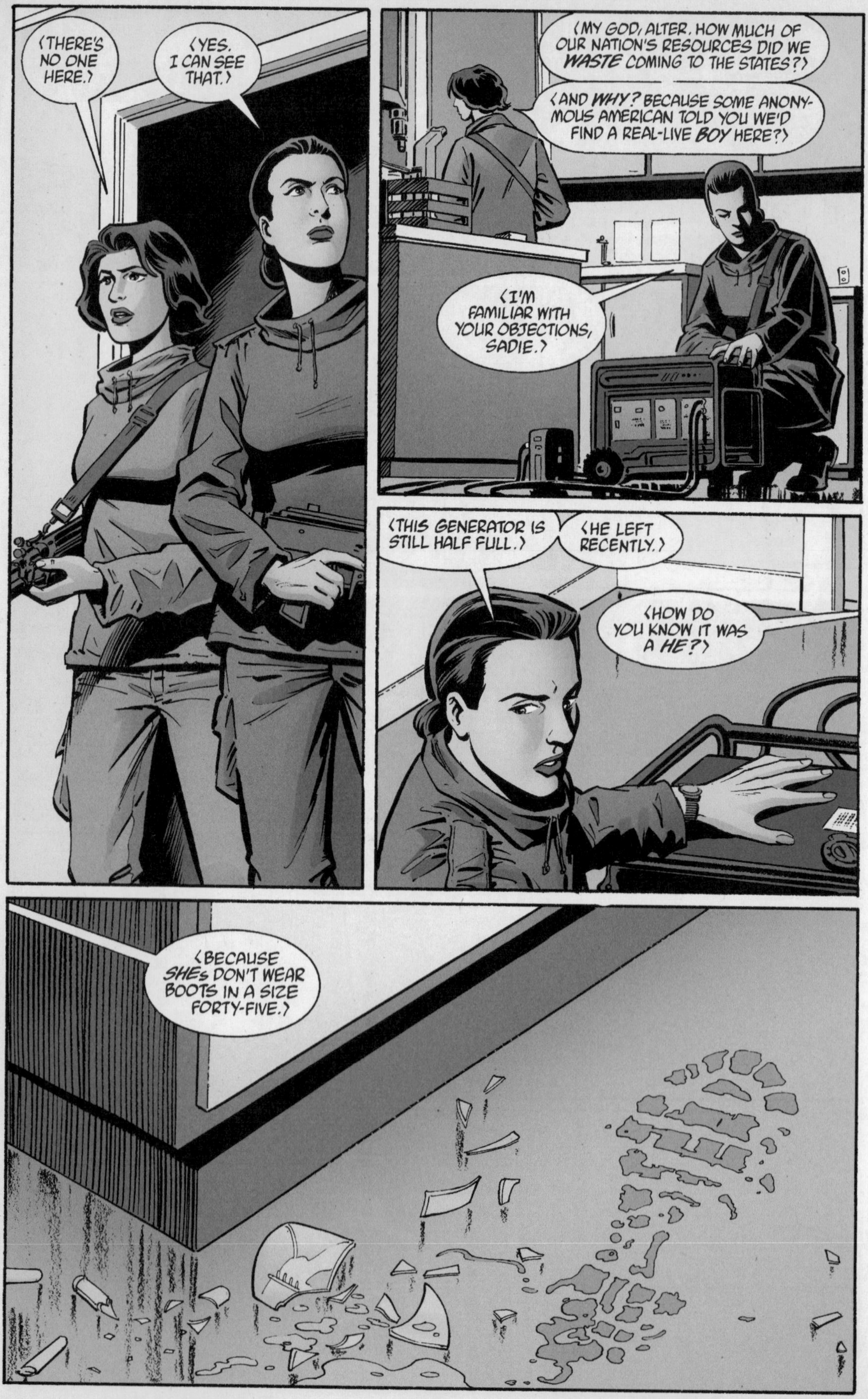
‹THERE'S NO ONE HERE.›
‹YES. I CAN SEE THAT.›
‹MY GOD, ALTER. HOW MUCH OF OUR NATION'S RESOURCES DID WE WASTE COMING TO THE STATES?›
‹AND WHY? BECAUSE SOME ANONYMOUS AMERICAN TOLD YOU WE'D FIND A REAL-LIVE BOY HERE?›
‹I'M FAMILIAR WITH YOUR OBJECTIONS, SADIE.›
‹THIS GENERATOR IS STILL HALF FULL.›
‹HE LEFT RECENTLY.›
‹HOW DO YOU KNOW IT WAS A HE?›
‹BECAUSE SHEs DON'T WEAR BOOTS IN A SIZE FORTY-FIVE.›

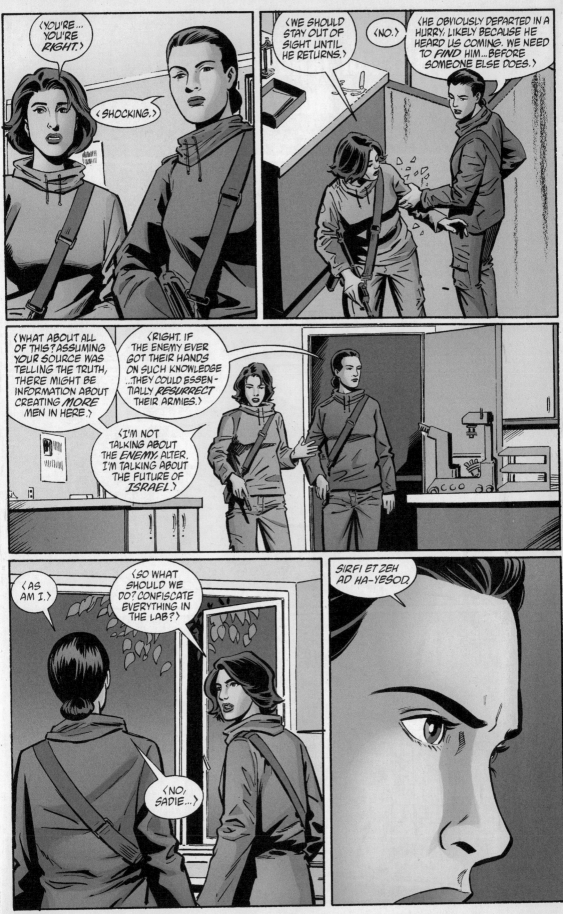

‹YOU'RE... YOU'RE *RIGHT*.›

‹SHOCKING.›

‹WE SHOULD STAY OUT OF SIGHT UNTIL HE RETURNS.›

‹NO.›

‹HE OBVIOUSLY DEPARTED IN A HURRY, LIKELY BECAUSE HE HEARD US COMING. WE NEED TO *FIND* HIM...BEFORE SOMEONE ELSE DOES.›

‹WHAT ABOUT ALL OF THIS? ASSUMING YOUR SOURCE WAS TELLING THE TRUTH, THERE MIGHT BE INFORMATION ABOUT CREATING *MORE* MEN IN HERE.›

‹RIGHT. IF THE ENEMY EVER GOT THEIR HANDS ON SUCH KNOWLEDGE ...THEY COULD ESSEN-TIALLY *RESURRECT* THEIR ARMIES.›

‹I'M NOT TALKING ABOUT THE *ENEMY*, ALTER. I'M TALKING ABOUT THE FUTURE OF *ISRAEL*.›

‹AS AM I.›

‹SO WHAT SHOULD WE DO? CONFISCATE EVERYTHING IN THE LAB?›

‹NO, SADIE...›

SIRFI ET ZEH AD HA-YESOD.

123

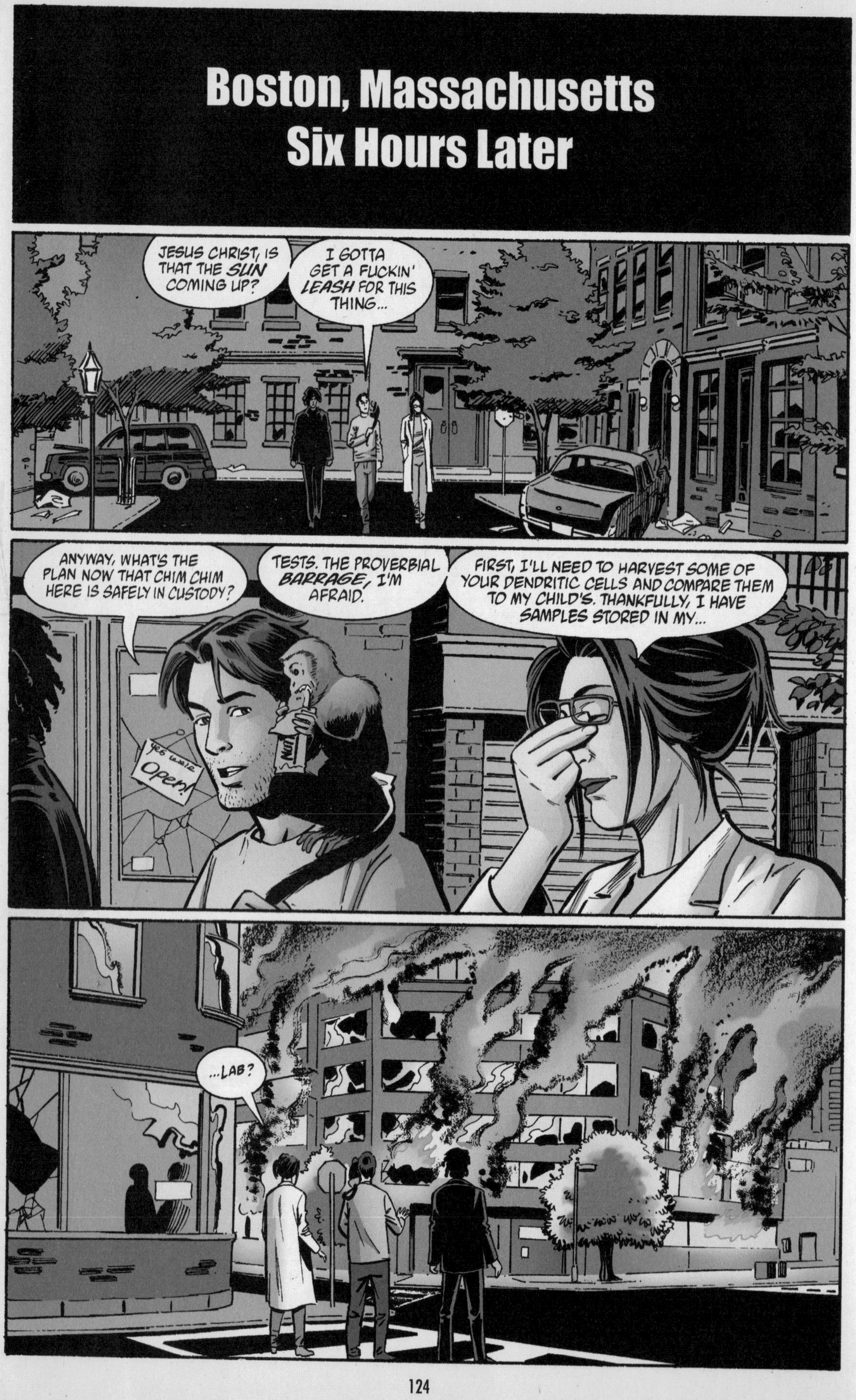
Boston, Massachusetts
Six Hours Later
JESUS CHRIST, IS THAT THE SUN COMING UP?
I GOTTA GET A FUCKIN' LEASH FOR THIS THING...
ANYWAY, WHAT'S THE PLAN NOW THAT CHIM CHIM HERE IS SAFELY IN CUSTODY?
yes we're Open!
TESTS. THE PROVERBIAL BARRAGE, I'M AFRAID.
FIRST, I'LL NEED TO HARVEST SOME OF YOUR DENDRITIC CELLS AND COMPARE THEM TO MY CHILD'S. THANKFULLY, I HAVE SAMPLES STORED IN MY...
...LAB?

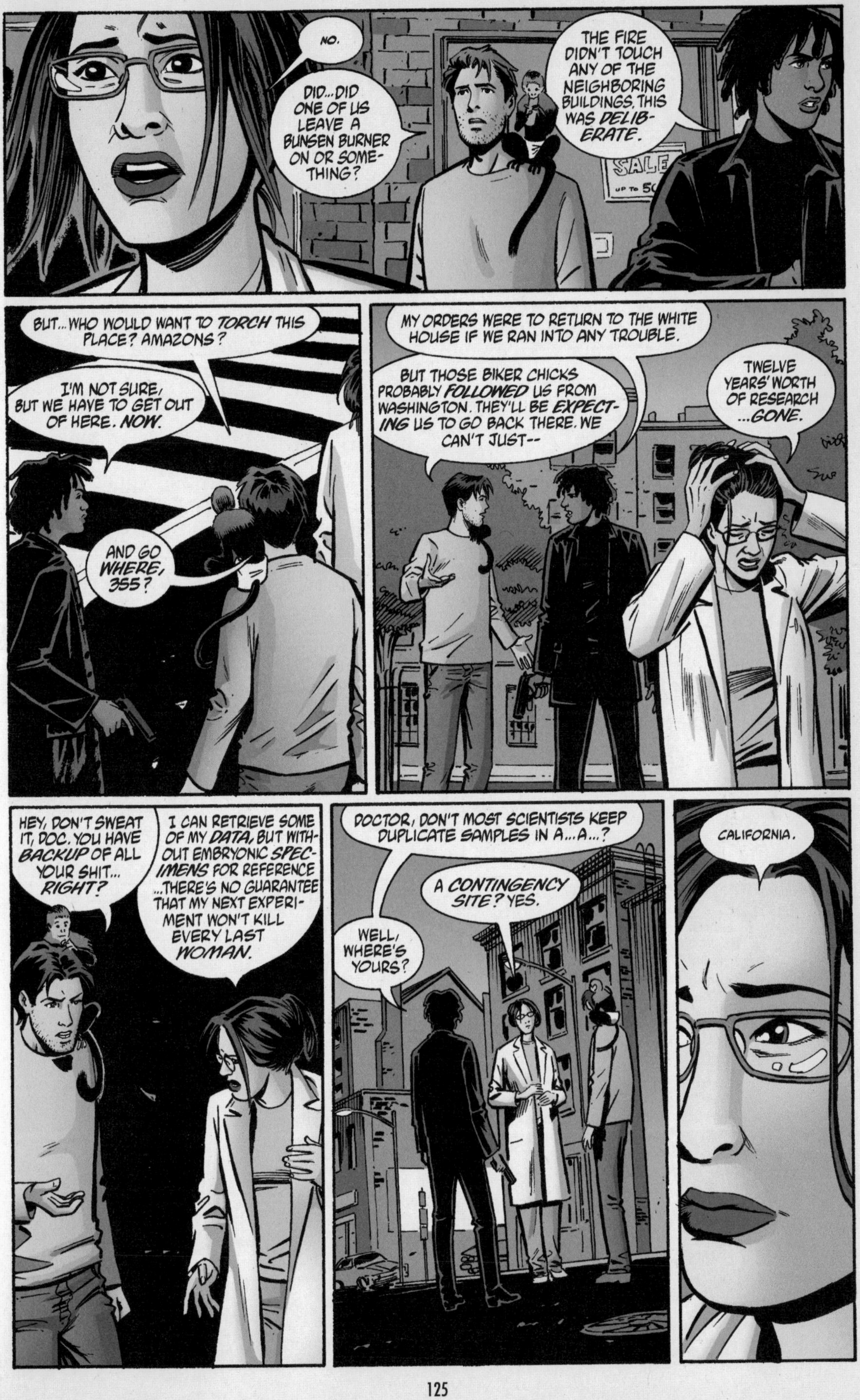
DID...DID ONE OF US LEAVE A BUNSEN BURNER ON OR SOMETHING?
NO.
THE FIRE DIDN'T TOUCH ANY OF THE NEIGHBORING BUILDINGS. THIS WAS DELIBERATE.
SALE UP TO 50
BUT...WHO WOULD WANT TO TORCH THIS PLACE? AMAZONS?
I'M NOT SURE, BUT WE HAVE TO GET OUT OF HERE. NOW.
AND GO WHERE, 355?
MY ORDERS WERE TO RETURN TO THE WHITE HOUSE IF WE RAN INTO ANY TROUBLE.
BUT THOSE BIKER CHICKS PROBABLY FOLLOWED US FROM WASHINGTON. THEY'LL BE EXPECTING US TO GO BACK THERE. WE CAN'T JUST--
TWELVE YEARS' WORTH OF RESEARCH ...GONE.
HEY, DON'T SWEAT IT, DOC. YOU HAVE BACKUP OF ALL YOUR SHIT... RIGHT?
I CAN RETRIEVE SOME OF MY DATA, BUT WITHOUT EMBRYONIC SPECIMENS FOR REFERENCE ...THERE'S NO GUARANTEE THAT MY NEXT EXPERIMENT WON'T KILL EVERY LAST WOMAN.
DOCTOR, DON'T MOST SCIENTISTS KEEP DUPLICATE SAMPLES IN A...A...?
A CONTINGENCY SITE? YES.
WELL, WHERE'S YOURS?
CALIFORNIA.

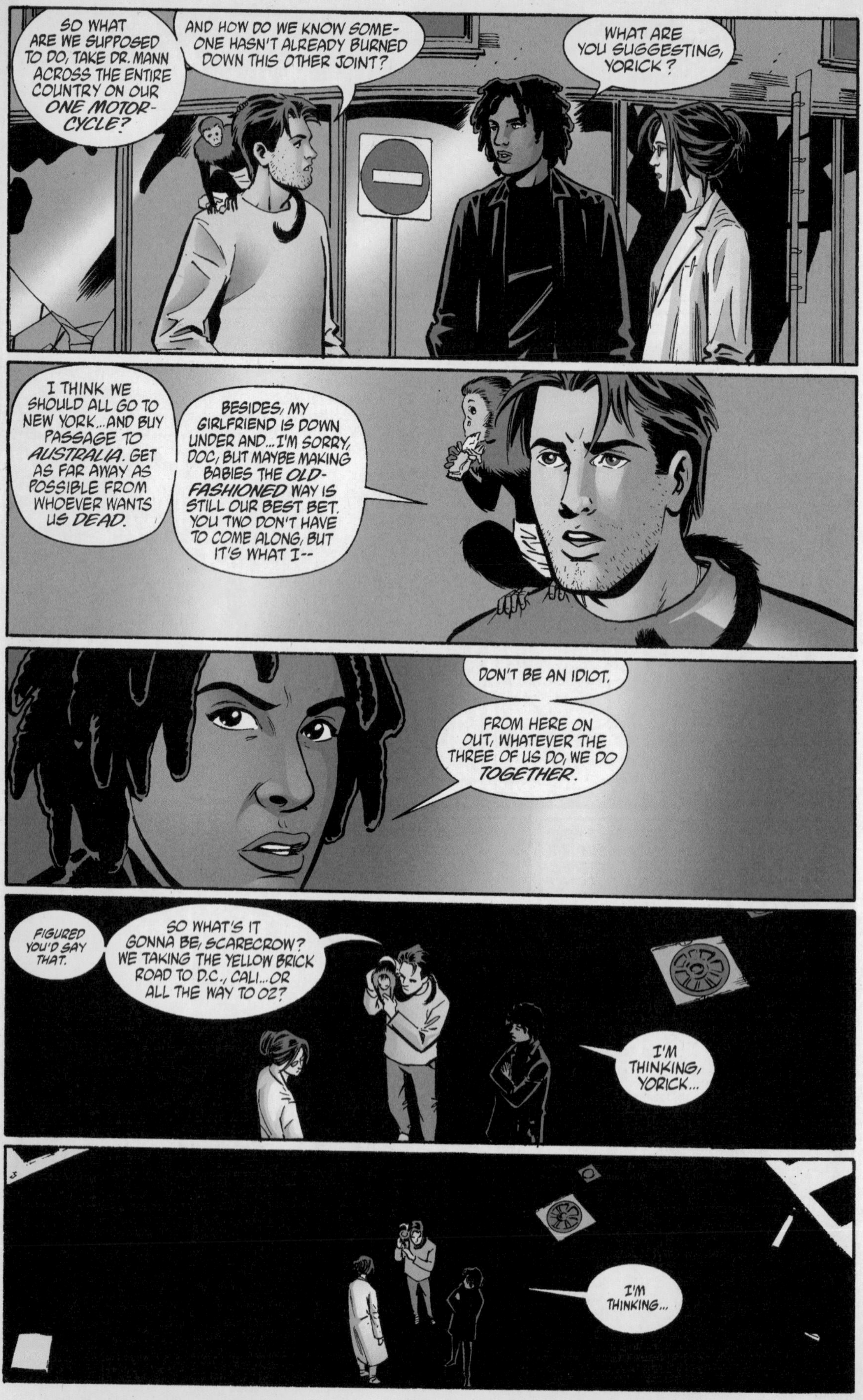
SO WHAT ARE WE SUPPOSED TO DO, TAKE DR. MANN ACROSS THE ENTIRE COUNTRY ON OUR ONE MOTOR-CYCLE?
AND HOW DO WE KNOW SOME-ONE HASN'T ALREADY BURNED DOWN THIS OTHER JOINT?
WHAT ARE YOU SUGGESTING, YORICK?
I THINK WE SHOULD ALL GO TO NEW YORK...AND BUY PASSAGE TO AUSTRALIA. GET AS FAR AWAY AS POSSIBLE FROM WHOEVER WANTS US DEAD.
BESIDES, MY GIRLFRIEND IS DOWN UNDER AND... I'M SORRY, DOC, BUT MAYBE MAKING BABIES THE OLD-FASHIONED WAY IS STILL OUR BEST BET. YOU TWO DON'T HAVE TO COME ALONG, BUT IT'S WHAT I--
DON'T BE AN IDIOT.
FROM HERE ON OUT, WHATEVER THE THREE OF US DO, WE DO TOGETHER.
FIGURED YOU'D SAY THAT.
SO WHAT'S IT GONNA BE, SCARECROW? WE TAKING THE YELLOW BRICK ROAD TO D.C., CALI...OR ALL THE WAY TO OZ?
I'M THINKING, YORICK...
I'M THINKING...

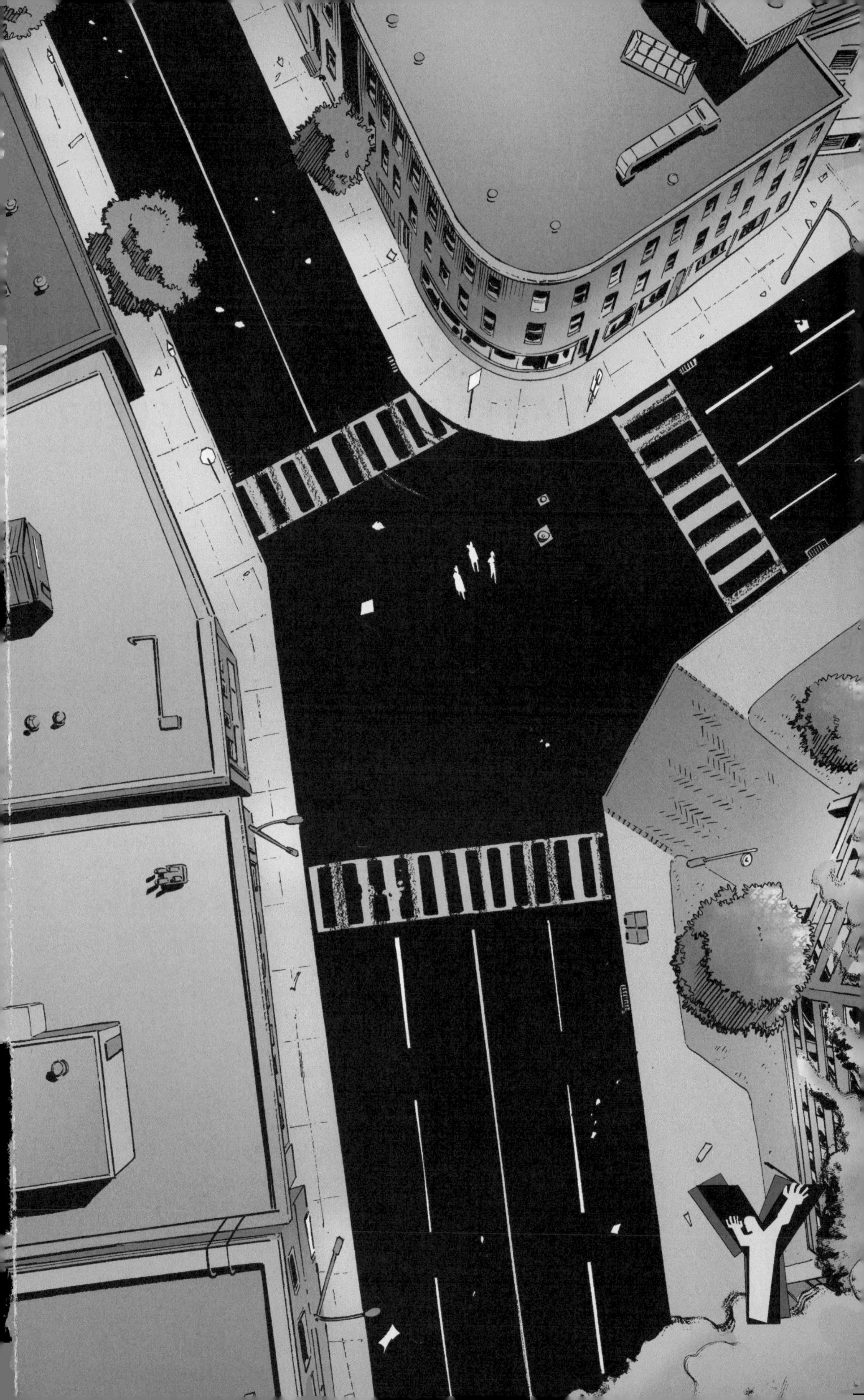